NEW EDITION

ECONOMIC ANALYSIS OF ENVIRONMENTAL IMPACTS

JOHN A DIXON

LOUISE FALLON SCURA

RICHARD A CARPENTER

PAUL B SHERMAN

ECONOMIC ANALYSIS OF ENVIRONMENTAL IMPACTS

John A. Dixon, Principal Environmental Economist and Chief, Indicators and Environmental Valuation Unit, with the World Bank Environment Department, is widely published on the topics of applied economic analysis of environmental impacts and natural resources management. Formerly with the Environment and Policy Institute of the East-West Center, Honolulu, he holds a Ph.D. in economics and has extensive field experience in Asia and Latin America. His address is: The World Bank, 1818 H Street, N.W., Washington, DC 20433, USA.

Louise Fallon Scura, Natural Resources Management Specialist with the World Bank Environment Department, specializes in economic analysis of natural resource and environmental impacts, natural resources management and coastal zone management, and has significant practical experience in Asia, Africa and the Americas. She has a Ph.D. in agricultural and resource economics, a B.S. in environmental sciences and aquaculture, and worked as a biologist before switching to economics. Her address is: The World Bank, 1818 H Street, N.W., Washington, DC 20433, USA.

Richard A. Carpenter, formerly a Research Associate at the Environment and Policy Institute of the East–West Center, Honolulu, is an independent consultant based in Virginia. He has a master's degree in chemistry and specializes in environmental assessment. His address is: Route 5, Box 277, Charlottesville, VA 22901 USA.

Paul B. Sherman, formerly with the East–West Center Environment and Policy Institute and the State of Hawaii Department of Business, Economic Development and Tourism, obtained a Ph.D. in economics and a master's degree in environmental management. His work focused on applied economic valuation, and economics of protected areas and drylands management.

ECONOMIC ANALYSIS OF ENVIRONMENTAL IMPACTS

JOHN A DIXON

LOUISE FALLON SCURA

RICHARD A CARPENTER

PAUL B SHERMAN

PUBLISHED IN ASSOCIATION
WITH THE ASIAN DEVELOPMENT BANK
AND THE WORLD BANK

EARTHSCAN
Earthscan Publications Ltd, London

First published in 1986 by
The Asian Development Bank

First Earthscan edition published in 1988

Second edition published 1994 by
Earthscan Publications Ltd
120 Pentonville Road, London N1 9JN
email: earthinfo@earthscan.co.uk
website: http://www.earthscan.co.uk

Reprinted 1996, 1997

A catalogue record for this book is available from the British Library

ISBN: 1 85383 185 9

Typeset by Florencetype Ltd, Stoodleigh, Devon
Printed and bound in Great Britain by
Biddles Ltd, Guildford and King's Lynn

Earthscan Publications Ltd is an editorially independent subsidiary of Kogan Page
Ltd, and publishes in association with the International Institute for Environment and
Development and the World Wide Fund for Nature.

Contents

List of Illustrations

FIGURES

TABLES

BOXES

Foreword

The past several decades have witnessed a growing realization that economic development and environmental management are mutually supporting goals. Accompanying this realization has been an important transition in the policies and implementation strategies of major international development and finance organizations such as the Asian Development Bank (ADB) and the World Bank. Both the World Bank and ADB are now actively involved in the effort to promote development which is both economically and environmentally sustainable. The World Bank has created a Vice Presidency for Environmentally Sustainable Development and the ADB has an Office of the Environment to lead the efforts. More generally, the environmental knowledge and skills of the banks' staffs have been enhanced through recruiting new staff and offering expanded training on environmental topics.

Both banks have supported the preparation of guidelines and procedures to ensure that environmental aspects are integrated into development projects. This book, which grew out of work originally commissioned by the ADB, focuses on methods for economic valuation and analysis of environmental impacts. The application of these analytical tools will contribute to the essential transition from environmental policy to practice.

The Asian Development Bank and the World Bank are pleased to make this important and timely material available.

Bong-Suh Lee
Vice President
Projects
Asian Development Bank
Manila

Ismail Serageldin
Vice President
Environmentally Sustainable Development
The World Bank
Washington, DC

Authors' Preface

In the early 1980s, the East–West Center's Environment and Policy Institute, Honolulu, Hawaii, under the initial leadership of Maynard M. Hufschmidt, undertook a research project on applied benefit-cost analysis that led to the publication of two books (Hufschmidt et al., 1983, and Dixon and Hufschmidt, 1986) and other applied materials.

In 1985 the authors, then at the East–West Center, were commissioned by the Asian Development Bank (ADB) to prepare a report based on these earlier publications. The report was published as ADB Economic Staff Paper Number 31 in 1986, and was revised into the first commercial Earthscan edition in 1988, as *Economic Analysis of the Environmental Impacts of Development Projects* by John A. Dixon, Richard A. Carpenter, Louise A. Fallon, Paul B. Sherman and Supachit Manopimoke.

In the 6 years since the original Earthscan edition was published there has been a major expansion in applied research and thinking on the subject of economic valuation and economic analysis of environmental impacts. This led to the decision to revise and update the earlier volume. Many new reference and case-study examples have been included and, in addition, the various valuation techniques have been re-grouped to reflect recent field experience with their applicability; some parts of the original book have been deleted. The change in focus and the contributions to the new edition are reflected in the new title and new authorship.

The book was prepared by John A. Dixon and Louise Fallon Scura of the Environment Department of the World Bank. Richard A. Carpenter contributed new material for Chapter 2 and Julian Lampietti helped draft several case studies. Both the ADB and the World Bank have supported this effort; the ADB through its sponsorship of the first edition and the World Bank by facilitating the work of the lead authors for this new edition. At the ADB the assistance of Bindu Lohani, Robert Salamon, Barun Roy and George Liu is noted. At the World Bank, financial support for the initial revision was provided by the Environment Department, the Training Office, and the Economic Development Institute. Colin Rees has been supportive in both institutions – at the ADB where the initial report grew out of a series of seminars that he organized for ADB staff, and, in his new position as Division Chief in the World Bank Environment Department.

We dedicate this volume to Maynard M. Hufschmidt who was the inspiration behind the original work at the East–West Center, and to Paul B. Sherman, whose valuable contributions to the first edition are retained in this volume and whose untimely death is a personal and professional loss to us.

Although the authors have benefitted from the support of both the ADB and the World Bank, the opinions contained in this book are those of the authors and should not be attributed to the ADB, the World Bank or any of their affiliates.

John A. Dixon
Environment Department
The World Bank

Louise Fallon Scura
Environment Department
The World Bank

Richard A. Carpenter
Charlottesville
Virginia

Dedication

To
Maynard M. Hufschmidt
mentor, colleague, friend

and

Paul B. Sherman
in memorium, 1959–1991

PART I

FROM THEORY TO PRACTICE

CHAPTER 1

Development, Environment and the Role of Economic Analysis

If the 1972 Stockholm Conference on the Human Environment can be considered the official start of international environmental awareness, the 1992 Rio Earth Summit (the United Nations Conference on Environment and Development, UNCED) represented a partial 'coming of age' of the international environmental movement. Increasingly it is recognized that environmental issues are fundamental to both social and ecosystem well-being, as well as to sustainable economic development. The links between improved environmental management and economic development were at the core of the UNCED agenda.

There have been many other important environmental 'benchmarks' of the past decade. These include the Brundtland Commission's 1987 report, *Our Common Future*, that made the concept of sustainable development fashionable. The idea that sustainable development means 'meeting the needs of the present generation without compromising the needs of future generations' explicitly recognizes the limited nature of environmental resources, intergenerational equity issues, and the need to evaluate trade-offs, both for the current generation as well as between resource use and environmental quality now and in the future.[1]

In 1992 the World Bank's *World Development Report* focused on the links between development and the environment, and highlighted opportunities for 'win-win' policies that are good both for the environment and for economic development. The Global Environment Facility (GEF) was set up to support, with grant funds, the cost of incremental activities that have global benefits that would not be economically justified on a narrower, national accounting framework.[2] Numerous post-UNCED activities have sought to operationalize the concepts of sustainable development.

Fortunately, the growth and sophistication of environmental awareness has been matched by a rapid increase in both theoretical and applied economic

---

1 The concept of sustainability has proved very difficult to define and operationalize. The issue is discussed in a 1989 *Society and Natural Resources* article, *The Concept of Sustainability* by Dixon and Fallon, in Pezzey's World Bank Environment Paper *Sustainable Development Concepts: An Economic Analysis* (1992), and in Pearce and Warford (1993) among others.

2 The GEF's initial phase (slightly more than $1 billion for the period 1991–94) focused on four specific project areas: biodiversity protection, reduction of greenhouse gas emissions, reduction of CFC emissions to protect the ozone layer (the Montreal Protocol), and controlling the pollution of international waters. The GEF is supported by countries around the world and is implemented by the World Bank, the United Nations Development Programme, and the United Nations Environment Programme.

analysis of these issues. In recent years there has been an explosion of writings on economics and the environment.[3]

And an equal number of major new works are appearing in 1994, including several based on research and training projects supported by both the United Nations University (UNU)-affiliated World Institute of Development Economics Research (WIDER) in Helsinki and the Swedish Royal Academy's Beijer Institute in Stockholm.[4] Interest in 'ecological economics', an amalgam of environmental and economic analysis that is still being defined, has resulted in the formation of an international society, and a journal (*Ecological Economics*).[5]

Valuation (the placing of monetary values on environmental goods or services or the impacts of environmental quality changes), the focus of this book, has also received increased attention. Governments realize that to evaluate alternative investment measures requires the placing of monetary values on the benefits and costs, both direct and indirect, of different actions. Valuation is thus essential to a fuller economic analysis of alternatives. Although valuation began with a narrower project focus on direct environmental impacts of activities, its use has broadened to include analysis of impacts of macro policy changes as well as the evolving concept of natural resource accounting – so-called 'green accounts'.[6]

As reflected in the developments since Stockholm and much of this recent work, environmental concerns and management have also shifted from being

---

3 Of note are edited volumes by Schramm and Warford, *Environmental Management and Economic Development* (1989), Markandya and Richardson, *Environmental Economics: A Reader* (1992), Munasinghe (1993a), and Weiss, *The Economics of Project Appraisal and the Environment* (1994). Major new texts include Pearce and Turner, *Economics of Natural Resources and the Environment* (1990), Tietenberg's third edition of his popular text (1992), Pearce and Warford's *World Without End* (1993), and numerous volumes by Pearce, Barbier and others working in London. These include *Blueprint for a Green Economy*, Pearce, Markandya and Barbier (1989); *Elephants, Economics and Ivory*, Barbier, Burgess, Swanson and Pearce (1990); *Sustainable Development: Economics and Environment in the Third World*, Pearce, Barbier and Markandya (1990); *Valuing the Environment*, Barde and Pearce, eds. (1991); and *Economics for the Wilds: Wildlife, Wildlands, Diversity and Development*, Swanson and Barbier, eds. (1992).
4 These books include a major text by Maler and Dasgupta (tentatively titled *Economic Analysis of Environment and Development*) and an edited volume *Environment and Emerging Development Issues* (1994); *The Economics of Transnational Commons*, Maler, Dasgupta and Vercello, eds. (1994); and two edited volumes dealing with biodiversity issues: *Biodiversity Loss: Economic and Ecological Issues*, and *Biodiversity Conservation: Policy Issues and Options*, both Perrings, Maler, Folke, Holling and Jansson, eds. (1994).
5 See also writings by Daly (1977, 1991), Daly and Cobb (1989), Costanza (1991), Folke (1991) and others.
6 The applied valuation literature has grown considerably and includes such earlier work as Pearce (1978), Sinden and Worrell (1979), Hufschmidt *et al*. (1983), Dixon and Hufschmidt (1986), and more recent work including our earlier Earthscan volume (Dixon *et al*. 1988), Bojo, Maler and Unemo (1990), Winpenny (1991), and publications by Pearce (1991, 1993), Munasinghe (1993b) and various reports from the OECD, the Paris-based Organization for Economic Co-operation and Development.

seen as rich country problems to ones that are important to all nations – rich and poor alike.

Governments in developing countries have become increasingly aware that environmental and natural resource degradation endangers the potential for long-term development. As a result, they are more receptive to the implementation of measures which ensure that development projects take both the environment and natural resources into account.

Many countries have experienced instances where the degradation of their natural resource base has resulted in the impairment of long-term growth. One common instance is that of fisheries, both inland and marine, damaged by water polluted by domestic and industrial effluents. In some areas this damage has reduced the traditional primary source of protein. Another example is the deforestation of upland regions produced by both changes in agriculture practice and excessive timber extraction for fuel and wood products. This has led to the disruption of the hydrological cycle of major watersheds and has caused erosion, siltation of rivers and reservoirs, and increases in both the incidence and severity of flooding. Productivity, health and aesthetic costs have been the result. For example, there has been a significant reduction in the productivity of many forests, agricultural lands, and fisheries. There have also been decreased returns from major investments in hydroelectric power and irrigation schemes.

Many people in developing countries work on the land and are directly dependent on natural resources for their food, shelter, and employment. Their welfare in both the short and the long term is inextricably tied to the productivity of natural systems. Thus the socioeconomic effects of degraded environments often hit the poor hardest.

In addition to the 'green' natural resource management agenda traditionally associated with environmental issues, there is an equally important set of concerns focused on urban environmental issues, especially the pollution of air and water – the so-called 'brown agenda'. Urban populations are large and growing rapidly: for example, over 70 percent of the population in Latin America lives in cities; for Asia the share is over 30 percent. In many urban areas, the impact of pollution on health, both sickness and premature death, is the most important consequence of urban environmental degradation. And, as in rural areas, the poor are usually the most seriously affected by pollution. The capital and operating costs of air and water pollution control can be very high, however, and careful analysis of these costs and expected benefits (largely from improvements in health) is therefore essential to the wise allocation of scarce financial resources.

It is clear that successful economic development depends on the rational use of environmental resources and on minimizing, as far as possible, the adverse impacts of development projects. This can be done by improving project selection, planning, design and implementation.

Both bilateral and multilateral institutions devoted to funding development projects and programmes see their role as promoting the most efficient use of available resources within the context of the socioeconomic priorities of individual developing countries. Valuation, as described earlier, allows fuller economic analysis of alternative development projects to assess the whole range of direct and indirect benefits and costs of proposed actions from a broader perspective.

Most lending institutions feel that the direct economic costs of a project are relatively easy to quantify, except where significant externalities such as environmental impacts are involved. Even in these cases, they realize that the costs of such effects should be quantified as far as possible, but the difficulties involved in this process have prevented this quantification; hence environmental effects have often been described and evaluated only in qualitative terms. The real question, therefore, is: How can the environmental impacts of development projects be identified, quantified, and valued?

There are two major elements in assessing environmental impacts: first, they have to be identified and measured; second, ways must be found to place monetary values on these impacts so that they can be included in the formal analyses of projects. Only when a monetary value cannot be given to a particular environmental impact should it be dealt with qualitatively within the analyses.

Both components are reviewed in this book, and suggestions are given as to how economic measurement of environmental impacts generated by development projects may be undertaken. The approach and techniques presented are based on work done by economists around the world; this book's contribution is to synthesize existing information and provide a practical application of the techniques to handle environmental quality effects of development projects.

This book focuses on the better economic analysis of environmental and resource impacts. Although much of the emphasis is on project-level impacts, we recognize the major importance of macro-level government policies on the patterns of resource use. Such policies as pricing of fertilizer, pesticide, and water have major impacts, both good and bad, on resource use and the environment. Similarly, trade policies, foreign exchange rates, the use of taxes or subsidies all have far-reaching impacts. Nevertheless, the development, analysis, and funding of discrete projects is the major form of economic development in all parts of the world.

THE ANALYTICAL SEQUENCE

Projects are frequently identified and developed in a process known as the project cycle. Figure 1 illustrates the main components of the project cycle used by the Asian Development Bank, but similar patterns are used by the World Bank and the other major regional development banks (Rees, 1983). There are numerous places within the project cycle where environmental and resource concerns may be injected. It is crucial, however, that these concerns are taken into account early in the cycle, during the design stage. Only in this way can alternatives be considered before too much time and effort have been invested in one concept. The project designers must work in a multidisciplinary team to

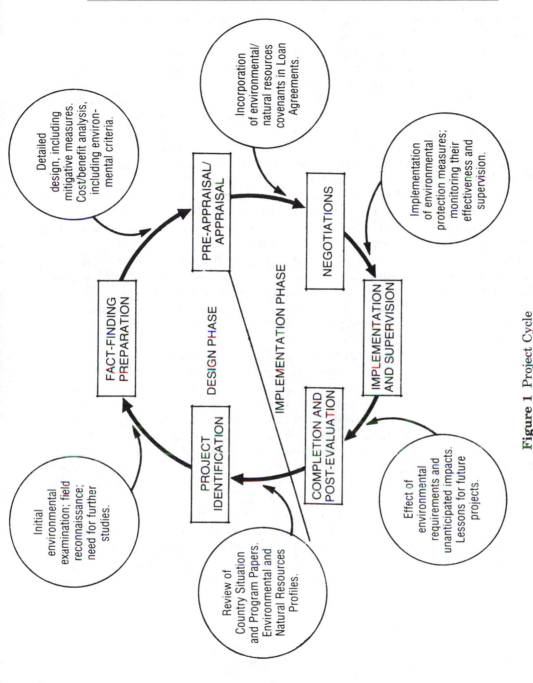

Figure 1 Project Cycle

Source: Asian Development Bank (1986), *Environmental Planning and Management*

design projects that consider a variety of goods and services – economic, social, environmental – at the same time.

The purpose of this book is to demonstrate the use of this analytical approach and to provide a range of techniques with which to determine the monetary values for the impacts of projects on the environment. The use of environmental assessment procedures, valuable at the early stages of project identification and priority setting are discussed in Chapter 2. The remaining chapters of Part One of the book deal with attributing monetary values to environmental impacts. The basic theoretical assumptions underlying our proposed approach to valuation are outlined in Chapter 3. The techniques themselves are presented in Chapters 4, 5, and 6; Chapter 4 focuses on techniques that are generally applicable to project analysis, while Chapters 5 and 6 concentrate on techniques which are more difficult to apply and whose use in project analysis has therefore been limited. Chapter 5 covers selectively applicable techniques that rely on the existence of surrogate markets or the use of survey-based approaches, a rapidly growing part of the valuation literature. Chapter 6 presents the use of other surrogate market techniques and discusses the use of mathematical models, natural resource accounting, and analysis of economy-wide impacts within the broader context of economic development and environmental management. The limitations of the economic measurement of environmental impacts are discussed in Chapter 7.

We have changed the placement of techniques based on experience with the application of different approaches in the field. Whereas in the previous Earthscan volume the contingent valuation approaches were placed in the 'potentially applicable' category, the positive experience with their use has led us to move them to the 'selectively applicable' category in Chapter 5. Similarly, many of the hedonic approaches, especially land and property value approaches, have been shifted to Chapter 6 with other less frequently applied techniques. These approaches, in spite of their theoretical elegance and academic appeal, are little used because their formidable data requirements are hard to fulfill in most developing countries. For similar reasons, the previous discussion on input-output analysis has not been included in this volume.

In the main text we briefly summarize each technique, discuss its applicability and illustrate its use. Case studies, which illustrate complete economic analyses as well as the use of individual techniques, are presented in Part Two.

CHAPTER 2

Assessing Impacts and Setting Priorities

Environmental and natural resource degradation can be caused by both too little and by too much economic development. Rural poverty and population pressure often combine to exert stress on productive natural systems: examples include the degradation of range and pasture lands as a consequence of overgrazing; loss of productive soils as a result of inappropriate agricultural practices such as cross-contour tilling on steeply sloping lands; and loss of productive forests as a consequence of shifting agriculture and fuelwood collection. Urban areas are also affected as population growth (including the influx of people from the countryside), urban sprawl and industrialization give rise to polluted water and air, congestion and increased incidence of disease. To the extent that these problems are the result of inadequate development, part of their solution lies in well-planned economic growth. On the other hand, economic growth itself frequently results in environmental and resource degradation. For example, many large infrastructure projects, including dams and reservoirs or urban road and service development, can require the resettlement of large numbers of people with accompanying social, environmental and economic problems.[1] Rapid economic growth often exacerbates urban pollution and congestion.

It is rarely the case, however, that a choice must be made between development and the environment (see the 1992 *World Development Report* for a careful presentation of this position); rather it is generally a question of understanding and incorporating cost-effective measures to restore, sustain and protect natural systems and maintain environmental quality at the earliest stages of planning. Environmental Assessment (EA)[2] is the information gathering and analytical process that helps to ensure environmentally sound development. The EA process attempts to identify potential problems so that the economic feasibility (and environmental impact) of alternative approaches can be assessed while there is still time to make changes. As such, EA complements the conventional package of engineering, socioeconomic, and financial and economic analyses and provides practical advice to planners.

---

1 Involuntary resettlement, although often considered as a social problem, is quickly becoming one of the major 'environmental' issues to be addressed in both urban and rural areas. Problems associated with resettlement have been a principal focus of the controversy over the Narmada dam projects in India, for example. For a discussion of the issues see Cernea, *Involuntary Resettlement in Development Projects*, 1988, and *The Urban Environment and Population Relocation*, 1993.

2 EA is sometimes referred to as Environmental Impact Assessment (EIA).

UNDERSTANDING ENVIRONMENTAL ASSESSMENT

Economic valuation of environmental impacts relies on careful identification and measurement of the biophysical changes produced by a project or alternative project designs. The systematic methodologies of EA are designed to produce this information.[3] Natural systems are holistic and interconnected.[4] Consequently, it is essential from the very beginning of the planning process to determine carefully which natural systems will be affected. A 'scoping process' may be used to set appropriate boundaries – the geographical limits, time horizon, and the range of issues, actions, interrelationships, alternatives and impacts that need to be considered. When appropriate, natural boundaries should be used: for example, the watershed is often a good planning and management unit.

Three criteria for identifying significant impacts on the environment were suggested in the World Conservation Strategy.[5] The first concerns the *length of time and geographic area* over which the effect will be felt. This criterion would include an assessment of the numbers of people affected, how much of a particular resource would be degraded, eliminated or – depending on what action is taken – conserved. The second criterion is that of *urgency*. It is important to establish just how quickly a natural system might deteriorate and how much time is available for its stabilization or enhancement. Finally, it is important to assess the *degree of irreversible damage* to communities of plants and animals, to life-support systems, and to soil and water.

There are several other criteria which are relevant to this impact identification process. One important consideration is the nature of the effects for example, on human health, or productivity, or changes in the structure and function of a natural system. The assessment should also take into account the cumulative and synergistic effects of the various components of the project and other projects.[6] The effects of individual projects or of their component parts may be small, but cumulatively they may become considerable, even far greater than could be predicted by the sum of their individual effects.

---

3 See, for example, the World Bank's *Environmental Assessment Sourcebook*, that includes separate volumes on policies, procedures and cross-sectoral issues (Volume 1), sectoral guidelines (Volume 2), and guidelines for environmental assessment of energy and industry projects (Volume 3). For a more detailed, sector-specific approach to EA, see *How to Assess Environmental Impacts on Tropical Islands and Ecosystems*, by Richard A. Carpenter and James E. Maragos, prepared under the auspices of the Asian Development Bank, Manila, in 1989.
4 A natural system, or ecosystem, is a dynamic arrangement of plants and animals with their surroundings of soil, air, water, nutrients and energy. For example, lakes, rainforests, mangrove forests, and grasslands are ecosystems; so are rice paddies, oil palm plantations, fish ponds, pastures and home gardens. As the latter are all modified by human beings, they are called 'managed systems' and are often less complex than undisturbed environments.
5 International Union for the Conservation of Nature and Natural Resources (IUCN), 1980: *World Conservation Strategy* (Geneva).
6 Regional master plans examine the ecosystem linkages among various projects and

The next step is to quantify, as far as possible, all the important biophysical and socioeconomic changes that are likely to result from the project. These might include, for example, the intrusion of salinity into groundwater; price changes induced by new energy policies, programmes and projects; the impacts on fisheries' productivity of disposal of industrial effluent; deforestation as a result of building new highways, and so on. When such effects cannot be quantified, they should at least be noted qualitatively and preserved in the analysis.

Project impacts cannot be meaningfully quantified without a basis for comparison, that is, likely conditions in the absence of the project. This baseline information should include quality of the air and water supplies, the fertility of the soil, and condition of habitats. These data on conditions and trends make possible the assessment of those changes produced specifically by the development project as compared to any natural changes which might occur at the project site. These are the 'with' and 'without' project scenarios used in economic analysis.

The objective of environmental assessment is to predict alternative future states of resources and environments depending on the project design chosen (including the option of no development at all – the 'without project' baseline condition). These biophysical changes are then assessed for plausible impacts on human health and welfare, natural resource productivity and ecosystem integrity by asking the questions 'who cares?', and 'why?' For example, a pulp and paper mill may discharge wastes that reduce the amount of dissolved oxygen in the receiving river. One likely impact is that fish would be killed as a result of oxygen deprivation. The assessment then proceeds to generate corrective actions such as installation of an oxidation pond to treat the waste water before it enters the river. Options are later analysed economically to determine if the benefits exceed the costs.

Industrial wastes may make water unsuitable for livestock, cutting mangroves for charcoal may ruin fish spawning grounds and thus reduce catches, or particulate emissions from a power plant may cause an increased incidence of respiratory diseases. Some changes have more indirect impacts on human welfare, for example, conversion of forests to agricultural land may endanger wild species and reduce genetic diversity. Understanding the physical system and potential health and resource impacts sets the stage for economic valuation and expanded benefit-cost analysis – the value of the lost catch of fish, the cost of an oxidation pond or other mitigative measures, the costs of ill-health or death. (Table 1 illustrates typical economic damages from environmental impacts.). The valuation of these types of impact is the focus of the rest of this book.

---

sectors. In Asia, the Asian Development Bank has sponsored the development of a series of plans for the Han River Basin, Korea; Palawan, The Philippines; and Songkhla Lake Basin in Thailand, among others. At the national level, many governments around the world are developing national environmental action plans (NEAPs); these are discussed later in this chapter.

Table 1 Examples of Economic Damages from Environmental Impacts

Impact	Damages – Health, Productivity, Aesthetics
Pollution	
Air	
Respiratory illness	Lost work days, medical expense
Vegetation effects	Lower crop yields
Soiling of materials	Cleaning costs, more frequent painting
Aesthetic degradation	Lowered visibility, odours leading to devalued property
Water	
Pathogenic organisms or toxic materials in drinking water	Lost work days, medical expenses, expenses of alternative supply
Fisheries effects	Lowered catch
Affects water-contact recreation	Loss of tourism revenues
Noise	Lowered property value
Ecosystem degradation	
Forest lands	
Harvesting effects	Sedimentation - shortened life of hydroelectric reservoirs
	Lowered water quality
Monoculture plantations	Loss of services from intact diverse forest (e.g. predators of pest insects)
	Loss of biodiversity
Wetlands	
Filling and dredging	Greater flood damage, loss of unique habitat
Coral reefs	
Toxics or sediment effects	Reduced fishery production
	Loss of recreation values, loss of biodiversity
Ground water	
Contamination	Cost of alternative supply
Lowered water table	Subsidence of land, structural damage

Environmental assessment identifies potential problems and opportunities and is thus an essential part of the project cycle. By itself, however, it is insufficient for decision making. As mentioned earlier, the economic and financial analysis helps the planner to decide among possible options so as to eliminate or reduce negative environmental effects in a cost-effective manner. Balancing costs and benefits, private and public considerations, is where difficult decisions have to be made. In some cases, the result of the ecological and economic analysis is to abandon the proposed project; most times, however, a compromise is possible whereby development proceeds, but in a more environmentally sound manner.

EXAMPLES OF ASSESSING IMPACTS

EA of a multipurpose dam

Consider a plan to build a multipurpose dam. Conventional analysis would concentrate on the dam, the reservoir, the irrigated land and the production of electricity. The benefits of the dam would be thoroughly evaluated: power, water storage, flood control, fisheries, recreation and irrigation. The costs would be those of construction, operation and maintenance together with attention to resettling those people to be moved from the area to be inundated (see Figure 2).

However, the natural boundary of the project is the entire river basin and this should, whenever appropriate, be reflected in the analysis. The displaced people may move in a number of directions: to the steeper lands, to the now protected flood plain, or to the new lake shore. If the uplands already support people engaged in activities like logging, tree-crop cultivation and shifting agriculture, the arrival of the displaced lowlanders may produce the sort of pressure on resources that will lead to shorter fallow periods, farming of marginal lands and the penetration, by means of logging roads, of steeper and yet more erodible areas.

An increase in soil erosion is thus virtually certain. Some of the resulting sediment will be carried downstream to the new reservoir, where it can cause damage by abrasion to hydroelectric turbine blades, and turbidity which may interfere with fish spawning. Nutrients washed out of the uplands may fertilize the growth of aquatic weeds which, as they die and decompose, reduce the dissolved oxygen in the water and thereby adversely affect fish production. Ultimately the sediment displaces the water in the reservoir, directly decreasing its storage capacity and reducing the useful life of the generating facility.

A reduction in the storage capacity of the reservoir due to sedimentation means that less storm water can be intercepted by the dam. In periods of heavy rain the spillways must be opened, thus negating the promise of flood protection which originally attracted residents and investment to the flood plain.

Irrigation water is delivered to fields under intensive agriculture, which

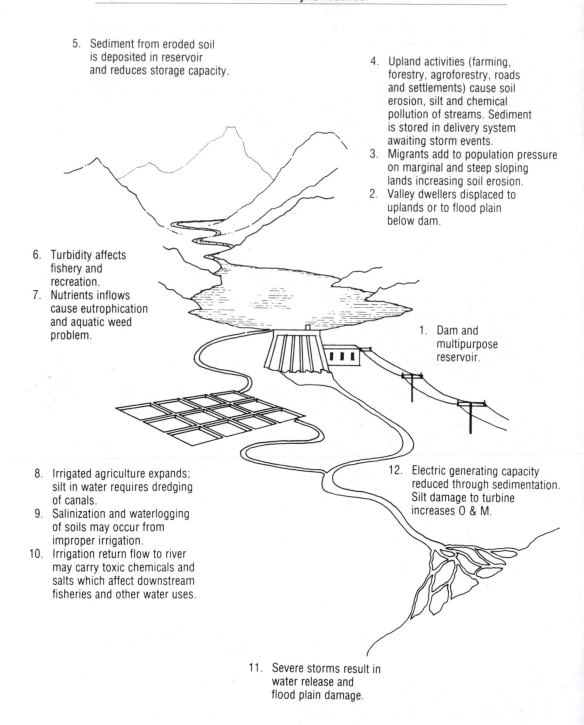

5. Sediment from eroded soil is deposited in reservoir and reduces storage capacity.

4. Upland activities (farming, forestry, agroforestry, roads and settlements) cause soil erosion, silt and chemical pollution of streams. Sediment is stored in delivery system awaiting storm events.

3. Migrants add to population pressure on marginal and steep sloping lands increasing soil erosion.

2. Valley dwellers displaced to uplands or to flood plain below dam.

6. Turbidity affects fishery and recreation.

7. Nutrients inflows cause eutrophication and aquatic weed problem.

1. Dam and multipurpose reservoir.

8. Irrigated agriculture expands; silt in water requires dredging of canals.

9. Salinization and waterlogging of soils may occur from improper irrigation.

10. Irrigation return flow to river may carry toxic chemicals and salts which affect downstream fisheries and other water uses.

12. Electric generating capacity reduced through sedimentation. Silt damage to turbine increases O & M.

11. Severe storms result in water release and flood plain damage.

Figure 2 Multipurpose Dam Project: Loss of Economic Development Opportunities

14

includes the use of fertilizers and chemical pesticides. The runoff and irrigation return flow to the lower river basin may be substantially contaminated and thus affect fisheries and plant growth in the estuary and delta regions, with a consequent loss of income for the local communities.

The numbers of migratory fish may be reduced because the dam prevents them from moving upstream to spawn. Downstream fisheries may also be affected by changes in the water temperature from the impoundment of the river. In addition, the changes in nutrient and sediment delivery as a result of the alteration in the hydrologic regime may adversely affect coastal mangrove forests and marine fisheries.

In fact, as seen in Table 2, the environmental effects of dams and their economic impacts (sometimes benefits, more often costs) are numerous and can be divided into two broad categories: the effect of the upstream environment on the dam (largely through soil erosion and deposition), and the more numerous effects of dams on the surrounding and downstream environment and its human impact via resettlement. Negative environmental effects reduce both the total economic benefits from the dam, and the useful life of the reservoir. Most of these effects can be expressed in monetary terms, and representative valuations techniques that can be used to estimate these values are given in the last column of Table 2. These techniques are explained in later chapters.

Such effects have already occurred in numerous multipurpose dam projects. For example, in power projects in both Fiji and Western Samoa service roads built for transmission equipment opened up formerly inaccessible forest and hence made possible both poaching and deforestation. Changes have also been documented in hydrological patterns, soil erosion, siltation and flooding, with consequent losses in forestry, agricultural land, and fisheries. A reduction in the useful life of downstream hydropower facilities, loss of property and increased incidence of disease have also been observed.

In a hydropower project in Papua New Guinea, the river-driven generator was built in a catchment area already under heavy pressure from other development projects which had changed the area's hydrological patterns and increased soil erosion rates. As a result there have been instances of storm events causing extreme river flows which brought heavy loads of silt which, in turn, have affected the operation of the power station. In this case neither the project's design nor the estimates of its useful life took into account the surrounding environmental conditions which, although not a consequence of the project, considerably affected its operation. It is increasingly possible to estimate the economic costs of these changes: examples of such analysis for soil erosion in Indonesia and China (Magrath and Arens, 1989; Magrath, 1992) are reported on in later chapters.

Similar problems have been reported with major dam projects in Latin America (for example, loss of genetic diversity, upper watershed encroachment and increased soil erosion) and Africa (for example, health problems associated with the reservoir of the Aswan dam project in Egypt or involuntary resettlement issues in many countries).

In other projects considerable progress has been made in alleviating these

15

Table 2 Selected Environmental Effects and their Economic Impacts

Environmental Effect	Economic Impact	Benefit (B) Cost (C)	Representative Valuation Technique
Environment on dams			
Soil erosion – upstream, sedimentation in reservoir	Reduced reservoir capacity, change in capacity, change in water quality, decrease in power.	B, C	Change in production, preventive expenditures, replacement costs.
Dams on the environment			
Chemical water quality – changes in reservoir and downstream	Increased/reduced treatment cost, reduced fish catch, loss of production.	B, C	Preventive expenditures, changes in production.
Reduction in silt load, downstream	Loss of fertilizer, reduced siltation of canals, better water control.	B, C	Replacement costs, preventive expenditures avoided.
Water temperature changes (drop)	Reduction of crop yields (esp. rice).	C	Changes in production.
Health – water related diseases (humans and animals)	Sickness, hospital care, death; decreased meat and milk production.	B, C	Cost of illness.
Fishery – impacts on fish irrigation, spawning	Both loss and increase in fish production.	B, C	Changes in production, preventive expenditures.
Recreation – in the reservoir or river	Value of recreation opportunities gained or lost, tourism.	B, C	Travel cost approach, property value approach.
Wildlife and biodiversity	Creation or loss of species, habitat and genetic resources.	B, C	Opportunity cost approach, tourism values lost, replacement costs.
Involuntary resettlement	Cost of new infra-structure, social costs.	B, C	Replacement cost approach, 'social costs', relocation costs.

Table 2 *cont.*

Discharge variations, excessive diurnal variation	Disturbs flora and fauna, human use, drownings, recession agriculture.	C	Relocation costs, changes in production.
Food attenuation	Reduces after flood cultivation; reduces flood damage.	B, C	Changes in production, flood damages avoided.

Source: Dixon, Talbot and Le Moigne (1989)

types of adverse effect. The Kirindi Oya Irrigation and Settlement Project in Sri Lanka, for example, was located in a watershed that was in good condition. To ensure that the watershed would not deteriorate and adversely affect the project, a watershed management covenant was written into the loan agreement. In phase two of the project, land-use studies and the designation of a protected area around the reservoir will help to ensure that water continues to be available.

Irrigated agriculture: soil salinization and effects on human health

Soil salinity, which is often caused by poorly designed or mismanaged irrigation schemes, has undermined, to varying degrees, the productivity of much irrigated land. Excessive irrigation, inadequate drainage, or inadequate quantities of water for effective flushing are the principal causes of soil salinization.

A systematic analysis of the sources of salt within an area being developed, and of ways of removing it, will often permit the prevention of salinization and thus avoid costly rehabilitation programmes later. The salt balance equation is illustrated pictorially in Figure 3. The information needed in order to calculate the net change in salt content is not difficult to obtain. Once the factors are known, salinization may usually be reduced or prevented altogether by improving the design and management of irrigation systems to reduce salt inflows or increase salt outflows. The costs of such measures can then be compared to the benefits of greater agricultural production on salt-free soil and the avoided costs of rehabilitation at a later date.

Other unintentional and unforeseen consequences of irrigation projects include the effects on human health. Although there are undeniable public benefits from making available increased supplies of water, there can also be negative impacts. The construction of water impoundments for irrigation and for other purposes in areas with endemic water-related diseases (for example malaria or schistosomiasis) has increased levels of infection and created new areas of transmission. Physical measures, such as drainage, flow modification, the lining of irrigation canals, and the use of molluscicides and insecticides, can be taken to render the habitat less suitable for disease vectors.

17

Figure 3 The Salt Balance

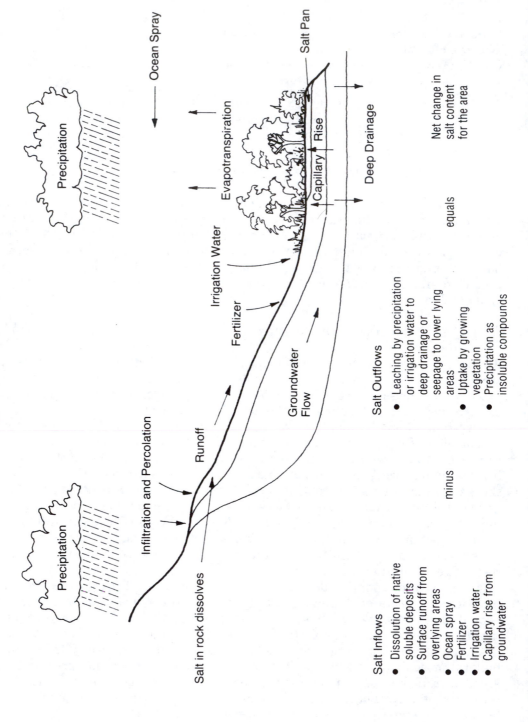

Salt Inflows

- Dissolution of native soluble deposits
- Surface runoff from overlying areas
- Ocean spray
- Fertilizer
- Irrigation water
- Capillary rise from groundwater

minus

Salt Outflows

- Leaching by precipitation or irrigation water to deep drainage or seepage to lower lying areas
- Uptake by growing vegetation
- Precipitation as insoluble compounds

equals

Net change in salt content for the area

Urban and industrial development projects in coastal zones

Coastal zones support a number of land uses including agriculture, fisheries and settlements, and provide a base for transport and trade. As both urban and industrial uses of coastal zones increase, it is becoming clear that many of these uses are incompatible.

Environmental impacts in coastal zones occur during both the construction and operation phases of economic development projects. Typical construction activities include earthmoving, dredging and filling. Direct impacts are destruction of shoreline habitat for water birds and spawning grounds for fish. Indirect impacts, perhaps somewhat removed from the construction site, are the result of soil erosion and suspension of solid materials that are then deposited as sediment or cause turbidity in coastal waters. Sedentary shellfish may be smothered, coral reefs that serve fisheries may be damaged and primary productivity may decrease as a result of reduced light penetration.

During the operation phase of coastal projects, water pollution from waste discharge may occur. Heavy industry, industrial parks, electric power plants, and petroleum refineries are typical coastal zone installations and may release oil and grease, toxic metal compounds, and industrial sewage into the coastal environment. Even if waste treatment facilities are installed, there is a risk of accidental release of pollution.

Coastal ecosystems that are important and subject to adverse impacts include coral reefs, seagrass beds, mangrove and other wetlands, estuaries and lagoons. These waters are the most productive of all marine areas. Their role goes beyond merely providing a location for fishing. Many species of fish and crustaceans are dependent on near-shore waters during at least part of their life cycle. Mangrove swamps and inshore waters, for example, provide nursery areas and breeding grounds for many species which are commercially exploited in deeper waters later in their lives.

Fish, as well as being an important export product, are a vital source of protein in most developing countries. The artisanal fisheries and small-scale fish-processing are also important sources of income in many coastal areas. Any reduction in the productivity of fisheries therefore has considerable socio-economic consequences that need to be taken into account.

Air pollution from industrial facilities

Industrial air pollution can seriously affect people as well as crops, livestock and materials. Pollution damage may occur at some distance from the source because its distribution depends on the vagaries of wind and terrain. Since emission controls are usually more costly to install after the initial design and construction of an industrial facility, it is important that control options be evaluated during the early stages of project planning and design.

One valuable tool for estimating the effects of emissions from facilities such as coal-fired power stations or fertilizer manufacturing plants is the definition of an air quality control region (AQCR). The region's boundaries are set either

19

by measuring ambient conditions at a number of distances and directions from an existing source of pollution or by producing models which predict the dispersal of pollution from some future source, taking into account terrain, wind, temperature and plume characteristics.

Population centres, transportation networks, topographical features and sensitive areas are all identified in the AQCR. The patterns of pollution generation and distribution are calculated by the model for each major pollutant, based on assumptions about the source of pollution and the location of affected populations or property. Prevailing wind direction and speed, land forms, turbulence and atmospheric stability patterns, chemical changes of the pollutants during transport, removal mechanisms such as settling or rainfall, and receptor response are all considered. Local governments are frequently responsible for setting the boundaries of the AQCRs and for determining emissions limits. Figure 4 illustrates an AQCR for the Batu Caves area, near Kuala Lumpur, Malaysia; in this case the pollutant being considered is dust created by local quarrying operations that adversely affects surrounding human and animal populations, a temple and a public park. The information on dust concentrations can then be linked to health and other impacts to evaluate the 'external' costs created by the quarrying operation.

The rapidly growing field of urban air pollution analysis in developing countries relies on similar data on pollution emissions, ambient concentration levels, and populations exposed in order to develop physical (and economic) estimates of health impacts. Whether pollution is from fixed sources such as industries and power plants, or mobile sources such as automobiles and buses, data on total pollution generated, its sources, and ambient levels is essential to developing cost-effective and efficient policy responses.[7]

SETTING PRIORITIES

While assessing and mitigating negative impacts of development projects is important, project-level actions are not sufficient to reduce all environmental problems. The underlying causes of many environmental problems are not directly related to specific projects, but rather stem from policy and market failures.[8] In these cases government action is required to correct these failures

---

7 For an example of the analytical approach to urban air pollution see Ostro (1992), Eskeland (1992, 1994a, b, c) and the 1992 *World Development Report*. Suspended particulates (also referred to as TSP and 'dust'), particularly the fine particles referred to as PM10, have been identified as one of the major public health problems associated with urban air pollution. In Latin America, for example, a number of cities where air pollution is particularly severe, including Mexico City and Santiago, Chile, are making large investments to address the particulate problem.

8 *Market failures* refer to the inability of market prices, under certain conditions, to reflect accurately the value of environmental goods or services. For example, land markets fail to capture the value of the wide variety of goods and services provided by mangrove areas. This is because property rights to these areas are ill-defined; subsistence uses, rather than

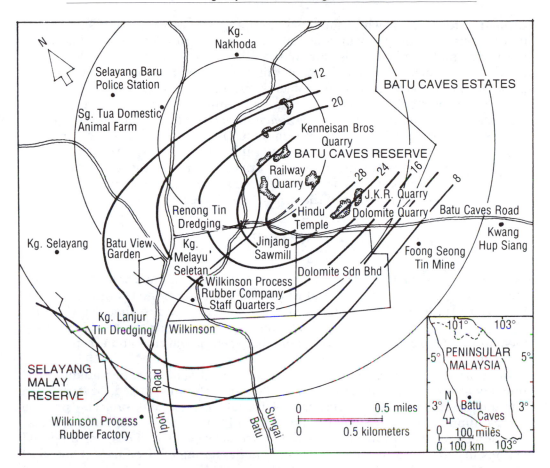

Figure 4 Dust Fall Concentration Near Batu Caves, Kuala Lumpur, Malaysia, 1973–5 (in metric tons/km²/month)
Source: R.A. Carpenter (ed.), *Natural Systems for Development: What Planners Need to Know* (New York: Macmillan, 1983).

commercial exploitation, predominate for extracted products such as fuel wood, tannin and fish, and benefits from the in situ ecological and shoreline protection services provided by mangroves accrue to a large and widely dispersed group (see Hamilton, Dixon and Miller, 1989, and Dixon and Lal, 1994, for details on the economics of mangrove and other wetland systems). Similarly, an industry that emits damaging air or water pollution has no incentive to reduce those emissions if pricing or regulations do not force it to internalize the values of the external damages created (economic externalities). *Policy failures* refer to instances when government policies have unintended, perverse side effects or cause resource-use behaviour inappropriate from a societal perspective. For example, governments often subsidize the use of resources including water, energy, and key agricultural inputs such as pesticides and fertilizers, encouraging overuse of these resources, resulting in environmental degradation (at substantial financial cost to the national treasury).

through interventions which may include changes in property rights and other institutions governing resource use; policy instruments such as market-based incentives and regulatory measures; and direct public investments. Valuation techniques, which are the subject of this book, are essential to establishing priorities among environmental problems and possible interventions.

Many governments, especially in the environmentally more aware post-Rio world, are developing *national environmental action plans* (sometimes referred to as NEAPs) to identify priority areas for investment and policy change. In other cases the analysis may be done at the sectoral level to identify, for instance, what are the priority investments in urban areas, or in the agricultural sector. Planning for integrated area or special area management, such as coastal zone planning, is another example of the priority setting process.[9]

SUMMARY

These examples illustrate the importance and utility of environmental assessment as an essential component of project design and its importance in setting priorities. At the project level, without EA the chances are that externalities will not be recognized in sufficient time to take the least costly counter-measures, nor to calculate the trade-offs between prevention and acceptance of damage.

Environmental assessment is now well developed to identify and quantify the impacts of projects on the environment. These techniques, used together with an understanding of the ecological setting of development projects, provide critical inputs into the economic analysis of alternatives. In this way the social economic analysis can include a wider range of benefits and costs of proposed actions in order to determine if the benefits (including environmental benefits) exceed the costs (including environmental costs.) Similarly, EA plays a critical role in establishing regional, sectoral and national priorities. This information, in turn, helps governments develop better environmental and resource management policies.

Priority setting builds on the results of environmental assessment and economic analysis and is a simple recognition that the problems to be addressed are numerous and the resources, both financial as well as human/institutional, are limited. It is therefore essential to identify which environmental problems are the most severe and require the most urgent attention, and which interventions are the most effective and economically efficient. The criteria applied to determine priorities will vary depending on the issue addressed. Economic values are useful for identifying priorities when environmental problems result in resource productivity effects or affect human health. Economic analysis is poor, however, for assessing priorities in other areas such as the value of

---

9 For an application of both ecological and economic principles to coastal area management see *Integrative Framework and Methods for Coastal Area Management*, Chua and Scura, eds., 1992. Manila: ICLARM.

biodiversity or cultural factors. Still, recent advances in methodology mean that economic analysis and environmental assessment can play a role in even these difficult valuation areas, as will be discussed later.

CHAPTER 3

Economic Measurement of Environmental Impacts – Theoretical Basis and Practical Applications

The valuation methods introduced in this chapter have broad application. However, a project focus is adopted here for ease of presentation. Both economic and financial analyses are commonly employed in project evaluation. Whereas financial analyses focus primarily on market prices and cash flows, economic analyses should include the total economic value of the effects that development projects have on the environment, whether or not they are reflected in the marketplace.[1]

NEOCLASSICAL WELFARE ECONOMICS

It is useful to review the theoretical basis of economic, as opposed to financial, analysis. Neoclassical welfare economics, as developed by Pigou (1920) and Hicks (1939) among others, is concerned with the total welfare of society and evaluates alternative projects or actions on the basis of changes in social welfare. A number of important assumptions are implicit in this approach. These include:

- societal welfare is the sum of individual welfare;
- individual welfare can be measured (measurement was originally conceived in terms of units of utility called 'utiles' and, more conveniently, as reflected in the prices paid for goods and services); and
- individuals maximize their welfare by choosing that combination of goods, services and savings that yields the largest possible sum of total utility given their income constraints.

Of particular importance when valuing environmental effects subject to an income constraint are the following assumptions:

- Utility and welfare can be obtained from goods and services even if they are

---

1 For a full discussion of the roles of and the distinctions between economic and financial analysis, see Dixon and Hufschmidt (1986) *Economic Valuation Techniques for the Environment*, Chapter 2. Total economic value (TEV) is a relatively new concept that is based on the idea that the TEV of any good or service is composed of direct and indirect use values as well as less tangible non-use values, such as option and existence values. While a wide range of methods can be used to make monetary estimates of use values, non-use values are usually estimated using survey-based techniques. For a more comprehensive discussion of TEV see Pearce and Turner, 1990, and Pearce and Warford, 1993.

provided free or at minimum cost. The difference between the amount paid for a good or service, and the total utility enjoyed, is called 'consumer's surplus' or CS.[2] Total utility for any good is the combination of the amount paid for the good plus any consumer's surplus. Graphically, this relationship can be derived from total utility and marginal utility curves and the related, easily observed, individual demand curve (graphs 1, 2, and 3, respectively, in Figure 5). As illustrated in the third graph in Figure 5, the area of consumer's surplus for good X is area PAB when the price is at P and the individual purchases quantity Y. If good X were free (price = 0), the entire area OAC would be consumer's surplus and would measure the benefit to the individual from consuming good X. Since many environmental goods and services have low or zero prices, the CS component in total utility of those goods and services may be very large. In turn, if these 'free' environmental goods and services are lost, the loss of welfare (CS) is large. In the Bonaire case study in Part Two, an estimate was made of the CS of visiting recreational divers as part of a survey of their willingness to pay user fees. The results indicated that the CS was over $500,000 per year, and that the proposed (and later introduced) user fee captured only about a third of the total.

- Initially, we assume that the marginal utility of income is the same for all individuals. This means that all individuals get the same amount of increased utility from an additional dollar of income. This is obviously a very strong assumption and one that has to be relaxed in many situations. The discussion of the impact of development projects on income distribution mentioned in Chapter 1 is part of this issue. The assumption of a common marginal utility of income allows aggregation across individuals and the use of prices observed in one part of the economy to place values on unpriced goods and services that may occur elsewhere. To aggregate individual demand curves into market demand curves, we need either no change in income distribution or an income elasticity of demand which is the same for individuals.

- In reality, the marginal utility of income usually decreases as income increases. That is, the utility from an extra dollar's income for a rich person is less than that for a poorer individual. In practice we cannot compare utility across individuals, so for simplification we assume a constant marginal utility of income. One way to avoid the implications of this assumption is the use of 'weights'. This topic will be discussed further in Chapter 7.

- Total individual welfare (and, in turn, societal welfare) is equal to the sum of expenditures and consumer's surplus. Both of these components are appropriate indicators of welfare and should be measured and included in the analysis.

- Using 'willingness to pay' measures in benefit-cost analysis implies two

---

2 CS can be measured in two ways: compensating variation (CV) and equivalent variation (EV). These measures are discussed in Chapter 5.

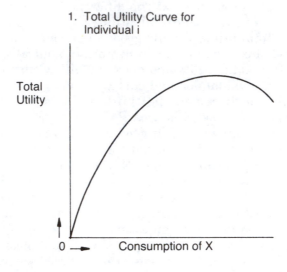

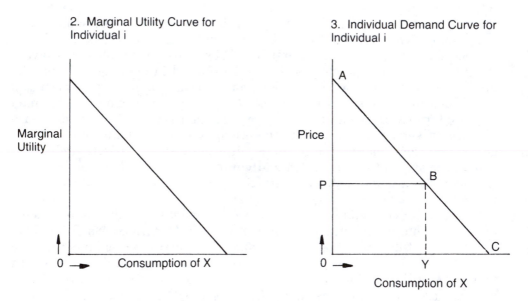

Figure 5 Total and Marginal Utility Curves and Individual Demand Curve
for Good X

value judgements: individual preferences count; and individual preferences
should be weighted by some factor correlated with income, either the status
quo or by some other criterion.

The implications of the previous assumptions have frequently been overlooked.
Project analyses have usually focused on the easily measured direct benefits
and costs (also used in financial analyses) and often ignore the economic

externalities – some of which may be measured directly by using market prices, but many of which consist of losses (or, more rarely, gains) of consumer's surplus.

The identification and inclusion of economic externalities is at the basis of much of environmental economics. As noted previously, for a proper B/CA, the analyst must take into account both the location of goods and services and their valuation. This dichotomy between location and valuation is illustrated in Figure 6; the figure was developed for the specific case of mangroves, but can be used to analyse most environmental problems. This matrix defines the location of goods and services on one axis (on-site and off-site) and the valuation problem on the other axis (whether or not market prices are available). Traditional analyses of mangroves tended to focus on those resources included in Quadrant 1 – those goods and services that are found on-site and are marketed, e.g. mangrove poles or crabs. Some of the Quadrant 2 resources – those found off-site (outside of the mangrove in adjacent waters) but with market prices – are also included, especially in more recent evaluations. The explicit valuation and inclusion in the analysis of fish or shellfish that depend on the mangrove for part of their life cycle but are caught in adjacent waters is an excellent example.

The resources in the last two quadrants are usually largely ignored.

		Location of Goods and Services	
		On-site	*Off-site*
Valuation of Goods and Services	*Marketed*	**1** Usually included in an economic analysis (e.g. poles, charcoal woodchips, mangrove crabs)	**2** May be included (e.g. fish or shellfish caught in adjacent waters)
	Nonmarketed	**3** Seldom included (e.g. medicinal uses of mangrove, domestic fuelwood, food in times of famine, nursery area for juvenile fish, feeding ground for estuarine fish and shrimp, viewing and studying wildlife)	**4** Usually ignored (e.g. nutrient flows to estuaries, buffer to storm damage)

Figure 6 Relation Between Location and Valuation of Environmental Goods
and Services
Source: Hamilton and Snedaker, eds. (1984).

Quadrant 3 includes the important goods and services found in the mangrove, some of which may be collected and used by local communities, that do not enter into the market (for example, medicines, other minor forest products, fish 'nursery' values). Recreational uses of mangrove may also fall into this quadrant. The fourth quadrant, off-site and nonmarketed goods and services, includes such difficult to measure and value impacts as nutrient flows to estuaries and the storm surge benefits that mangroves provide to coastal areas. The problems inherent in the identification and monetization of such effects pose a major valuation challenge for those concerned with more correctly identifying the total contribution of mangrove ecosystems to social welfare.

The matrix in Figure 6 serves as a useful checklist for the analyst who is investigating the economic value of an environmental resource (for example, a mangrove, a fishery, a farming system), or the impacts of some environmental problem (for example, pollution of air or water). It is clear that the environmental assessment process is crucial to developing the matrix (a theme developed in Chapter 2) and that the economist must work with natural and social scientists to identify, quantify and value the varied goods and services produced by a natural ecosystem or identify the impacts of some pollutants.

Since a proper economic analysis of a project or activity should include all benefits and costs, on-site as well as off-site, the matrix in Figure 6 helps organize information and identify those areas where additional work is needed, especially when attempting to place monetary values on certain benefits and costs. Accordingly, this book focuses on techniques for placing monetary values on environmental externalities so that a comprehensive social welfare analysis may be undertaken.

PRACTICAL APPLICATIONS

To conduct the expanded economic analysis advocated here, the analyst has to accept both the implications derived from welfare economics and the need for multidisciplinary work. It would be unusual for any one person to have the necessary breadth of knowledge to assess properly both the 'economic' and 'environmental' effects of any given project. The role of the environmental specialist in helping to identify these effects was discussed in Chapter 2. This book will not discuss this topic further, but the importance of multidisciplinary work cannot be overstated.

The hardest task for the economist or project analyst is to decide which of the environmental and resource impacts to include and then how to quantify and monetize them. There is no 'cookbook' answer, yet the analysis should not be done *ad hoc*. Our approach is one which requires the analyst to think through each problem, identify important impacts, make selections, and make all assumptions explicit. Some general guidelines that should be of help in setting up the analysis follow:

* *Start simply with the most obvious, most easily valued environmental impacts*. This may mean looking for impacts on the environment resulting in changes in productivity that can be valued using market prices. A land

development project, for example, may create soil erosion and sedimentation that disrupt a traditional downstream fishery or some agricultural activity. The net change in fish or crop production can be identified and valued. The change in the quantity and quality of water flowing downstream and its effect on the coastal mangroves or on offshore coral reefs is a secondary effect. Secondary effects may be very important, both ecologically and economically, but the analyst would do best to start with the fishery or the agricultural activity. In short, start with the effects that have directly measurable productivity changes that can be valued by market prices.

- There is a *useful symmetry in benefits and costs*: a benefit forgone is a cost, while a cost avoided is a benefit. The analyst should always look at both the benefit and cost sides of any action and approach valuation in the most feasible and cost-effective way. The value of improved industrial waste water treatment could be approached from both the direct cost side (largely capital and operation, maintenance and replacement costs) or the 'costs avoided' side – the benefits of reduced needs for downstream water purification expenditures or reduced morbidity. The distinction between benefits (costs avoided) and costs is the reference point from which changes are measured. If a decision is made to take some action (for example, pollution control) even though the benefits are not measured, the approach is a form of cost-effectiveness analysis which is discussed in Chapter 4.

- The economic analysis itself should be done in a *with-and-without-project framework*. It is important that only additional or incremental benefits and costs due to implementation of the project be considered. Sunk costs – costs already spent directly or indirectly on the project – should not be included. A series of alternative 'with-project' options (for example, of varying scale or with mitigating measures) may need to be considered. The El Nido study in Palawan discussed in Chapter 4 is a good example of a with-and-without-project analysis. In this case the 'without project' scenario was a continuation of present logging practices, and the 'with project' scenario included a logging ban.

- *All assumptions should be stated explicitly*. This is particularly important in valuing effects on the environment because other analysts may wish to challenge the results or make comparisons with other areas and can do so only if the assumptions and the data are clearly presented.

- When market prices cannot be used directly, it may be possible to use them indirectly by means of *surrogate-market techniques*. In these approaches, the market prices of substitute or complementary goods are used to value an unpriced environmental good or service. For example, the value of an unpriced environmental amenity, such as clean air, may be a factor in the price of marketable assets, such as housing or land. Analysis of the price differentials of such assets in areas of varying air quality may give an indication of an implicit price for the unpriced environmental amenity.

Table 3 presents a menu of valuation techniques, examples of the types of effects valued, and the underlying basis for the valuation. For example, the cost-of-illness approach can be used to value the health impacts of air pollution; the approach is based on underlying damage functions which related the degree

Table 3 Menu of Valuation Methods

Valuation Method	Effects Valued	Underlying Basis for Valuation
Objective Valuation Approaches		
1 Changes in productivity	Productivity	Technical/physical (behaviour assumed)
2 Cost of illness	Health (morbidity)	Technical/physical (behaviour assumed)
3 Human capital	Health (mortality)	Technical/physical (behaviour assumed)
4 Replacement/ restoration costs	Capital assets, natural resource assets	Technical/physical (behaviour assumed)
Subjective Valuation Approaches		
1 Preventive/mitigative expenditures	Health, productivity, capital assets, natural resource assets	Behavioural (revealed)
2 Hedonic approaches		
Property/land value	Environmental quality, productivity	Behavioural (revealed)
Wage differential	Health	Behavioural (revealed)
3 Travel cost	Natural resource assets	Behavioural (revealed)
4 Contingent valuation	Health, natural resource assets	Behavioural (expressed)

of physical health impact (e.g. incidence of respiratory disease) to the level of pollution. Among the hedonic approaches, the travel cost approach is used to measure consumer's surplus of visitors to recreational sites and parks. The approach used observed information on travel costs to derive a demand equation and thereby estimate CS.

Two distinct sets of approaches can be distinguished in Table 3. The first set are the *objective valuation approaches* (OVA) that are based on physical relationships that formally describe cause and effect relationships and provide objective measures of damage resulting from various causes. Included in this set of techniques are the changes-in-productivity, cost-of-illness, opportunity-cost, and replacement-cost approaches discussed in Chapter 4.

The OVA use 'damage functions' which relate the level of offending activity (for example, the level and type of air pollutants) to the degree of physical damage to a natural or man-made asset (for example, soiling of buildings), or to the degree of health impact (for example, incidence of respiratory disease). Data for the development of damage functions come from two sources: uncontrolled field studies, which are referred to as epidemiological studies in the case of health impacts, and controlled experimental trials.

Damage functions for ecological processes and natural resources such as forest and fisheries can be extremely complex and are often highly speculative with regard to magnitude and timing of impacts. For man-made assets, such as buildings, and natural resource assets, such as agriculture crops, damage functions, while less complex and uncertain, are often fairly site-, process- and crop-specific. However, the relationships, once determined, are sometimes transferable for use in other areas. More care must be exercised, however, when analysing health impacts. Although damage or dose-response functions derived for developed countries can and have been borrowed for use in developing countries, this must be done with caution. These limitations are discussed in more detail in Chapter 7.

The approaches in the general category of OVA provide measures of the gross benefits – in the sense of losses avoided – of preventive or remedial actions. It is implicitly assumed in the use of these methods that the net value of averting damage is at least equal to the cost which would be incurred if the damage actually occurred. With OVA, it is assumed that rational individuals, in order to prevent some damage from occurring, would be willing to pay an amount less than or equal to the costs arising from the predicted level of environmental effects. However, because preferences for more or less damage are presumed rather than discovered, OVA estimates are not directly related to individuals' utility functions, and therefore may be biased in certain instances.

In contrast to the OVA, the second set of approaches, *subjective valuation approaches* (SVA), are based on more subjective assessments of possible damage expressed or revealed in real or hypothetical market behaviour. Using revealed behaviour involves examination of real markets for goods or services which are affected by environmental impacts, such as air or water pollution, in which people actually make trade-offs between the environmental impact (pollution) and other goods or income. For example, people sometimes take actions to prevent damage from pollution, such as boiling water before consuming it to prevent transmission of water-borne diseases. Also, examination of housing markets has revealed in many cases that property values are higher in areas where air quality is good as compared with areas where air quality is bad. The difference in the property values between these two areas is a proxy measure of willingness to pay for good air quality. These market transactions are used as surrogate markets for environmental goods and services. The preventive expenditures method discussed in Chapter 4, the travel cost approach described in Chapter 5, and the hedonic approaches in Chapter 6 are included in this category.

In other cases environmental impacts cannot be valued, even indirectly, through market behaviour. The alternative is to construct hypothetical markets for various options to reduce environmental damages, and to ask directly a sample of people to express how much they would be willing to pay for various reductions in environmental impacts. These are the so-called contingent valuation methods (CVM) discussed in more detail in Chapter 5.

The SVA are based on expressed or revealed preferences, and are directly related to individuals' utility functions. However, in the case of SVA, information constraints may introduce bias. Whereas OVA are based on the best objective knowledge about cause and effect relationships relating the level of offending activities to expected damage, SVA are highly dependent on the extent of knowledge or the amount of information individuals have with regard to the actual damages imposed by various activities. If people have inadequate information on which to base perceptions of potential damage or if they for other reasons incorrectly perceive risks of damage, their willingness to pay to avoid damage may either underestimate or overestimate actual damages costs.

The choice of a particular method of measurement will obviously depend on what is being measured: Figure 7 presents a valuation flowchart that suggests where one might begin an analysis. The figure starts with any environmental impact and determines whether or not there is a measurable change in production, or if the primary effect of the impact is a change in environmental quality. Those impacts that result in a change in production (for example, changes in crop yields, or fishery catch) are fairly easy to handle. Environmental quality changes are usually more difficult to value. In the case of habitat change, for example, the analyst may use the opportunity-cost approach, replacement-cost approach, land-value approach or contingent valuation method to estimate benefits and costs. Similarly, air and water quality can be valued by several cost-based approaches and health impacts are handled with other methods. Non-use values and less tangible impacts (for example, recreational or aesthetic effects) are frequently valued by contingent valuation methods. Nonetheless, in Figure 7 there are some methods which are listed more frequently than others. Although a wide range of measurement/valuation techniques have been developed by economists, this book will concentrate on those which are more easily applied to the probable environmental effects of standard types of development projects.

Table 4 lists these techniques by chapter. The first set, those thought to be generally applicable, are presented in Chapter 4. These are fairly standard and straightforward approaches that rely largely on changes in physical production or on direct cash expenditures (for example preventive expenditure, cost-effectiveness). Opportunity-cost, cost-of-illness, and replacement (and relocation)

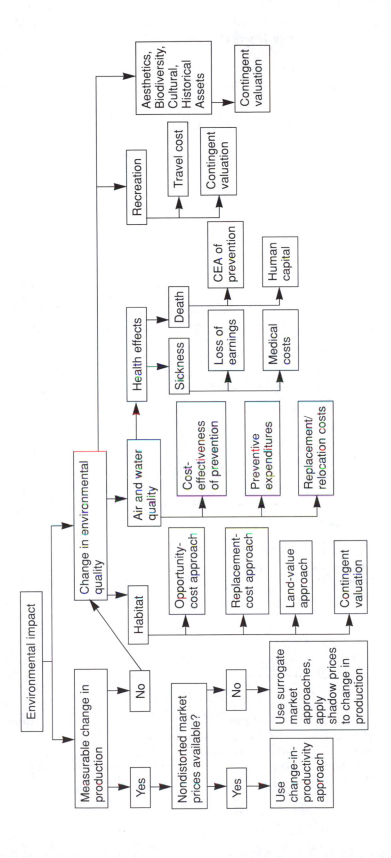

Figure 7 A Simple Valuation Flowchart
Adapted from: Dixon and Sherman (1990).

Table 4 Measurement and Valuation Techniques

Generally Applicable (Chapter 4)

Approaches that use market values of goods and services:
- Changes-in-productivity
- Cost-of-illness
- Opportunity-cost

Cost-side approaches that use the value of actual or potential expenditures:
- Cost-effectiveness
- Preventive expenditures
- Replacement costs
- Relocation costs
- Shadow-project

Selectively Applicable (Chapter 5)

Surrogate-market techniques:
- Travel-cost
- Marketed goods as environmental surrogates

Contingent valuation methods:
- Bidding games
- Take-it-or-leave-it experiments
- Trade-off games
- Costless choice
- Delphi technique

Potentially Applicable (Chapter 6)

Hedonic methods
- Property and other land-value approaches
- Wage-differential approach

Macroeconomic models:
- Linear programming
- Natural resource accounting
- Economy-wide impacts

cost approaches look at economic costs associated with environmental impacts. These approaches provide powerful tools for measuring many of the effects that development projects have on the environment.

A second set of techniques, presented in Chapter 5, are 'selectively' applicable because they can be used only in certain situations. These approaches are usually more indirect and rely either on surrogate markets (for example travel costs) or contingent valuation methods. The scope for using both sets of techniques is elaborated in the text.

Chapter 6 presents information on the use of macroeconomic models, natural resources accounting, and the analysis of economy-wide impacts. Although these approaches currently have more limited immediate usefulness in many developing countries, there are cases when such approaches can be, and have been, used.

Besides the major task of identifying the impacts on the environment and determining their monetary values, three important conceptual problems remain: determining the *boundary* of the analysis; setting an appropriate *time horizon*, and choosing a *technique* for project evaluation.

The *boundary* of the economic analysis refers to the choice of what to include and what to exclude. The identification of externalities implies an expansion of the conceptual and physical boundaries of the analysis. How far to expand will depend on each individual project. An oil palm mill will generate waste water which will adversely affect downstream uses of water – including drinking, irrigation and fishing. We will argue that the economic analysis of the project should include these effects in a with- and without-project frame-work.

Other impacts on the environment may be more distant or more difficult to identify. The effect of emissions from a power plant on creation of acid rain is one example. The interaction of upland agricultural development with its attendant soil and chemical runoff, and lowland and coastal ecosystems provide another example of a complicated, extended relationship. No single rule can be used to draw lines for the analysis. As with valuation, we believe that it is best to start with the directly observable and measurable effects. The project engineer, the economist and the environmental specialist will collectively have to determine the boundaries. Initial attempts have been made to establish 'protocols' for representative types of project. For example, see discussion of the World Bank's *Environmental Assessment Sourcebook* in Chapter 2. Ideally each protocol should outline the impacts on the environment likely to be produced by given projects which should be considered in the analysis. A significant contribution to the development and updating of such protocols would be the results of *ex post facto* evaluations of similar projects as well as the checklists and guidelines developed by environmental specialists.

Setting an appropriate *time horizon* is the next major conceptual problem. Usually the time chosen should be long enough to encompass the useful life of the proposed investment – thus a factory will have a defined 'life of project'. In other kinds of project in which benefits are expected to accrue over very long periods (for example, a dam or reservoir with a life expectancy of some 300 years) a time horizon is chosen which will capture most of the benefits and costs – say some 30 to 50 years. At any positive discount rate the present-day magnitudes of benefits and costs will, after 50 years, be very small in the calculations of net present value. A discount rate of 10 percent, for instance, would mean that most benefits and costs would become inconsequential after only 20 years. (Discounting and discount rates will be discussed later in this chapter.)

The environmental impacts of development pose a special challenge. If the duration of the impact is less than the expected economic life of the project, then there is no problem – the effects on the environment can be included in the standard economic analysis. For example, an oil palm plantation with a project life expectancy of 25 years may involve road construction during its initial phase. The construction of the roads may cause an increase in soil erosion, with consequent sedimentation downstream in irrigation canals. After five years the road cuts have been stabilized, erosion has stopped and extra costs for dredging the canal have come to an end. In such a case the project's impacts on the environment can be included in the standard analysis with a time horizon equal to the project's expected life.

If, on the other hand, the effects on the environment are expected to last beyond the lifetime of the funded project, the time horizon over which the project must be considered must be extended. For example, consider a new port to be developed by means of dredging. The process is expected to destroy an established fish breeding ground and its associated fishery. The port project is expected to last for 25 years and is evaluated over that period. However, as the fishery will never be re-established, its loss of fish production beyond the 25 years should also be included in the analysis.

There are two ways in which the extended time horizon to be considered can be accommodated within an analysis. One is to *extend the cash-flow analysis* beyond the normal end-of-project period for an additional number of years. This course is feasible if what is being considered has a clearly defined expected life (a teak forest, once cut, may need 60 years to regenerate, for example). The second way is to add a *capitalized value* of net benefits (or costs) at the normal end of the project period. This approach implicitly assumes that the impact on the environment (either a benefit or a cost) extends to infinity. In essence the second method is the establishment of a kind of 'environmental salvage value' for the project and is likely to be a negative – although it can be a positive – number. As with the determination of the analytical boundary, the setting of the appropriate period is a multidisciplinary task which will require the cooperation of various specialists.

Beyond all this there are some impacts on the environment which are almost impossible to quantify and sometimes even difficult to identify. Aesthetic, socio-cultural and historical factors are all examples of intractable types of impacts. Effects on biodiversity and gene pools present similar problems. Such factors may be important, but they are not easily handled by economic analysis. They are discussed in Chapter 7.

Once the appropriate conceptual and temporal analytical boundaries have been set for a project, the next step is the choice of *technique* for evaluation of the relative economic attractiveness of alternatives. Three methods are commonly used for comparing costs and benefits: the internal rate of return (IRR) or economic internal rate of return (EIRR), the benefit/cost ratio (B/CR), and net present value (NPV).

All three evaluation criteria depend on the same information – the yearly generation of benefits and costs associated with the project over the appropriate time horizon. Box 1 presents some basic information on the three criteria; they are also covered in detail in any standard project evaluation text (for example Gittinger, 1982; Mishan, 1982; Ward *et al*, 1991).

BOX 1
CRITERIA FOR PROJECT EVALUATION

Perhaps the single most widely used formula in project analysis is that which calculates the *net present value* (NPV) of a project. Also known as net present worth, the NPV determines the present value of net benefits by discounting the streams of benefits (B) and costs (C) back to the beginning of the base year (t=0). Two formulas can be used; both yield identical results:

$$NPV = \sum_{t=0}^{n} \frac{B_t - C_t}{(1 + r)^t}$$

or

$$NPV = \sum_{t=0}^{n} \frac{B_t}{(1 + r)^t} - \sum \frac{C_t}{(1 + r)^t}$$

The *internal rate of return* (IRR) is defined as the rate of return on an investment which will equate the present value of benefits and costs. It is found by an iterative process and is equivalent to the discount rate (r) that satisfies the following relationship:

$$\sum_{t=0}^{n} \frac{B_t - C_t}{(1 + r)^t} = 0$$

or

$$\sum_{t=0}^{n} \frac{B_t}{(1 + r)^t} = \sum_{t=0}^{n} \frac{C_t}{(1 + r)^t}$$

The IRR is widely used by financial institutions, but there are some theoretical and practical problems associated with its usage. These are discussed in Hufschmidt *et al.* (1983).

The IRR is the discount rate that would result in a zero net present value for a project. If the IRR calculated is 15 percent and the cost of project funds is 10 percent, the project would be financially attractive. If project funds 'cost' 18 percent, however, the project would be financially unattractive. The IRR does not give one the discount rate; it merely finds the value of r that meets the set condition of a zero net present value. The calculated IRR must then be compared to some other financial interest rate or discount rate to determine whether the project is financially or economically attractive.

The *benefit/cost ratio* (B/C ratio) is a simple derivative of the net present value criterion:

$$\text{B/C ratio} = \frac{\sum_{t=0}^{n} \dfrac{B_t}{(1 + r)^t}}{\sum_{t=0}^{n} \dfrac{C_t}{(1 + r)^t}}$$

This ratio compares the discounted benefits to discounted costs. If the B/C ratio is exactly equal to 1, the project will produce zero net benefits over its lifetime – the discounted benefits just equal discounted costs. A B/C ratio of less than 1 means that the project generates losses from an economic perspective.

Both NPV and B/CR require that a discount rate be chosen. The determination of this rate for development projects is a policy decision and detailed discussion of it is therefore beyond the scope of this book. However, important factors governing the choice of a discount rate include the opportunity cost of capital, the social rate of time preference, the requirements of the donor or lending agency, and the developing country's view of the consumption-investment mix of the private and public sectors. Box 2 presents additional information on discount rates.

BOX 2
DISCOUNT RATES

Whereas in financial analysis the interest rate used normally reflects market rates for investment and working capital and is therefore sensitive to current or expected inflation rates, the discount rate used in economic analysis is usually not readily observable in the economy. Economists have developed a number of approaches for determining and justifying a discount rate.

Several explanations are given of possible choices of a discount rate for use in economic analysis (see Schramm and Warford, 1989; Pearce and Turner, 1990; and Pearce and Warford, 1993). They are all based on economic or social phenomena:

Opportunity cost of capital

This approach is based on the forgone production that results when capital is invested in one project rather than another, or invested in a particular project by government rather than by the private sector. In this sense the opportunity cost of capital is directly related to the theory of capital productivity. Invested in plant or equipment, a dollar's worth of investment should yield net benefits over time. The discount rate reflects this rate of return.

This approach is also closely related to the financial (or nominal) interest rate, although the latter may include an upward adjustment for inflation. The real (inflation-adjusted) opportunity-cost rate is affected by changes in real income, the distribution of wealth, taste, and technology (Hyman and Hufschmidt, 1983).

The opportunity-cost approach appears to be used (implicitly) by many international development banks in requiring that, to be eligible for loans, proposed projects promise an annual rate of return at least equal to a specified rate – which appears to be based on the opportunity cost of capital.

The cost of borrowing money

Governments frequently have to borrow money, either domestically or internationally, to finance development projects. The financing mechanisms used include government debt from borrowing, inflation, or taxation on private consumption. Especially when a country expects to borrow abroad, this approach may be used to set the discount rate.

A danger in this cost-of-borrowing-money criterion is that extremely favourable loans (at very low, subsidized interest rates) will favour projects with long-term net benefits and, conversely, a high discount rate will favour short-term-pay-off projects. To the extent that these extremes represent distortions of true scarcity in the economy, they will lead to misallocation of scarce resources.

The social rate of time preference

A third school of thought relies on the ability of society to reflect more accurately than the private market the trade-offs between present and future consumption. If, from society's viewpoint, individuals overconsume in the present rather than save for investment and increased future production, the social rate of time preference will lead to a lower discount rate than that exhibited by individuals in private markets (the lifetime of an individual is much shorter than the relevant time horizon of society). How this rate is actually set depends upon the circumstances in the particular country involved. If the social rate is determined by the political process, this in turn is influenced by elected officials who may have a very short time horizon – namely, until the next election.

In summary, the actual rate to be used in economic analysis will be country-specific and will probably be established as a matter of government policy. Important factors governing the choice of rate will be the opportunity cost of capital, donor or lending agency requirements, cost of money to the government, and government's current views of the private-sector consumption-investment mix in relation to its concerns for future generations. The following points are important:

- Only one discount rate will be used in any single economic analysis, although the analysis may be repeated several times using different discount rates (sensitivity analysis).
- The discount rate used does not reflect inflation; all prices used in the analysis are real or constant dollar prices.
- In theory, the discount rate can be positive, zero, or negative. However, ignoring the concept of discounting (in effect, adapting a zero discount rate) does not do away with the problem of trade-off between present and future consumption (time preference).

When in doubt, project analysts should seek guidance from responsible government policy-making agencies on the discount rate to be used. In the absence of such guidance, analysts should undertake project economic analyses using a range of rates reflecting those recently or currently in use in the country for public and private investment projects. It is important to re-emphasize that these rates should be on a real-cost, inflation-adjusted basis.

The EIRR technique does not require the pre-selection of a discount rate, but in effect it calls for a very similar sort of judgement, since a particular interest rate or discount rate is used as a cut-off point for determining the economic attractiveness of the project at issue.

In the case of many development banks (including the ADB and the World Bank), it is standard to use EIRR with a cut-off rate of 10 percent to 12 percent to determine the economic attractiveness of a project. In other funding agencies, the NPV or B/C ratio criterion is commonly used. Although all three criteria are based on the same data, if multiple projects are being considered the different criteria may yield different rankings. The B/C ratio, for example, focuses on the generation of benefits per unit of costs, not on the absolute magnitude of net benefits generated. The NPV criterion, on the other hand, measures the overall size of net benefits (contributions to social welfare) generated by a project. A fuller discussion of this topic is presented in Gittinger (1982) and Dixon and Hufschmidt (1986).

CHAPTER 4

Generally Applicable Techniques of Valuing Environmental Impacts

This chapter presents generally applicable valuation techniques. Each of these techniques is in common use. The selection of the appropriate technique will be influenced by many factors including the effect to be valued and the availability of data, time and financial resources. The challenge, as outlined in Chapters 2 and 3, is to identify the enviromental effects of the projects concerned and to incorporate correctly the valuation of their benefits and costs within the project analysis.

All the techniques presented in this chapter use market prices to determine values. The implicit assumption, therefore, is that these prices reflect economic scarcity and hence are economic efficiency prices. If there are distortions in the market prices, then appropriate adjustments will be required. Distortions often arise as a result of taxes, subsidies, fixed exchange rates, or mandated wage or interest rates. The derivation of adjusted prices (commonly called shadow prices) is discussed in detail in standard project analysis handbooks (for example, Squire and Van der Tak, 1975; Gittinger, 1982; Little and Mirrlees, 1974; Ward *et al*, 1991).

In this and the following chapters, each technique is described briefly and examples are provided. References to standard works which present fuller explanations of the approach are also included. The focus is on fairly simple techniques that are most easily applied given the data and time limitations common to project analysis.

TECHNIQUES IN WHICH MARKET PRICES ARE USED TO VALUE IMPACTS

The techniques discussed here are those of straightforward benefit-cost analysis. The emphasis, however, is on the economic valuation of the environmental impacts of development projects. Impacts on environmental quality or on the sustainability of renewable resources are frequently reflected in changes in productivity of the systems involved and these, in turn, are used to assign values. Many of the valuation techniques listed in Table 3 rely on market prices as a basis for estimating values.

Both natural and human systems may be affected. Natural systems include fisheries, agriculture and forests; human systems would include buildings, materials and products both in the producer and household sectors, as well as human health and productivity.

The sustainability of resource use and the quality of the environment are treated as factors of production. Changes in these factors often lead to changes in productivity and/or production costs which may, in turn, lead to changes in prices and levels of output which can be observed and measured. These techniques are attractive because physical changes in production are easily observed and measured, and the use of market prices avoids some of the difficult questions of valuation arising from environmental effects which are not marketed. Before market prices can be used to value changes in productivity, assumptions must be made about the relevant supply and demand curves. Two situations may be distinguished:

- If the increase (or decrease) in the output of a commodity is small relative to the total market for it, and the change of inputs is small relative to the market for variable factors, then it can be assumed that product and variable factor prices will remain constant after the change in production. This, the 'small project' assumption, eliminates the need for further assumptions about the direction and magnitude of price changes. For most projects this partial equilibrium view is a realistic assumption and is used implicitly in most of the techniques presented here.
- Sometimes, however, the change in output of a commodity will be large enough to affect either the output prices, factor prices, or both. In such cases, information is needed about the shape of both demand and supply curves and then appropriate adjustments need to be made.

Three sets of techniques are considered. Each set uses market prices to value a change in the production of some good or service. The first deals with *changes in productivity and the value of output*; the second with *cost of illness*; the third with the *opportunity costs* of different actions.

Changes in productivity

Techniques using changes in productivity as the basis for measurement are direct extensions of traditional benefit-cost analyses. Physical changes in production are valued using market prices for inputs and outputs or, when distortions exist, appropriately adjusted market prices. The monetary values thus derived are then incorporated into the economic analysis of the project. This approach is based directly on neoclassical welfare economics and the determination of social welfare. The boundaries of the analysis are broadened so as to include all benefits and cost of an action regardless of whether they occur within the project's ordinary boundaries or beyond them.

Several steps must be taken in order to use this technique:

- Changes in productivity caused by the project have to be identified both on site and off site. Changes on site are typically the outputs for which the project was designed and are included in any project analysis. Changes off site (both positive and negative) include all the environmental or economic externalities which were frequently ignored in the past. These off-site effects must be included to give a true picture of project impacts.
- The effects on productivity both of proceeding with the project and of not

going ahead should be assessed. Even if alternative projects are being considered, the 'without-project' option should be retained. The reason for this is simple: we have to be able to specify the changes which will be brought about by the project as compared to what would happen if no project were undertaken. For example, a proposed agricultural development project in an upland area may cause soil erosion and increase damage to irrigated rice fields downstream. The environmental 'cost' of the project is not the total damage to the rice fields, but only that caused by the additional load of sediment produced by the project. An analysis which postulates both 'with' and 'without' scenarios will help to clarify the degree of damage or the damage avoided as a result of the project.

In the evaluation of the without-project alternative, care must be taken to account for what might be expected to occur without the project. In many cases, this will not be a simple continuation of current levels of output. If the resource would be expected to degrade over time if no action were taken, this decline over time must be taken into account. We want to compare the actual differences of the with-project and without-project alternatives over time, not just a comparison to the current situation.

- Assumptions have to be made about the time over which the changes in productivity must be measured, the 'correct' prices to use, and any future changes expected in relative prices.

Several examples of this approach are provided here. Case Study 1 in Part Two is taken from a soil-conservation project in Nepal. In it, changes in production of grass and fodder are valued in terms of the value of the milk and dung produced by livestock. A slightly different approach to the valuation of the on-site and off-site costs of soil erosion on Java, Indonesia, is provided in Box 3. Bojo (1991) also provides a careful and detailed application of this technique to valuation of the economic costs of land degradation in Lesotho, specifically in terms of expected crop losses.

In a study of the impacts of logging in a coastal area near El Nido in the island of Palawan, the Philippines, Hodgson and Dixon (1988, 1992) used the change in production approach to estimate the generation of gross revenues by three established industries linked by the coastal ecosystem: logging, an artisanal fishery, and resort development based on scuba diving. Bacuit Bay is the focus of the study since it supports the tourism and fishery industries and also receives the sediment produced by the logging operations carried out, in part, in the Bay's watershed. Logging can be fairly erosive and eroded soil is carried into the Bay and damages the coral reefs and seagrass beds, thereby affecting the food chain, the fish catch, and the attractiveness of the Bay to visiting divers.

The study compared two scenarios: continued logging with consequent damage to the Bay's ecosystem and resulting losses of fishery and tourism income (the 'without project' scenario), and a logging ban with loss of forestry income but sustainable or increased fishery and tourism revenues (the 'with project' scenario). The analysis examined the changes in revenues due to changes in production (trees harvested, fish caught, tourists visiting) under the two scenarios. Lack of cost-side data for the three industries prevented carrying out a traditional benefit-cost analysis; rather, the analysts estimated the generation of gross revenues for all three industries, with and without the logging ban. The estimates covered a 10-year period and used a 10 percent discount rate.

As seen in Table 5, the logging ban clearly yielded larger gross revenues: $42.7 million versus $25.2 million with continued logging. The loss of logging income with the ban was more than made up for by increased fishery and tourism revenues. Although continued logging would have reduced fishery revenue by half, the biggest cost of continued logging was the loss in tourism revenue, both from existing facilities and planned expansion that would not take place.

Table 5 Ten-Year Sum (1987–1996) of Gross Revenues, and Present Values of Gross Revenues ($1,000) (at a 10% Discount Rate) for each Industry Sector under Option 1 (logging ban) and Option 2 (continued logging)

	Option 1: Logging Ban	Option 2: Continued Logging	Option 1 less Option 2
Gross revenue			
Tourism	47,415	8,178	39,237
Fisheries	28,070	12,844	15,226
Logging	0	12,885	−12,885
Total	**75,485**	**33,907**	**41,578**
Present value			
(10%)			
Tourism	25,481	6,280	19,201
Fisheries	17,248	9,108	8,140
Logging	0	9,769	− 9,769
Total	**42,729**	**25,157**	**17,572**

Source: Hodgson and Dixon (1992).

Despite the clear message of the economic analysis, the logging company had a legal right to log and a clear financial incentive to do so. The analysis does indicate the size of the economic costs of continuing to log, however, and provides important information for decision makers who may want to consider alternative logging policies or compensatory measures.

BOX 3
COSTS OF SOIL EROSION ON JAVA

To estimate the economic significance of soil erosion on the island of Java in Indonesia, a recent study developed a model of the physical extent of erosion and linked these to on-site changes in crop production or the production of other goods and services, as well as off-site costs attributable to sedimentation downstream.

The method for quantifying the physical extent of erosion involved the use of computerized geographic information systems (GIS) to identify and classify areas by their susceptibility to erosion, and to record their spatial distribution. The output of the GIS analysis is an overlay of three maps: slope and soil type, erosivity, and land use, thus classifying areas with various combinations of these three variables. The erosion rates corresponding to these various combinations were taken from experimental and empirical estimates of erosion under comparable conditions elsewhere.

The erosion/yield relationships used in the study are based on controlled experiments and interpolations based on knowledge of soil properties. The study included 25 soil types and two groups of crops (sensitive and insensitive). The estimates of erosion/yield relationships, along with the estimates of the extent of erosion given the predominance of different types of upland farming practices, produce estimates of the severity of physical production loss. These estimates are in the order of 6.7 percent for sensitive crops (e.g. maize), and 4.2 percent for insensitive crops (e.g. cassava).

Representative farm budgets were used to value estimated productivity changes. The results of the study indicate the overall impact of erosion-induced productivity loss leading to progressively lower farm profitability, and gradually to the adoption of less and less profitable crops. This is estimated to result in an annual cost of about $315 million, or about 4 percent of the value of agricultural output.

Magrath and Arens also estimated the off-site costs of soil erosion, largely due to removal of sediment from irrigation systems, reservoirs, and harbours. These costs turned out to be quite small in comparison to the on-site, productivity based cost estimates. Table 6 presents the results of the analysis showing the annual costs of on-site and off-site effects (using the high-end estimate of off-site costs). Of the total of slightly more than $400 million per year, over three-quarters of the costs is due to on-site reductions in agricultural production.

Source: Magrath, W. and P. Arens. 1989. *The Costs of Soil Erosion on Java: A Natural Resource Accounting Approach*. Environment Department Working Paper No. 18, The World Bank, Washington, D.C.

Table 6 Total Estimated Annual Costs of Soil Erosion on Java
($000,000)

	West Java	Central Java	Jogyakarta	East Java	Java
On Site	141.5	29.1	5.7	138.6	315.0

Off Site
  Irrigation
  System
  Siltation
	5.7	2.7	0.5	4.0	12.9

Harbour Dredging (1984/85)	0.9	0.3		2.2	3.4
Reservoir Sedimentation	41.3	16.3		17.3	74.9
TOTAL	**189.4**	**48.4**	**6.2**	**162.1**	**406.2**

Source: Magrath and Arens (1989).

In another study Lal (1990) used the change-in-productivity approach to evaluate the alternatives of conservation and conversion of mangroves in Fiji. Markets, when they exist for mangroves, often fail to properly value these areas because they fail to incorporate the values of many goods and services produced there, some of which are harvested within the mangrove (for example, mangrove crabs and wood products) while others are caught outside the mangrove forest (for example, fish and shrimp that are dependent on the mangrove for part of their life cycle). In addition, many of the products collected in mangrove areas are not marketed, but rather are used for subsistence consumption by those who collect these products. There may also be important benefits from ecological processes like filtering of waste water and shoreline protection. All these benefits of mangroves accrue to a large and widely dispersed group, and may not be easily captured by market transactions; hence, these values, which are often substantial, are ignored.

Lal estimated the market values associated with mangroves in Fiji and found that the minor value of forestry production within the mangrove (about F$ 9 per ha per year) was less than 10 percent of the off-site fishery benefits attributable to the mangrove (estimated at about F$150 per ha per year). And yet, conversion decisions are all too often made on the basis of the narrow measurement of on-site benefits, thereby losing the much more valuable off-site fishery and ecoservice benefits. The economic analysis indicates the magnitudes of benefits and costs; political action, however, is needed to prevent excessive loss of mangrove forests.

Many other examples exist and they all have one common characteristic: designed for one particular purpose, each project causes unintentional damage to another productive system. The value of this unintended 'cost' can be estimated by using the simple technique of valuing the change in productivity caused by the disturbance.

Cost of illness

The cost-of-illness approach is often used to value the cost of pollution-related morbidity (Lave and Seskin, 1977; Freeman, 1979; Krupnick and Portney, 1991). As with the change-in-productivity approach, this approach is based on an underlying damage function. In this case, the damage function relates the level of pollution (exposure) to the degree of health effect.

Few epidemiological studies have been done to determine the health effects of various pollutants in developing countries, and those which have been done to date are somewhat inconclusive. The alternative to development of site-specific dose-response functions for developing countries is to use ones derived for developed countries. However, this approach raises some methodological concerns. Dose-response functions from developed countries may produce inaccurate results when used in developing countries because baseline concentration of pollutants, both indoors and outdoors, and the general health status of the populations differ considerably. Therefore, use of dose-response functions from developed countries would likely bias results downwards, underestimating possible damage.

With this approach, costs are interpreted as a (lower-bound) estimate of the presumed benefits of actions which would prevent the damage from occurring. Costs to be counted include any loss of earnings resulting from illness, medical costs such as for doctors, hospital visits or stays, and medication, and any other related out-of-pocket expenses.

The cost-of-illness method disregards the affected individual's preference for health versus illness, for which they may be willing to pay. Also, the method assumes individuals treat health as exogenous and does not recognize that individuals may undertake defensive actions (such as flu shots or other immunizations, special air or water filtration systems) and incur costs to reduce health risks. In addition, the method excludes non-market losses associated with sickness, such as the pain and suffering to the individual and to others concerned, and restrictions on non-work activities.

In general it is easier to value environmental effects using the cost-of-illness approach when the illness is relatively short, discrete, and does not have negative long-term impacts. Chronic illness is harder to handle; thorny moral and theoretical difficulties arise when periods of illness lengthen.

One example where the cost-of-illness approach might be useful is an urban potable water supply project which reduces the incidence of diarrhoea. It is fairly easy to establish a link between contaminated drinking water supplies and diarrhoea and the disease is not in general, except in children, life threatening. (There may, of course, be other transmission links such as contamination of foods via irrigation with polluted water, and direct hand to mouth transmission, that must be considered.) Many urban air pollutants also produce important health effects and these can be valued. Box 4 reports on some back-of-the-envelope calculations of the economic costs of air and water pollution in Mexico.

Some general guidelines for choosing projects for which the cost-of-illness approach may be used include the following:

- A direct cause-and-effect relationship can be established and the etiology of the disease is clearly identifiable.
- The illness is not life-threatening and has no chronic effects.
- An accurate estimate of the economic value of earnings and medical care is available. Unemployed labourers or subsistence farmers, for example, present problems in this context since a 'shadow price' for their earnings must be developed.

In applying the cost-of-illness approach the analyst needs to identify clearly the cause-and-effect relationship and its implications on net social welfare. Candidates for the use of this technique would include projects designed to improve public water supplies or waste disposal systems which will ultimately improve human health and productivity. Similarly, many air-pollution control investments produce important health benefits, especially from the fairly inexpensive technologies available to reduce suspended particulates and dust, major causes of respiratory diseases. The analyst must be careful in determining the net improvement in worker production or earnings (or the reduction in illness) and the net social costs of savings in medical care. For example, where the demand for medical services is less than or equal to the supply, the savings in medical care are less than the actual medical costs which have been avoided, since some facilities or services may go unused as a result even though there is a cost to supplying them. This is a short-run effect. If, on the other hand, the demand for medical services exceeds the supply, as it does in many developing countries, then the full value of the savings in medical services can be counted as a benefit

Applications of this techniques are presented in Box 4 and in Case Studies 3 and 9 in Part Two.

When loss of earnings is used to value the cost associated with mortality, it is referred to as the *human-capital approach*. It is similar to the change-in-productivity approach in that it is based on a damage function relating pollution to productivity, except that in this case the loss in productivity of human beings is measured. In essence, it is an ex-post, exogenous valuation of the life of a particular individual using as an approximation the present value of the lost (gross or net) market earnings of the deceased. In this usage, it is a controversial extension of the more standard human capital theory (Becker, 1960) which relates the demand for education to the potential payoff in terms of expected life-time earnings.

By reducing the value of life to the present value of an individual's income, the human capital approach to the valuation of life suggests that the lives of the rich are worth more than the lives of the poor (and, as a direct consequence, the lives of residents of rich countries are that much more valuable than the lives of those in poor countries). Specifically, narrowly applied, the human capital approach implies that the value of life of subsistence workers, the unemployed and retirees is zero, and that of the underemployed is very low. The very young are also valued little since their future discounted earnings are often offset by education and other costs that would be incurred before they enter the labour force. Furthermore, the approach ignores substitution possibilities that people may make in the form of preventive health care. In addition, non-market values such as pain and suffering are excluded.

At best, this method provides a first-order, lower-bound, estimate of the lost production associated with a particular life. However, the current consensus is that the societal value of reducing risk of death cannot be based on such a value. Although this method is not favoured by most economists for policy analysis purposes, it is often used to establish ex-post values for court settlements related to the death of a particular individual. An alternative method of valuing reductions in risk of death – the wage differential approach – is discussed in Chapter 6.

BOX 4
ENVIRONMENTAL DAMAGE COSTS IN MEXICO

A 1991 World Bank study on the cost arising from various environmental problems in Mexico employed the cost-of-illness approach to estimate air pollution costs. The study used damage functions – derived from both laboratory experiments and epidemiological studies done in the US – for air pollutants, including suspended particulate matter, ozone and lead, combined with local data on ambient concentrations and exposures to arrive at ballpark estimates of US$ 1.1 billion annually as likely costs of air pollution in Mexico City. This figure tends to be a lower bound estimate because it only includes direct costs such as medical expenses and lost wages, and not indirect costs of individual disutility (for example, discomfort, suffering, and the opportunity cost of time).

The study used a three step procedure consisting of:

- determining the ambient concentrations of various pollutants;
- given these concentrations and the age distribution of the population, using dose-response relationships to determine the incremental incidence of disease, including both morbidity and mortality, in the population; and
- estimating the costs of the increase in morbidity and mortality, as measured by treatment costs, loss of wages and loss of life.

The costs associated with suspended particulate matter relate to restricted activity days (RAD) and increased mortality. The RAD in Mexico City due to suspended particulate matter are estimated at 3 days per person per year. If concentrations of total suspended particulates (TSP) were reduced to the legislated standard, RAD would be reduced by 2.4 days. This figure was calculated by applying US dose-response relationships to Mexican conditions. Thus, the cost of not meeting the legislated standards can be estimated by valuing the RADs. With a estimated population of 17 million (55 percent adult), and assuming that one-half of the RADs were also days of lost work, the total number of lost work days caused by not meeting air quality standards for suspended particulate matter in Mexico City is 11.2 million days (17 million people $\times$ .55 adults $\times$ 2.4 RAD $\times$ .5 LWD/RAD). Multiplying this by a typical wage of $4 per hour yields an estimated cost of US$ 358 million annually from lost work days by adults alone, not to mention the costs due to sickness of children and discomfort that does not result in lost work days.

In the case of excess mortality from exposure to suspended particulate matter, dose-response relationships (also from the US literature) estimate that 6,400 lives are lost by not meeting legislated standards in Mexico City, and these lives are estimated to be cut short by an average of 12.5 work years. Using a human capital approach to value these lives, the discounted value of lost earning per person totals US$ 75,000, for a total cost from mortality at US$ 480 million. The total annual cost caused by excess concentrations of suspended particulate matter in Mexico City is thus estimated at US $850 million.

The major health consequence of ozone pollution is related to RAD. A calculation for RAD caused by ozone (using the same methodology as for particulate matter) yields an annual cost associated with ozone pollution of US$ 102 million.

Lead pollution is associated with high blood levels in children which can cause neurological damage, and with high blood pressure in adults which can cause cardiovascular disease. Since local data on these costs were not available, hospital, medication and treatment costs for children were assumed to be 1/15 of similar costs in the US. These unit cost estimates were multiplied by the number of cases predicted by the dose-response function to yield an estimated cost for children's treatment of US$ 60 million per year.

Children with high blood lead levels also have slowed cognitive development and require compensatory education. Assuming that three years of supplemental education would be required for the estimated 140,400 children with high blood lead levels, and, with average annual education costs of US$ 153 per child in Mexico City, yields a total cost in compensatory education of US$ 21.5 million.

It is estimated that elimination of lead in Mexico City's air would also lead to a reduction of 70,422 cases of adult hypertension, and 498 cases of myocardial infarctions. The total costs associated with the hospitalization and treatment of these illnesses and the value of lives lost is estimated at $48 million.

The annual estimated health costs associated with lead atmospheric pollution above zero concentration levels in Mexico City are thus about US$ 125 million, with total costs of the three major air pollutants in Mexico City (TSP, ozone, lead) of roughly US$ 1.1 billion.

Source: Margulis, Sergio. 1991. *Back of the Envelope Estimates of Environmental Damage Costs in Mexico*. Internal Discussion Paper, Latin America and the Caribbean Region, Agriculture Operations Division, Country Department II, The World Bank.

Opportunity cost

This approach is based on the concept that the cost of using resources for unpriced or unmarketed purposes (for example, preserving land for a national park rather than harvesting its trees for timber) can be estimated by using the forgone income from other uses of the resource as a proxy. Rather than attempting to measure directly the benefits gained from preserving a resource for these unpriced or unmarketed purposes, we measure what has to be given up for the sake of preservation. The opportunity-cost approach is, therefore, a way of measuring the 'cost of preservation'. This information, in turn, is used to evaluate the options open to a decision-maker. There are many instances where the opportunity cost of preservation is found to be low, resulting in a decision to preserve or to conserve the resource in its natural state.

The first step of the analysis is a conventional benefit-cost analysis of the proposed project. If the traditional project analysis shows the project to be uneconomic, the analysis need go no further. If, however, the proposed project does have positive net benefits, these must be weighed against the benefits of the preservation alternative which can be measured easily. If these measurable benefits of the preservation alternative outweigh the project benefits, the project should not be undertaken.

Where the benefits of the proposed project are slightly greater than the preservation alternative, we are left with a difficult choice. The preservation alternative will also have some less tangible benefits such as option value, quasi-option value and existence value (these are discussed in Chapter 7) which are not easily measured. These unquantified benefits must then be weighed qualitatively against the amount of benefits by which the proposed project exceeds the preservation alternative. When the difference in benefits between the two alternatives is low, prudence is advised since development projects usually have irreversible effects. However, such subjective decisions must be left to policy-makers; the economist can only lay out the relevant information.

52

One well-known example of the use of this technique is the Hell's Canyon Study in the United States of America (Krutilla, 1969; Krutilla and Fisher, 1985). It had been proposed to dam the canyon for the generation of hydro-electric power which would have altered, irrevocably, a unique area of wilderness. Rather than trying to value all the benefits of the canyon in its natural state, the analysts produced conventional benefit-cost analyses both of the proposed project and of its next cheapest alternative. The analysis showed that even under a variety of assumptions, the benefits of the project were not large enough to justify the irreversible loss of a unique natural area. The decision-makers chose not to build the dam since the opportunity cost of preservation – the additional expense of generating power from another source – was thought to be worth paying for the sake of preserving Hell's Canyon in its natural state.

Nominally, this technique is a cost-side approach, but it is actually used to evaluate the benefits of preservation, which are not themselves valued, by means of estimating the extra costs entailed in using an alternative. In this way it may be very useful in valuing unique natural resources whose benefits are difficult to identify, monetize, or both. Possible situations where this approach may be valuable include alteration of tropical rainforests, establishment and protection of wildlife sanctuaries, cultural or historical sites and natural vistas. The technique is relatively quick and straightforward and provides information valuable to decision-makers and to the public.

In terms of development projects it can also be used when deciding where major infrastructure projects or industrial facilities are to be sited. New ports, airports and highways all frequently require the use of open, undeveloped or sparsely developed areas. Where alternative locations exist, the opportunity-cost technique helps to clarify the additional costs of preserving one area over another.

Similarly, the effect on the environment of different technological options can be valued with this technique. For example, it is possible to choose between alternative ways of meeting the same need, such as cooling ponds or cooling towers for heated water, between overhead or underground facilities, between parking lots or parking structures, and so on. With this technique it is possible to quantify the extra costs involved in choosing an environmentally better, but more expensive, solution. Of course the final decision will always lie in the hands of the policy-maker, but the opportunity-cost approach is a powerful tool with which to illustrate the real cost differences between alternatives which may have very different impacts on the environment.

TECHNIQUES IN WHICH MARKET PRICES OF ACTUAL OR POTENTIAL EXPENDITURES ARE USED TO VALUE COSTS

The final techniques in this chapter rely on the use of market prices. The first, *cost-effectiveness analysis*, is a widely used economic and engineering technique to evaluate the cost of mitigation. The second is the technique of *preventive expenditures* which examines direct costs involved with certain actions taken to avert damage.

The last three techniques use information on *potential* expenditures to value a development impact on the environment. Each of these techniques – the *replacement cost approach*, the *relocation cost approach*, and the *shadow project technique* – examines the costs that would be involved if an environmental impact were to be mitigated by replacing the environmental services that were damaged or destroyed. This information is then used to decide whether it is more efficient to take preventive measures beforehand or compensatory measures after the event. These three techniques are similar; they are presented separately, however, because there are situations when one will be more appropriate than another. (Note that if the potential expenditures are *actually made*, then the information can be used in the preventive expenditure approach.)

Note that none of the approaches attempts to estimate a monetary value for the *benefits* produced by the project. For these cost-side approaches, therefore, the analyst must determine that the potential benefits justify the costs involved.

Cost-effectiveness analysis

When funds are limited, data inadequate, or the level of knowledge insufficient to establish the link between environmental damage and human health and welfare, it may sometimes be more useful first to set a goal and then analyse different means of achieving it. Conversely, if there is a certain level of funding available for a given project, then the policy-maker must decide which method of using those funds will be the most effective. Alternatively, it might be necessary to consider a number of goals and to decide which of them seems best after considering the cost of each. In all of these situations, cost-effectiveness analysis is involved. The major difference between it and other approaches is that no attempt is made to monetize benefits. Rather, the focus is entirely on meeting a predetermined standard or goal.

Cost-effectiveness analysis is also appropriate for social programmes dealing with health and population as well as for the analysis of environmental effects. In general, it is useful for all projects whose benefits are difficult to measure in monetary terms.

The first step in cost-effectiveness analysis is to fix a target. In the environmental field this may, for example, be a certain ambient quality, a maximum level of exposure to a waterborne disease agent or an emission standard for industrial facilities. The policy-maker must consider the possible trade-offs between different standards and the costs associated with achieving them. The standard economic principle normally applied to this kind of decision is the equation of marginal costs with marginal benefits, where standards are increased to the point at which the additional costs of raising the standard further are just equal to the additional benefits from raising the standard. However, when benefits are difficult or impossible to measure or monetize, this approach becomes primarily conceptual.

In many cases technology may dictate the options available for achieving a target: as standards for air quality become more stringent, the possible strategies for control become fewer. In cases where there are only a few alternatives with very different outcomes, analysing the incremental cost of adopting one rather than another may provide a clear indication of which strategy it is sensible to adopt. Where there are many possibilities it may be more difficult to choose the sensible standard and the corresponding strategy for achieving it.

Sometimes optimization techniques that can handle multiple objectives, such as linear programming, may be used to help to set standards (Russell, 1973; Russell and Vaughan, 1976). These can simultaneously take into account the level of the primary output, the environmental considerations and the costs associated with alternative strategies.

Once a target or standard is chosen, cost-effectiveness analysis is carried out by examining the various means by which that target can be achieved. This may involve analysing the capital and operating costs of different pollution-control technologies. In other projects it may be management practices which are the variables subject to change. Each project will involve different alternatives and must be dealt with differently. Analysts must ensure that a wide range of options is considered, but the basic goal is the same – identifying the least-cost alternative which will achieve the goal selected.

Although cost-effectiveness analysis seems to be a straightforward economic (and engineering) approach, in practice there is wide scope for further analysis. One of the main reasons for this can be seen in the example considered below. Frequently, alternative strategies may achieve different levels of control. For instance, if the 'target' level is an emission standard of no more than 100ppm and there are three technologies from which to choose, A, B and C, the cost-effectiveness analysis may yield the following information:

Technology	Installation Cost (million $)	Emission Level (PPM)
A	50	98
B	15	135
C	25	105

Technology A is the only one which meets the set standard; technology B is much cheaper to install, but is clearly inadequate. Technology C is the problem. It costs only half as much as A and falls short of the target by only a small amount. Which technology should be recommended? A strict regulatory approach might demand that A be adopted, even though C would save $25 million. Is the slight increase in emissions justified by the savings? The cost-effectiveness analysis should present these choices to the decision-maker and, as mentioned in Chapter 2, input from both economic and environmental analysts should be considered in reaching a decision. The choice will depend on the potential dangers of the higher rate of emission and on how much society can afford and is willing to pay to reach certain standards.

This last point, how much a society is able or willing to pay, has not previously been discussed, but is of considerable importance. Since cost-effectiveness analysis often does not even attempt to estimate the benefits derived from meeting a given standard or goal, it is possible that even the most cost-effective (or least-cost) option of meeting a strict standard is still too expensive. This is not an excuse for doing nothing, but suggests rather that the standard should be relaxed. Cost-effectiveness analysis can help in pointing this out too. The experience of other countries can be used as a guide to both the target level or standards for emissions, and for their expected costs.

Some general guidelines follow:

- Examine targets in a mix of countries, both developed and developing. Find out what levels the World Health Organization (WHO) recommends and how they are determined.
- Evaluate the seriousness of the environmental impact which is to be controlled. Discover if it is life-threatening (for example mercury poisoning), a health hazard (for example dust and particulates) or merely a nuisance (for example certain noise levels).
- Evaluate the effect of the most cost-effective method of control on the financial and economic return from the project. If the cost of the preferred choice is so great that the project will not be profitable, then the decision must be either not to go ahead or to reconsider the issue of pollution control. Determine the implications of cancelling the project. Consider the probable effects of reducing the levels of pollution control. Establish what lessons can be learned from other countries which have faced the same problems.
- Discover whether there is some compromise which will minimize environmental damage while still allowing the project at issue, or another project, to be built.

In sum, cost-effectiveness is a powerful tool but one which has to be applied carefully. Rigid adherence to a standard which is too strict or inappropriate can result in excessive control costs or even the cancellation of a project. Although such drastic measures may be necessary in some instances, in many cases some compromise can be developed to allow the project to go forward while still protecting the environment. Sensibly applied, cost-effectiveness analysis can be very helpful in providing environmental protection at a moderate cost while allowing development activities to continue.

Preventive expenditures

The expenditures people make in an attempt to avert damage from pollution or other offensive activities – preventive or mitigative expenditures – are sometimes used as subjective valuations of the minimum costs of these environmental problems. Whereas the cost-effectiveness approach examines the direct cost of meeting some predetermined target or standard, this technique examines actual expenditures in order to determine the importance individuals attach to environmental and health impacts. In other words, expenditures for the mitigation of environmental damage may be seen as a surrogate demand for environmental protection.

The substitution possibilities which are ignored in the change-in-productivity and other objective valuation approaches are the central focus of the preventive expenditures method. It is recognized that people may act preemptively to protect themselves from damage, and their expenditures for this purpose are thought to provide an estimate of their minimum subjective valuation of potential damages. The underlying premise is that an individual's perception of the cost imposed by damage is at least as much as the individual pays to avert the damage.

This approach gives a minimum estimate for two reasons: actual expenditures may be constrained by income, or there may be an additional amount of consumer's surplus even after the preventive expenditure has been made.

Valuation based on preventive expenditures may not unambiguously give a lower-bound estimate of the environmental costs, however. In some cases, the expenditures many not have been made exclusively or even primarily to avert costs. For example, bottled water may be perceived as a status drink and valued for that as well as any potential health benefits associated with its use. Clearly, individuals will commit their resources only if their subjective estimate of the benefits is at least as great as the costs. An indirect measure of individual perception of those costs can thus be derived by looking at the amount of resources allocated to avoiding them. However, an individual's willingness to incur costs is constrained by his or her ability to pay. Therefore this approach will only provide a minimum estimate of the benefits received.

The assumptions implicit in this kind of analysis are that:

- accurate data on the costs of the mitigating expenditures are available;
- there are no secondary benefits associated with the expenditures.

An example of the use of this method can be seen in a case study of environmental quality aspects of upland agricultural projects in Korea (Kim and Dixon, 1986). This study examined alternative soil-management techniques designed to stabilize upland soils and to enhance agricultural production. The study used information on lowland paddy farmers who were prepared to incur costs for the construction of dikes to divert water, thus preventing waterborne eroded soil from silting up their fields and damaging their crops. The lowland farmers' subjective valuation of the measures taken to prevent upland soil erosion would be at least as great as the cost they incurred to construct the dikes.

We could take an urban water supply project as another example. The preventive-expenditure approach would call for the examination of how much people pay to get water from sources other than the city supply, in order not to be exposed to pathogens. In a city like Jakarta, these sources include door-to-door sales, private wells and filtration systems, boiling water and even bottled water. Which method is chosen depends, in part, on individual income and ability to pay, but a realistic picture of the willingness of various groups of consumers to pay for potable water could be built up from a survey of those individual choices. This amount, summed across all residents and appropri-ately weighted by population and income distribution, may be substantial. Information like this can be very useful in assessing the social benefits of an improved urban water supply.

Other public services like electricity or garbage collection can similarly be analysed. In each case the analyst should examine how the goods and services to be provided by the project are being supplied at present.

Preventive expenditures are common and, if carefully used, can provide useful data. The strength of the approach is that it relies on observable market behaviour and is fairly easy to explain to decision-makers. However, in many developing countries the extent of preventive expenditure is more commonly constrained by income than by demand.

Replacement costs

The basic premise of the replacement-cost approach is that the costs incurred in replacing productive assets damaged by a project can be measured, and that these costs can be interpreted as an estimate of the benefits presumed to flow from measures taken to prevent that damage from occurring. The rationale for this technique is similar to that for preventive expenditures except that the replacement costs are not a subjective valuation of the potential damages but, rather, are the true costs of replacement if damage has actually occurred. The approach may thus be interpreted as an 'accounting procedure' used to work out whether it is more efficient to let damage happen and then to repair it or to prevent it from happening in the first place. It gives an estimate of the upper limit but does not really measure the benefits of environmental protection *per se*.

The assumptions implicit in this type of analysis are:

- The magnitude of damage is measurable.
- The replacement costs are calculable and are not greater than the value of the productive resources destroyed; and therefore it is economically efficient to make the replacement. If this assumption is not true, it would not make sense to replace the resource lost.
- There are no secondary benefits associated with the expenditures.

An example of the use of this approach may be seen in the case study by Kim and Dixon (1986), which examined the viability of alternative soil-stabilization techniques in upland agricultural areas in Korea. The damaged productive asset was the upland soil. The cost of physically replacing lost soil and nutri-ents was taken as a measure of the potential benefits of preventing soil erosion and nutrient loss. The implicit assumption (which may be a strong one) is that the erosion is worth preventing: that is, that the productive value of the soil is greater than the cost of replacement. In this case the costs of the proposed steps to prevent the erosion of the soil were lower than those of replacement, so the preventive measures were thought to be economically justifiable.

A forestry development project in Luzon, Philippines, is an example of a project where replacement-cost techniques could have been used. It involved the establishment of 10,700 hectares of tree plantations, measures to protect vegetation from fire and uncontrolled grazing on a further 1,300 hectares which are too steep for planting trees, and the development of pasture land, cut-and-carry fodder supply land, and agroforestry on a further 1,000 hectares.

The only benefit quantified in the project appraisal was that of wood production for various purposes. The slowing of severe soil erosion with a resultant reduction in the siltation of reservoirs, rivers and irrigation canals, the decreased incidence of flooding, were all regarded as non-quantifiable benefits. Much as in the Korean case cited above, the cost of replacing the lost soil and nutrients could have been used as the basis on which to estimate the value of the benefits from the reduction in soil erosion. In this case the decrease in soil erosion was a secondary benefit of the project, so the information derived from the replacement cost would not be used to evaluate the direct project costs but would be included as a benefit.

Both the Korean and Philippine examples could also be evaluated using a productivity approach, either to examine the potential loss in production if no replacement is carried out, or to estimate the value of present production. In either case the information obtained can be used to assess whether or not replacement is economically justified.

In general, the replacement-cost approach can be useful when an effect on the environment has caused, or will cause, money to be spent on replacing a physical asset. When that asset is a road, dam or bridge, the technique is straightforward. When it is soil, water or aquatic life, its application is the same but the problems of measurement are greater. The change-in-productivity approach can also be useful in these cases. When impacts on the environment result in physical economic externalities, then this approach can frequently be used to bring those externalities into the analysis.

Relocation costs

This is a variant of the replacement-cost technique. In it, the actual costs of relocating a physical facility because of changes in the quality of the environment are used to evaluate the potential benefits (and associated costs) of preventing the environmental change. For example, the construction of an oil palm mill would result in the discharge of waste water into a nearby stream. Of the various environmental costs associated with this discharge, one might be the need to relocate an intake for a domestic water supply which is, at present, downstream from the mill. If additional waste-water treatment equipment is installed in the downstream water intake rather than relocating the intake, then the equipment costs become an example of preventive expenditure.

Many examples of the relocation cost approach exist. In China, the government recently decided to relocate Shanghai's water intake. Shanghai, a city of 14 million inhabitants, was facing increasing difficulties in ensuring a safe potable water supply. The lower Huangpu River was heavily polluted by wastes from industries, ships and municipal sewage treatment plants. A number of options were considered: one was to clean up the industries and plants discharging wastes into the river; another was to move the municipal water intake up river to take advantage of cleaner water supplies, reduced treatment costs, and less risk of major pollution disasters. (A major accident in the lower reaches of the river could have meant cutting off water supplies to Shanghai for a number of days, at enormous economic and social cost.) Although the cost of the relocation and associated pollution and environmental control initiatives was high (supported in part by a World Bank loan of $160 million), these costs were judged less than the costs involved in cleaning up existing polluters sufficiently to be able to continue to rely on the present water intake and reduce the risks of a major pollution disaster to an acceptable level.

Another example of this approach is the decision recently made in connection with the almost completed 3000 MW Yacyreta hydropower project located on the Parana River between Argentina and Paraguay (World Bank, 1993a). A major concern was the optimal operating height of the reservoir – the original design calls for operation at 83 metres (above mean sea level). Lowering the level by seven metres would reduce the number of people to be resettled from 41,000 to 7,000, cut the flooded area in half, and reduce potential water quality problems. However, this would also cut energy production by half. The economic analysis compared the costs of relocating people and facilities with the higher operating level, to the economic costs of lost power production with the lower operating level. The results showed that the returns from the additional power generated at the higher level could easily justify the roughly $500 million expenditure needed to relocate facilities and resettle affected people. A phased process is therefore being implemented whereby revenues from sales of electricity are being set aside to pay the relocation and resettlement costs as the operating level is slowly increased.

Shadow projects

In an attempt to estimate the cost of replacing the entire range of environmental goods and services threatened by a project, the shadow-project technique was developed.

This is a special type of replacement-cost technique. If environmental services, the benefits of which are difficult to value, will be lost or diminished as a result of a development project, then their economic costs can be approximated by examining the costs of a hypothetical supplementary project which would provide substitutes. Take, for example, a project which requires harvesting a significant part of a mangrove forest. An alternative investment could be conceived which would, in principle, provide the same output of goods and services as does the mangrove forest. The total cost of the alternative can then be added to the basic resource cost of the project in order to estimate its full cost. It should be noted that the supplementary or 'shadow' project need only be conceptual and not actually built in order to arrive at an estimate of its costs. Inclusion of shadow-project costs gives some indication of how great the benefits of the new project must be in order to outweigh the losses it causes.

The assumptions implicit in this type of analysis are:

- The endangered resource is scarce and highly valued.
- The human-built alternative would provide the same quantity and quality of goods and services as does the natural environment.
- The original level of goods and services is desirable and should therefore be maintained.
- The costs of the shadow project do not exceed the value of the lost productive service of the natural environment.

In general, shadow-project analysis is used to give an estimate of the order of magnitude of the cost of replicating threatened environmental good or service. It may frequently be that recognition of the enormous cost, or even the impossibility, of replacing an environmental resource (a beach, a lake, a river, a tropical forest) will lead to greater concern about preventing the loss in the first place.

CHOOSING A TECHNIQUE

Cost-side approaches are frequently very useful because they involve tangible actions (actual or potential) which have directly observable market prices. All the techniques presented in this chapter have fairly wide applicability. The simplest and most powerful is the one which uses changes in productivity; this approach is useful once the effects of a project on the environment and their consequent effects on productivity have been identified. Similarly, the opportunity-cost and preventive-expenditure approaches are quite robust as they rely on actual (or potential) out-of-pocket expenses to determine values.

Both the replacement-cost and the relocation-cost techniques (and the associated shadow-project approach) use information on potential expenditures to decide whether it is more cost effective to *prevent* environmental damage or to *replace* the damaged resource after the damage has occurred. If the replaced or relocated environmental good or service is a perfect substitute for the damaged resource, then these techniques give an upper estimate of the economic cost of the damage. That is, if the cost of preventing the damage is less than the cost either of replacement or of relocation, then it is economically worthwhile to take action to prevent the damage. (This approach assumes that the benefits of preventing the damage are greater than the costs). On the other hand, if the replaced or relocated asset does not completely compensate for the environmental good or service lost, then the approach does not establish a true upper limit to the damage cost estimates.

Cost-effectiveness analysis is a strong approach if used in a sensitive way with realistic goals. As with the replacement and relocation techniques, the analyst must ensure that even the most cost-effective way of reaching a goal is likely to have benefits that exceed costs. The cost-of-illness approach uses observable information on treatment costs and can be helpful in assessing health-related projects like potable water supply, sewage disposal or air pollution control.

We cannot prescribe which technique is best for each situation since the choice is dependent on many factors. However, any of the techniques presented here, used appropriately, should produce results that can be defended and directly incorporated into project analyses.

CHAPTER 5

Selectively Applicable Techniques of Valuing Environmental Impacts

This chapter presents additional techniques and approaches which have been used to place values on the environmental impacts of development projects. We call these 'selectively applicable' either because they need greater care in their use, make more demands on data or on other resources, or because they require stronger assumptions than the more directly operational techniques presented in Chapter 4. This does not mean that these techniques cannot be used; many of them can add to project appraisal by explicitly incorporating the monetary costs of environmental impacts.

The seven techniques presented in this chapter (see Table 3) fall into two broad categories: those that use surrogate markets to determine values (either the travel cost approach or the use of marketed goods as environmental surrogates), and those techniques that are usually classified as contingent valuation methods (CVM), largely based on the use of surveys to elicit values. The degree to which each technique is directly operational is discussed at the end of the chapter.

TECHNIQUES IN WHICH SURROGATE MARKET PRICES ARE USED

Many aspects of the environment have no established market price. Things like clean air, unobstructed views, and pleasant surroundings are public goods; therefore direct market prices for them are rarely available. In many cases, however, it is possible to estimate an implicit value for an environmental good or service by means of the price paid for another good which is marketed.

Surrogate-market techniques, therefore, offer approaches which use an actual market price with which to value an unmarketed quality of the environment. The basic assumption is that the price differential, arrived at after all other variables except environmental quality have been controlled for, reflects a purchaser's valuation of the environmental qualities at issue. While there are some limitations to these techniques (to be discussed later), they can, in certain cases, be very useful in valuing a wide range of environmental qualities.

Travel cost

The travel-cost approach has been used extensively in developed countries to value recreational goods and services. First implemented in the late 1950s and 1960s (Clawson, 1959; Clawson and Knetsch, 1966) it is based on the simple proposition of renowned resource economist Harold Hotelling that observed behaviour can be used to derive a demand curve and to estimate a value (including consumer's surplus) for an unpriced environmental good by treating increasing travel costs as a surrogate for variable admission prices. Ward and Loomis (1986) provide a comprehensive review of theoretical refinements and empirical applications of the travel cost method.

The transaction price for most goods can be considered to be an expression of willingness to pay for the right to consume the good or the utility received from it. Recreational (or cultural, historic or scenic) goods are, however, a different case. Usually such goods (a public park will be used here as an example) are provided either free of charge or for a nominal admission fee. The value of the benefits or utility derived from a park, however, is often much larger than the fee, with the difference being equal to consumer's surplus. To estimate the total amount of consumer's surplus, we must derive a demand curve from the actual use of the park.

The present pattern of park use is determined by means of a survey of park visitors. Respondents are questioned about the time and money they spend travelling to the park, distance to the site, and a variety of other socioeconomic variables. The park users' zones of origin are usually defined in terms of increasing distance from, or cost of travel to, the park. A survey will normally show that the frequency with which people use the park (usually measured as a number of visits per thousand of population in each zone) is inversely related to their distance from the site. The more it costs, in time and money, to get there, the less frequently an individual will use the park, all other factors held equal. If plotted, this information will appear as in Figure 8.

In order to derive the demand curve, a number of assumptions must be made and a number of steps must be taken. The first assumption is that individuals can be grouped into residential zones where the inhabitants have similar preferences. Second, we assume that people will react to increasing travel costs in much the same way as they would react to increased admission charges at the park. This means that at some level of admission fee (or cost of travel) no one would use the park because, given other recreational options, it would be too expensive. Then we make a calculation of visitation rates from all origin zones, taking into account a number of variables related to income, cost of travel and other elements.

In its simplest form a regression equation is derived that relates visitation rates to the cost of travel. This is then used to determine the area of consumer's surplus for park users in each zone. This is calculated zone by zone using the travel-cost equation and the initial values for each particular zone. As the 'cost of travel' from each zone increases (by increasing the admission's price) the projected visitation rates drop. The objective is to determine consumers' willingness to pay, up to the point at which no one from a given zone would visit the park. In effect, a demand curve for the zone is traced out and the 'admission price' at which the demand for the park from that zone would equal zero is determined. The area below the calculated demand curve and above the cost curve is used as an estimate of the consumer's surplus of present park users

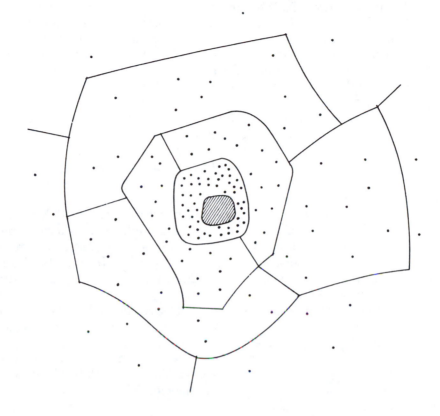

Figure 8 Plot of Hypothetical Survey Data Used in the Travel-Cost Approach

Note: Each dot represents 10 visitors to the park. For each zone a visitation rate (visitors per 1,000 population) is developed.

from that zone. This calculation is repeated for each zone and the consumer's surplus from all zones is added together to estimate the total consumer's surplus for users of the park.

It should be stressed that the amount of the travel cost *per se* is not equal to the value of the park. The travel-cost data are used only to estimate a demand curve for site visits. Further, the approach uses pre-established patterns of use in order to determine value and is heavily influenced by the existence of other sites. Numerous refinements of the approach are possible.

Although this approach would not at first seem applicable to many projects, it can often be used to place a value on a component of a larger project. The value of cultural and historical sites threatened by development projects could also be analysed by the travel-cost (TC) method. It is, however, most commonly used to value recreational benefits. For example, in a recent study on the economics of establishing the proposed Mantadia National Park in Madagascar, Kramer (Kramer *et al*, 1992; Kramer, 1993) used a modified travel-cost approach to estimate the importance of different attractions at an international travel destination (in this case, the country of Madagascar) to international tourists. (For more details on this study, see Case Study number 6 in Part Two.) The model (see Mercer and Kramer, 1992, for details) was modified to account for the multiple site visitation of international tourists; this correction is important since the traditional application of the travel-cost model is for national visitors to a single destination.

Kramer found that the average increased willingness-to-pay per trip as a result of the enhanced animal viewing and information facilities to be provided by the new Park was about $24 per visitor. Using a conservative assumption of 3,900 annual foreign visitors, this translates into an annual benefit of about $93,000, or, at a 10 percent discount rate, a net present value associated with the park of about $800,000 over a 20-year period.

The Madagascar study used the TC approach to estimate the addition to consumer's surplus from diversifying and enhancing facilities in a locale; another example of the application of the travel-cost method is its use to estimate the viewing value of Kenyan elephants. Box 5 summarizes the results of a study that tries to estimate the importance of different animals in total consumer's surplus of game-park visitors.

In all cases the values obtained should be clearly identified as a minimum valuation of only part of the total value of the resource. The travel-cost method only measures recreation benefits of the site, or natural resources being valued. Option values, related to future uses, or existence values are not included in the value estimated by the travel-cost method. These less tangible values may be significant for unique areas, habitats and species. These points are discussed further in Chapter 7.

Marketed goods as environmental surrogates

Sometimes a privately marketed good may be an adequate but imperfect substitute for some environmental service or publicly provided good. For example, private swimming pools may substitute for clean lakes and streams, or private parks for national parks. The potential benefits of an increase in the supply of an environmental good, such as national parks, may be deduced from the demand for the private good. If the two are close substitutes, the users' level of welfare will not change significantly.

Marketed goods, by definition, have quantities and market prices associated with them. The analytical difficulty is to determine to what degree the marketed good is an acceptable environmental surrogate. For some environmental goods this may not be an issue. For example, in the case of fresh water for use in an industrial process, it may matter little whether or not the water comes from a clean river flowing by the factory or from a treatment plant that extracts and purifies polluted river water. For other environmental goods and services, however, the marketed substitute will provide only a portion (and sometimes a very small portion) of the total value offered by the original environmental resource. This is particularly true for amenity and recreational resources, where

BOX 5
THE VIEWING VALUE OF ELEPHANTS

Elephants are unique natural resources which are valued for a number of reasons: their tusk ivory can be marketed; they are viewed and photographed as unique wildlife; and they are the embodiment of unique genetic resources which some value simply because they exist. Making monetary estimates of the total economic value of elephants would require summing estimates of all of the above categories of value. While the value of ivory can be measured from market transactions, the other two categories of benefits – viewing and existence value – are not easily quantified since easily observable markets for these goods and services do not exist.

The viewing value of elephants can be estimated using the travel-cost method. Safaris to Kenya to view and photograph elephants have become increasingly popular during the last decade. While viewing elephants in their natural habitat is a unique vacation opportunity, entrance fees to parks and reserves are typically very low and are not good estimates of the value of such an opportunity. For goods without close substitutes, such as a rare opportunity to view an elephant in the wild, consumer's surplus (the difference between the total benefit derived from the viewing experience and the admission fee) escapes appropriation by markets and must, therefore, be estimated by other means such as the travel-cost method.

This study used the travel-cost procedure in recognition that people coming from different locations face different costs for the same opportunity to view elephants. Estimates of these costs were obtained through interviews with 53 tourists from Europe and North America who came to Kenya for safaris during which they viewed or photographed elephants. These estimates were then grouped according to tourists' origin and were used to construct an inverse demand curve for safaris:

$$P = 4,023 - 1,674 \, Q$$

where P is price, defined as the sum of land costs, air fare and travel time costs, and Q is safari visits per 1,000 population. Demand curves for North American and European tourists were estimated separately.

The land costs of safaris vary considerably depending on their length and what amenities are provided. People take safaris of various durations in which they view small or large numbers of animals in one or more parks or reserves. Similarly, they can take a budget tour or travel in luxury. To control for this variability, a separate survey was made of 22 tour operators, and a quality weighted price index was estimated:

$$P_n = \text{Sum} \left((P_{nj} * N_{nj})/C_n \right) * P_{nj}$$

67

where n = origin of the visitor;
       j   = tour operators;
      C_n = total expenditures of visitors from the nth origin;
      N_{nj} = number of visitors from the nth origin that the jth tour operator served in last 12 months;
      P_{nj} = average price of tour offered by jth operator to visitors from the nth origin.

The consumer's surplus (CS) attributable to the total safari experience was calculated as:

$$CS = 0.5 * (4,023 - 3,535) = \$194 \text{ per tourist for North Americans}$$

and;

$$CS = 0.5 * (4,023 - 2,378) = \$822.50 \text{ per tourist for Europeans};$$

These two values result in a weighted average of $727 for both groups. If visitation is assumed to be 250,000 to 300,000 tourists per year, total consumer's surplus is in the range of $182 to $218 million per year.

Since viewing elephants is only one part of the total safari experience (although a very important one), not all of the value of a safari can be attributed to elephants. To isolate the contribution of elephants to the total value of the safari, survey respondents were asked to allocated the total 'value' of the safari over five categories:

1. seeing, photographing and learning about wildlife;
2. accommodation, staff and services, drivers;
3. observing and learning about Africa and its cultures;
4. rest, relaxation and shopping; and
5. other experiences.

Respondents allocated 50 percent of their total value to category 1, viewing wildlife of all types. Additionally, respondents were asked to allocate the viewing value over the various types of wildlife they hoped to see on a safari:

1. seeing big cats (lion, leopard and cheetah);
2. seeing large numbers of a variety of wildlife;
3. seeing African elephants;
4. learning about ecology and animal behaviour; and
5. other.

The respondents allocated 25 percent to category 3, viewing elephants.

The results of the two questions suggest that viewing elephants makes up about one-eighth, or 12.6 percent of the 'value' of an average safari. Therefore, the portion of consumer's surplus attributable to the viewing value of elephants is about $20–24 million per year.

Source: Gardner Brown, Jr. and Wes Henry, 1989. *The Economic Value of Elephants.* LEEC Paper 89–12. London: IIED/ The London Environmental Economics Centre.

the entire 'experience' must be considered in assessing values (and the ability of substitutes to replace them). For example, part of the thrill of a big-game safari is experiencing the majesty of the African landscape, a value not replaced by seeing the same animals in a zoo.

Therefore, in the case of perfect substitutes, the problem is reduced to the careful specification of the situation and the identification of the changes in use that might be expected. For imperfect substitutes, the value of the new environmental good may be somewhat different from that of the existing private substitute, making the valuation process more difficult.

This approach would appear to have most potential when the focus is on an environmental good or service that is an input into some other production system. The case of industrial water supply mentioned earlier is one example. Marketed goods can also yield valuable information on something as basic as domestic water supply. If an area is served by wells or small scale systems that rely on natural water sources, one way to estimate the value of this 'environmental service' (provision of potable water supply) is to examine the costs of replacing it with the least-cost alternative. This may be bottled water, home filtration systems, or roof top collectors. In other situations street water vendors provide a convenient, but high cost, service. These costs can be identified and used to assess the 'value' of maintaining and protecting the natural source.[1]

For natural ecosystem or amenity values, the use of the surrogate market approach varies. For example, one of the benefits of coastal wetlands such as mangroves is their role as a nursery for fish and as a source of shrimp larvae. Commercial hatcheries can be used to replace some of these services and, in fact, are increasingly common with the expansion of aquaculture and the destruction of natural breeding grounds. In this case the cost of the marketed good – commercial production of larvae – gives useful information on the value of the natural larvae production provided as an environmental service by an intact coastal wetland. Of course, the marketed good only replaces part of the total goods and services of the intact wetland. A complete valuation, within the framework of Total Economic Value, is needed to more fully assess the value of a healthy, functioning natural system.

If the environmental good in question is a recreational resource, this approach again provides useful, but limited, information. Pools, even wave pools, are not a complete substitute for an ocean beach, just as zoos do not replace seeing animals in the wild. Indoor ski runs (increasingly popular in Japan) are obviously no substitute for the real thing!

In conclusion, surrogate marketed goods can provide minimal estimates of the benefits from many environmental services (information that is useful

---

1 The poor often pay a high price and spend a very large share of their income on water. For example, in Port-au-Prince, Haiti, the poorest households sometimes spend 20 percent of their income on water; in Onitsha, Nigeria, the poor paid an estimated 18 percent of their income on water in the dry season while the rich paid only 2–3 percent. In some cases, households purchasing water from vendors pay as much as 25 to 50 times more per unit of water

in deciding whether to protect or replace an environmental good or service), but great care must be taken to ensure that other non-marketed or intangible benefits are not ignored.

CONTINGENT VALUATION METHODS

In some cases, where markets for environmental goods or services do not exist, are not well-developed, or where there are no alternative markets, it may not be possible to value the environmental effects of a particular project by using the market or surrogate-market techniques set out in Chapter 4 and at the beginning of this chapter. A viable alternative in these situations may be the use of contingent valuation methods (CVM), sometimes also referred to as hypothetical valuation.

CVM was proposed and first used in developed countries for valuation of public goods like access to parks, clean air or water, endangered species or un-obstructed views. The essential feature of public goods is that one person's consumption does not affect the amount available to the next person (although some public goods, such as recreational areas, may be subject to congestion beyond a certain point). Clean air or public defence are classic examples of public goods. Once provided, the marginal cost of an additional person using a public good is zero. Therefore, all respondents' willingness to pay rather than do without the good may be summed to provide an estimate of aggregate willing-ness to pay. In economic terms, this is analogous to the vertical summation of individual compensated demand curves.

However, use to date of CVM in developing countries has been most often for valuation of publicly or privately provided goods, such as water supply and sewerage in areas without existing services. In these cases CVM may be used as a type of market analysis, to guide systems design and setting of tariff rates.[2] An example of the use of contingent valuation for valuing a publicly-provided good, water supply, is given in Box 6.

These techniques involve the direct questioning of consumers to determine how they would react to certain situations. Unlike market and surrogate-market techniques, estimates are not based on observed or presumed behav-iour but, instead, by inferring what an individual's behaviour would be from the answers he or she expresses in a survey framework. This approach can be useful in evaluating components of development projects which cannot be measured using other methods Although they may not always yield precise estimates, they do provide an order-of-magnitude estimate which can be very valuable. Comprehensive reviews of survey-based valuation techniques are

---

than those connected to municipal systems. In Jakarta, for example, of some 8 million inhab-itants, only 14 percent are served by the municipal system and over 30 percent of the pop-ulation buy water from street vendors, who charge as much as $1.5 to $5 per cubic meter, a huge expense for those who can least afford to pay. (*Source: Water Resources Management, A World Bank Policy Paper.* Washington, D.C.: World Bank, 1993b.)

found in Cummings, Brookshire and Schulze (1986), and Mitchell and Carson (1989).

With the exception of the travel-cost method most of the techniques set out in Chapter 4 and this chapter examine changes in the quality of the environment in aggregated form and then place a value on the change. In contrast, the CVM techniques start with the individual and his or her perception of change. Once values for a representative set of people have been determined, they are aggregated to a total value directly dependent on the number of individuals affected. Whether or not an individual is benefited or hurt by the proposed change in environmental quality will have an impact on the valuations reported in a CVM. Box 7 explores the differences between compensating and equivalent variation, and the related concepts of willingness-to-pay (WTP) and willingness-to-accept-compensation (WTAC).

A description follows of the various contingent valuation methods in current use and the problems associated with them.

Bidding games

There are different varieties of bidding game, though they have certain features in common. In a bidding game, each individual is asked to evaluate a hypothetical situation and to express his or her willingness to pay (WTP) for, or willingness to accept compensation (WTAC) for, a certain change in the level of provision of a good. This technique is most often used in developed countries to value public goods like access to parks, clean air or water or unobstructed views.

There are two major types of bidding games: single bid games and iterative (or converging) bid games. In the former an interviewer, after describing a good (for example preservation of an endangered species, or a certain improvement in air or water quality) to a respondent, asks him or her to name the maximum price they would be willing to pay for the good or to name the minimum level of compensation they would accept in exchange for losing the option to purchase that good. The responses are then averaged and extrapolated to arrive at an aggregate willingness to pay or an aggregate level of compensation for the population as a whole.

For example, a recent study conducted in the Metropolitan Region of Rio de Janeiro (MRRJ) used a *single bid CVM* to elicit WTP for ambient surface water quality improvements (Scura and Maimon, 1993). The hypothetical market constructed for the study was modelled as a referendum whereby respondents could reallocate existing tax revenues to government interventions aimed at improving surface water quality.

---

2 This usage of contingent valuation is similar to conjoint measurement, which was developed by mathematical psychologists but found popular usage in the field of market research. Conjoint measurement is routinely used to analyse consumers' tradeoffs between bundles of attributes which make up different goods and the prices of the goods; this information is used as an aid in design and pricing of consumer products.

BOX 6
CONTINGENT VALUATION OF RURAL WATER
SUPPLY IN INDIA

In a recent study of the preferences of rural people for different levels of water supply service, Singh *et al* (1993) used the contingent valuation method to examine willingness to pay for yard taps or house connections in several rural villages in Kerala State, India.

Currently in Kerala, public water systems provide a low level of communal service with few private connections. The service is heavily subsidized and the monthly tariff for water from household connections is quite low. Little revenue is generated by the service, and the water authority cannot afford to maintain the system above a low level of reliability of service. Therefore, consumers are forced to supplement their piped water with water from traditional, often low quality, sources such as shallow wells, rivers, ponds, rainwater and vendors. Thus, the water supply is in a 'low-level equilibrium trap' – poor service generates little revenue thereby ensuring continuing poor service.

The research question posed was: is there potential for the system to rise out of its current trap? The use of CVM allowed respondents to consider hypothetical changes in water supply characteristics and to respond to questions about the effect of three variables – the cost of connection, the monthly tariff and improved quality of service – on their decision to purchase a yard tap (to become 'connectors' to the system).

The respondents' choices were modelled within a discrete choice random utility framework, in which an individual's response is the equal to the indirect utility that the respondent receives from choosing to purchase a yard tap rather than continuing to use existing sources. This choice is influenced by both the hypothesized water source characteristics and household characteristics. Of the variables affecting water use decisions, water policy decision makers can control only three: the connection charge, the tariff and the quality of service. An iterative bidding process was used, always starting with a pre-selected maximum possible bid. If a negative response was received, the interviewer worked down through a pre-arranged bid schedule.

The results of the analysis suggest that there is potential for the water system to rise out of its low-level equilibrium trap. A CVM survey of 1,150 households was carried out, and included both connectors and non-connectors in areas with improved water systems, and those living in areas currently without improved systems. The survey found that the constraint to new connections was the high up-front connection charge in combination with unfavourable credit market conditions. In addition, once connected, there was a high willingness to pay for improved quality of service.

Figure 9 shows the number of connections, revenue and consumer's surplus at the current tariff of 5 rupees per month. In contrast, Figure 10 shows the increased connections, revenue and consumer's surplus at an increased tariff of 10 rupees per month. (The demand curve was estimated from the survey results and assumed a connection charge of Rs. 100.) With increased connection at the Rs. 10 per month charge, those consumers who were already connected suffer a small loss in consumer's surplus (their costs go up from Rs. 5 to Rs. 10 per month), but this is more than offset by the very large increase in consumer's surplus from the large increase in those who now have private connections under the new tariff structure. As seen in Figures 9 and 10, the increase in consumer's surplus is roughly 450 percent, from about Rs. 5,500 in Figure 9 to Rs. 25,000 in Figure 10.

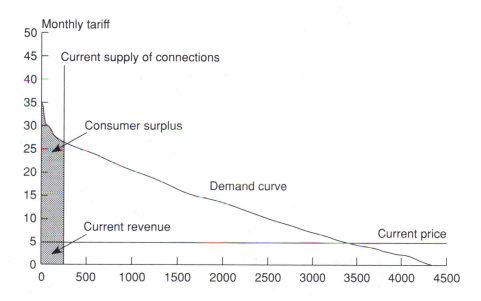

Figure 9 Current Availability of Yard Taps and Consumer Surplus

The results of this CVM application suggest that the local water authority can lead the way to a higher equilibrium by making some critical policy changes – encouraging private connections by folding the price of connection into the monthly tariff, charging a higher monthly tariff, and using the resulting increased revenues to invest in and maintain a higher quality of water service.

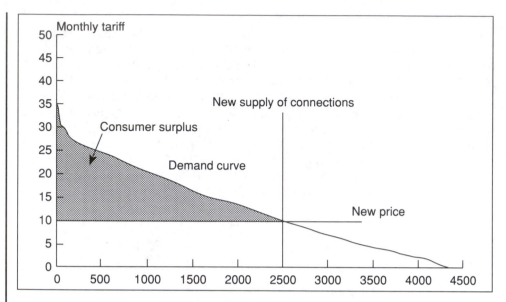

Figure 10 Simulated Change in Consumer Surplus with a Higher Price and Unconstrained Connections

Source: Singh, Bhanwar, Radhika Ramasubban, Ramesh Bhatia, John Briscoe, Charles Griffin and Chongchun Kim. 1993. *Rural water supply in Kerala, India: How to emerge from a low-level equilibrium trap. Water Resources Research*, vol. 29, number 7, July. pp. 1931–42.

The survey instrument, administered in 30-minute personal interviews to 100 households, contained 39 questions grouped into three sections. The first section contained a detailed description of the various water qualities that could be purchased in the hypothetical market, including visual displays such as written descriptions, photographs of sources and impacts of water pollution, and a water quality scale similar to that used by Carson and Mitchell (1984). The water quality scale compared various possible levels of water quality needed for different water uses such as boating, fishing and swimming. The next section included questions on demographic and socioeconomic characteristics of the respondents, such as income, education, literacy and type of housing and water supply. These data were compared with recent census information to give an indication of how representative the survey sample was of the total population in the area. In addition, the second section contained questions regarding frequency of and preferences for surface water uses, and perceptions of severity and importance of surface water quality problems. This information was used to help interpret the WTP responses. The final section was made up of questions to determine respondents' single bids for specific incremental improvements in surface water quality – for example, an improvement from boatable quality to fishable quality, or from fishable to swimmable quality.

BOX 7
WILLINGNESS TO PAY vs WILLINGNESS TO ACCEPT COMPENSATION

CVM techniques rely on standard neoclassical economic principles and use either of two Hicksian measures of consumer's surplus: compensating variation (CV) or equivalent variation (EV). Compensating variation is the amount of payment or change in income necessary to make an individual indifferent between an initial situation and a new situation with different prices. Equivalent variation may be viewed as a change in income equal to a gain in welfare resulting from a change in price. Alternatively, it may be considered as the minimum payment needed to persuade an individual voluntarily to forgo a price decrease. In the case of a price increase, EV is the maximum amount an individual will pay to avoid that increase. The difference between the two measures is that CV uses the initial level of utility as a reference point while EV evaluates the change from the *ex-post hoc* level of utility. Ordinary Marshallian consumer's surplus is sometimes used as an estimate of the more technically correct CV and EV. Freeman (1979) discusses the various consumer's surplus measures in depth.

While willingness-to-pay (WTP) is constrained by income, willingness-to-accept-compensation (WTAC) is not. Empirical evidence suggests that willingness-to-accept-compensation far exceeds willingness-to-pay for goods without close substitutes and for which individuals have legal or customary property rights. In numerous experiments Kahneman and Knetsch (e.g. 1992 a, b) have shown that the mere granting of ownership will cause individuals to value a good more highly than they would be wiling to pay to obtain the same item. This behaviour, which is not well-explained by economic theory, has strong psychological roots. In practice, it means that WTAC should be used when individuals are forced to give up something or suffer some damage (e.g. from increased air or water pollution). Similarly, WTP is the appropriate measure when an individual is being asked about an improvement from the present state. Actual experiments have shown this consistent asymmetry between WTP and WTAC for the same item, always dependent on the state of initial ownership. See Knetsch (1989, 1993) for an exploration of these themes.

The willingness to pay (WTP) responses were averaged and generalized to the total population of MRRJ to get an estimate of aggregate WTP for improvements in surface water quality. Although there were a significant number of zero WTP responses (30 out of 100), those who gave a non-zero response indicated that, on average, there is a significant willingness to pay for surface water quality improvements. Table 7 shows a summary of the willingness to pay responses (in dollars per household per month) for different levels of water quality, increasing in quality from 'boatable', the poorest, to 'swimmable', the highest. Assuming 2.4 million 4-person households, the total annual willingness to pay for increasing and maintaining surface water quality in MRRJ at the different levels is shown in the last column: for example, the total WTP to reach 'boatable' water quality is about US$ 133 million, while a 'swimmable' level of water quality is valued almost twice as much: US$228 million per year.

In *iterative bidding games* the respondent, rather than being asked to name a sum, is asked whether he should or would pay $X for the situation or good described. This amount is then varied iteratively until a maximum willingness to pay (or a minimum willingness to accept compensation) is reached.

For example, as part of a larger study of the ecology and economics of a Caribbean marine park in Bonaire, Netherlands Antilles, a small iterative bid CVM study was conducted to estimate WTP an entrance fee to the marine park by divers (Scura and van't Hof, 1993). In this survey, the respondents were a sample of 100 departing tourists who were familiar with the quality of diving conditions in the park – visibility (water clarity), reef conditions and abundance and diversity of fish and invertebrates.

The survey respondents were asked if they were willing to pay a $10/diver/ year entrance fee, the proceeds of which would go entirely to park management aimed at maintaining coral reef quality. Hypothetical charges (ranging from $20/diver/year to $100/diver/year) in the fee were proposed to elicit WTP increased entrance fees, until the maximum willingness to pay was determined. These responses were then averaged and extrapolated to the total visiting diver population to get an estimate of average WTP for park management which would maintain diving quality. The total WTP for park management can be interpreted as a minimum estimate for the viewing value of the coral reefs in the waters surrounding the island of Bonaire. More details of this application of CVM are presented in Case Study 7 in Part Two.

Although the Bonaire example illustrates the use of this approach with an educated, sophisticated population, CVM has also been successfully used in low income countries as seen in the water demand example reported earlier in Box 6 and in a study on establishing a national park in a rural, poor area in Madagascar. In the latter study, Kramer *et al.* (1992, 1994) used a simple iterative bidding game to determine villagers' willingness-to-accept compensation to forgo traditional extractive forestry uses in the proposed national park. The respondents were asked their WTAC in the form of amounts of rice, their staple food. This information was used to estimate a bid function in a logistics regression framework. The responses to the CVM questions indicate

Table 7 Willingness to Pay for Improved Surface Water Quality in MRRJ

Water quality level	WTP Avg. respondent (CR [$] / household / month)	WTP MRRJ population (CR x 10^12 [$ × 10^6]) / year
Boatable	CR 32,000 ($4.64)	CR 0.92 ($133)
Fishable	CR 38,060 ($5.52)	CR 1.10 ($159)
Swimmable	CR 54,500 ($7.90)	CR 1.57 ($228)

Source: Scura and Maimon, 1993.

that on average a compensation of about 240 kg of rice per year would make the respondents as well off with the park as without it. This translates into a monetary value of about $108 per household per year. More information on this can be found in Case Study 6 in Part Two.

Although both types of bidding game (single and iterative) may be useful, survey practitioners are split over their relative merits. One objection to the iterative technique is the potential existence of 'starting-point bias'. This is the idea that the interviewer may bias the respondent's answer by establishing a reference point for an acceptable range of bids. Another disadvantage is that although single bid games can be conducted either in person or through a mail survey, iterative bidding games can take place only in face-to-face interviews. One advantage of iterative bidding games is that answers often have a lower standard deviation around the mean as compared with single bid games.

'Hypothetical bias' is another problem inherent in bidding games and in survey techniques in general. People may not give answers which reflect their true values, particularly if they have no incentive to answer correctly questions which take time and thought. Another source of bias may be if people try to act strategically. This 'strategic bias' will reflect what respondents feel will be done with their answers. If they feel they may actually have to pay the amount they answer, they may undervalue their true response. If they feel that high answers will bring about changes they would like to see but they know they will not actually have to pay this amount, they may overstate the amount they would actually be willing to pay.

It is commonly thought that problems due to the hypothetical nature of CV questions arise more frequently and are more serious in the case of choice between goods with which people are not familiar. As a result, contingent values elicited for private goods (such as improved water supply) are expected to exhibit greater reliability and predictive validity than those elicited for public goods. This issue is thought to be even more problematic in developing countries, where various cultural factors may come into play.

For example, it is widely hypothesized that cross-sectional samples of populations in developing countries would be less likely than their developed country counterparts to be informed enough about environmental goods to be able make reliable estimates of WTP for these goods. It is also hypothesized that familiarity with and confidence in institutions governing the public good in question may be weak. These and other hypothesized limitations of CVM in developing countries are now being tested as the approach is increasingly being applied to valuation of both private and public goods. The initial results indicate much greater scope for the use of CVM in developing countries than previously thought. The studies reported previously from Madagascar and India are just two of the recent uses of CVM approaches. More are being reported each year in the literature.

Bidding games and possible biases are discussed in Rowe and Chestnut (1982) and Mitchell and Carson (1989). Although their discussion focuses on the valuation of visibility benefits, much of the information is applicable to valuation of other environmental goods and services.

These problems notwithstanding, surveys can be of great value in estimating economic values for effects which cannot otherwise be easily measured. Carefully worded surveys, properly conducted, can also provide a great deal of information regarding relative preferences from those people who will actually be affected by a proposed project.

Take-it-or-leave-it experiments

In a take-it-or-leave-it experiment, respondents are randomly divided into sub-samples or cells. Each sub-sample is then asked the same question, but each is offered a different amount of money and is asked either to take it or leave it. For example, an experiment attempting to find out people's willingness to accept a decrease in air quality might ask different groups of respondents if they would be willing to accept $10, $20, or $50 to allow the air in their neighbourhood to become more polluted. Each person is given only one amount to respond to, and the various amounts are randomly distributed over the entire surveyed population. The end result is a number of cells each with a certain proportion of people who would or who would not accept the payment offered. These answers can then be analysed using a logit model which will yield a willingness to pay for the average consumer. The aggregate willingness to pay can then be arrived at by multiplying this level by the number of people affected.

One advantage of this technique is that it more closely simulates an actual market. Respondents are offered something at a given price and can then decide whether or not to 'purchase' it.

Trade-off games

In trade-off games participants must choose between different bundles of goods. What is offered will, most often, be a mix of money and differing levels, or quantities, of an environmental good. The respondent is given a situation with a base level of an environmental good provided. Next she or he is offered an alternative in which the environmental good is increased, but at a price.

The respondent may then choose between these. The price of the increase is then varied until the respondent sees no advantage in one alternative over the other.

For example, in a situation attempting to determine willingness to pay for a larger neighbourhood park, the choices might be to pay no money and keep the original park or to pay a certain amount and get a five-hectare addition. The question would be repeated with different amounts of money until the point is found where the respondent is indifferent between paying no money and keeping the original park or paying a certain amount of money and receiving the park addition. The result may then be interpreted as the marginal compensated demand price for the environmental good.

Costless choice

Costless choice involves offering participants two or more alternatives, each of which is desirable and will cost nothing, and then questioning them directly to determine which they would prefer. One example might involve a choice between a certain sum of money or some unpriced environmental good (a reduction in air or noise pollution, or improved availability of public recreation facilities). If the individual chooses the environmental good rather than the money, then that would establish the minimum value of the environmental good to that individual. If the money were chosen rather than the good, then it would be established that the individual thought the good to be worth less than the sum of money.

Another version of this technique is to offer the respondent the choice between several well-known goods with established but differing values, and an unpriced environmental good. In a developed country, such goods might be a soft drink, a movie ticket, a dinner for two at a fine restaurant as compared with the opportunity to spend a day at a nearby lake. By calculating the value of those well-known goods which the respondent would reject in favour of the environmental good, it is possible to establish a range of values for the latter. Care must be taken to ensure that the goods are familiar and of approximately the same value to all respondents.

Costless choice may be useful in a developing country where actual market prices are not well established and few things are exchanged for money. In this situation, choices might include a kilo of rice, a day's worth of firewood, or other commonly traded goods. Such an approach may be more realistic to the respondent than the more abstract bidding game approach.

Delphi technique

Delphi techniques differ from the survey techniques described so far in that 'experts' rather than consumers are questioned. These experts, by an iterative process, try to place a value on a particular good. The Delphi technique has been used to place values on a diverse set of resources including the preservation values for endangered species, allocation of limited budgets

across competing areas, determination of minimum habitat size for preservation of genetic diversity, and the appropriate mix between development and
conservation.

The technique involves asking each of a group of experts to value or price a
particular good. The values chosen are then circulated with that member's
explanation for his/her choice. After seeing these opinions, the experts are then
asked to reconsider their estimates and to come to a new decision. Ideally, each
successive round should bring the values closer together until they cluster
tightly around a mean value.

Normally members of such a group are not assembled, or, if they are, then
the individual estimates are communicated in writing and not orally. This
prevents direct confrontation between the experts and helps to prevent any one
person from dominating the group. The results of the Delphi process will
depend on the quality of the experts involved, their ability to reflect societal
values and the manner in which the process is undertaken.

The limitations of contingent valuation

Because the contingent valuation methods do not analyse actual behaviour, the
most important question concerns their accuracy in simulating the conditions
of the real world. Surveys are, by their nature, hypothetical and, furthermore,
people have little experience in making explicit decisions about the value of
environmental goods.

Survey techniques are subject to a number of biases, including those
described in the section on bidding games. In addition to those previously
described, other biases may affect the reliability of the results.

An *information bias* can arise either as a result of providing too little
information about the choices offered or from misleading statements by the
interviewer. Ideally, survey respondents should be provided with clear,
complete and unbiased specifications for the choices. In a study on WTP to
protect humpback whales, an endangered marine mammal in Hawaii, 240
student respondents were divided into two equal groups that were surveyed
using a single bid format twice, once before and once after seeing a film
(Samples, Dixon and Gowen, 1986). Identical questionnaires were used before
and after seeing the film; the only difference was increased information on
whales from seeing the film, and a chance to reflect and make a second bid. The
experimental group increased its average reported WTP by 33 percent (to $57)
after seeing a conservation film on humpback whales. (Interestingly, the control
group that saw a film completely unrelated to whales also increased its bid an
average of 20 percent to $43, reflecting an increased value possibly due to just
having time to think about whales, even without any new information.)

Another form of information bias is referred to as the *embedding phenomena*
whereby respondents, commonly asked about their WTP to protect a particular
endangered species, give some dollar response, very commonly in the $8 to $10
per year range. When queried about their WTP to protect ALL endangered
species, the response is only marginally higher (often $15 or less). The first

species has effectively 'captured' most (often 60–80 percent) of the entire WTP for preservation or protection. It often does not matter which endangered species is the focus, just who asks first. This helps explain, in part, the steady stream of appeals for donations to protect one species or another that one receives in the mail!

In some types of survey, an *instrument bias* can arise if the respondent is hostile to the means by which payment would be collected. The vehicle chosen for payment – various forms of taxation, entrance fee or user fee – may result in different willingness-to-pay responses. Moreover, some people accustomed to certain public goods being provided free of charge may protest at any kind of payment and be unwilling to pay anything. Adding an additional question to make sure that any zero bid from the respondent actually reflects zero value to them, rather than a 'protest' against payment, can often eliminate this kind of bias.

One last problem is how to decide whether compensating variation or equivalent variation is the most appropriate measure of consumer's surplus. In theory, in most cases they should provide similar estimates, differing only in the effect on income caused by whether payment is made or received, and by the fact that willingness to pay is constrained by income. In practice, however, estimates obtained by using willingness to accept compensation as a measure are often much larger than those obtained from using willingness to pay (see Box 7).

The appropriate measure largely depends on property rights. Willingness to pay would be the correct measure if the right at issue is vested in the polluters, whereas willingness to accept compensation may be the preferred alternative if consumers have the 'property right' of a clean environment.

Properly planned and conducted surveys can, however, eliminate most of these problems. Since the costs of surveys increase with the number of people surveyed, the decision about their size must weigh the benefits of greater accuracy from larger samples against the additional costs. Care must also be taken that the sampling technique is statistically valid.

The level of accuracy is also affected by the way in which the hypothetical situation is described to the respondent. This should be as specific as possible and the alternative should be equally clearly outlined. The clearer the hypothetical situation, the less the effort called for from the respondent. Since in most cases little incentive is offered for an accurate answer, enough information must be given to allow the respondents to visualize the alternatives without undue effort.

Despite limitations, the methods of contingent valuation may, at times, be the best way to measure the effects of changes to the environment on social welfare. They may also be helpful in validating estimates of consumer's surplus obtained by more conventional methods.

CHOOSING A TECHNIQUE

The techniques presented in this chapter are called 'selectively applicable' because greater care has to be used in applying these approaches than was true for the generally applicable approaches presented in Chapter 4. Nonetheless, these techniques are increasingly being used to assess environmental impacts. In fact, some of these techniques (e.g. travel-cost and certain CVM approaches) are now becoming the standard approach for assessment of certain types of environmental goods and services.

The choice of technique, as always, is dependent on data and resource availability and the particular context. Surrogate-market techniques have proved particularly useful in valuing amenity benefits, among other environmental goods and services. The class of travel-cost approaches, for example, are very robust when used to estimate consumer's surplus from visitation to parks and protected areas, especially when visitors come from a number of different areas, and when the purpose of the trip is primarily to visit one site, or a group of similar sites. Travel-cost studies are being used in Africa to estimate the 'value' of certain recreational destinations, and to analyse the relative importance of different attractions within one locale. With the international increase in tourism, both within regions and between regions, the travel-cost approach will become increasingly useful. Not only does it allow planners to estimate the consumer's surplus associated with visits, but it also provides valuable information that can be used to set user fees, and thereby better manage and protect the very natural resources that attract visitors.

Other surrogate-market-based techniques are useful but, because they use indirect measures of value, have to be interpreted cautiously. They frequently give partial valuations, and hence are useful in providing a *minimum estimate* of the value of the resource in question.

Similarly, the rapid increase in the use of various CVM approaches, especially single and iterative bidding games, reflects the growing confidence in the use of this approach and its ability to provide initial answers for difficult valuation questions. In theory CVM should allow estimation of a wider variety of values than other approaches that focus on a subset of selected goods or services.

CVM techniques are particularly useful in two settings: first, when one wants to estimate willingness-to-pay for improvements in concrete social services like potable water supply, sewage disposal or solid waste collection. In these cases the objective of the CVM survey is easy to identify, and respondents have a good idea of what they are being asked to value (e.g. provision of in-house potable water supply, or, increasing system reliability from 8 to 24 hours per day.)

CVM is also increasingly being used in a very different valuation situation – identification of the WTP by individuals and societies to protect or preserve ill-defined or very difficult to value benefits. The valuation of biodiversity, or preserving natural areas are examples. The benefits are often grouped into categories like existence values, bequest values or option values, all terms used by economists to describe the values individuals place on just knowing that a resource exists and is protected, or can be preserved for possible use by the individual (option value) or one's children (bequest values). In these cases CVM is about the only way that economists can estimate WTP to protect and preserve. Because of the abstract nature of the resource being valued (and the uncertainty about its true value) the use of CVM in this case is more problematic and requires greater skill than in the previous case of the provision of concrete services. It may also be harder to use this approach in economic or cultural settings where such hypothetical surveying is less familiar. Still, this is one of the exciting 'frontier areas' in the valuation field.

CHAPTER 6

Potentially Applicable Methods of Valuing Environmental Impacts

Two distinct classes of techniques are presented in this chapter. The first class – hedonic value methods – uses market prices for goods or services to estimate an environmental value that is 'embedded' in the observed price. Property and land prices, and wages, are both used to place implicit values on environmental factors that are difficult to value in the abstract. For example, differences in property values are used to estimate people's willingness-to-pay for scenic views, or lower air pollution levels.

The second class of techniques are grouped under the heading of macro-economic variables and models. Although most of the valuation approaches discussed in this book are project focused, there is growing awareness of the impacts of broader macroeconomic variables (e.g. exchange rate changes, sectoral pricing policies) on the environment. We discuss briefly the use of linear programming and analysis of economy-wide impacts to identify likely environmental problems or benefits from policy changes. In a related vein, the use of natural resource accounting has gained increasing popularity as one way to help countries identify changes in both the flow and the stock of natural resources and environmental pollution. This information is then linked to the more traditional SNA – System of National Accounts – to present a fuller picture of economic growth over time.

Although the techniques presented in this chapter are all potentially applicable, their actual use to date in developing countries is mixed. The hedonic approaches are fairly data-intensive, and this has limited their use. Similarly, formal linear programming models have only been selectively applied. Natural resource accounting, on the other hand, has attracted considerable attention around the world and there is a growing literature on the application of this approach.

HEDONIC VALUE METHODS

The theory of hedonic prices (Rosen, 1974) is based on an alternative to neoclassical consumer theory in which a class of differentiated products is completely described by an array of objectively measurable characteristics (Lancaster, 1966). In general, goods and services consist of the bundle of attributes and characteristics that they contain, and prices reflect these differences. A basic car model, for example, can be customized by the addition of various options such as size of engine, finish, and number of accessories that it contains. Each different option has a price associated with it, and the consumer can easily identify what one is paying for as one selects various options. When goods or services contain an environmental dimension, however, it is difficult to explicitly price the environmental attribute by itself. It is 'embedded' in the overall sales price. In this context, observed prices and the levels of various attributes, environmental and non-environmental, contained in each good or service provide a measure of the implicit values consumers place on each of the attributes that make up the good or service, including the unpriced environmental attribute.

Two valuation techniques fall in the general category of hedonic methods: property and other land-value approaches, and wage-differential approaches. A discussion of each follows.

Property and other land-value approaches

In practice, property values are a prime example of the surrogate-market approach. The value of a house, for example, is affected by many variables including size, construction, location and the quality of its environment. When the variables of size, construction and location (in terms of proximity to work and shops) are controlled for, much of the price differential between similar units reflects the remaining variables related to environmental quality. A house built by a beach or with a beautiful view is an example. The information gathered from the consequent variations in house price may be used as a surrogate for measuring the unpriced variable.

The basic assumption is that purchasers of property will reveal their attitude to a bundle of attributes (some structural, some environmental, some aesthetic) by their willingness to pay. This is commonly true of residential properties. If no values were placed on environmental or other non-marketed attributes, then one would expect the value of a house to be equal to its construction costs plus an appropriate mark-up. In reality, of course, house prices reflect a very large range of attributes, only some of which are physical. The property-value approach is designed to control for certain variables so that any remaining price differential can then be assigned to the unpriced environmental good. Similarly, environmental 'bads' can be measured using this technique, as with a drop in property value due to increased noise or air pollution, or view obstruction.

As usually applied, the property-value approach needs extensive data on the selling prices of individual units and on a host of physical characteristics. Most of these variables, like the number of rooms, the floor space, construction materials and so forth, are easily measured. But in addition there will be one, unpriced, environmental variable like the levels of noise or air pollution.[1]

---

1 An excellent, although anecdotal, example of this effect is found in a neighbourhood in suburban Washington where one of the authors lives. There are about 350 homes in the area and they were all developed at the same time. They are very similar in all aspects – home size, construction, lot size, surroundings – except one. Some homes are on the edge of a major highway, the famous Interstate 495, the Washington Beltway. Although the homes are visually protected by trees there is considerable, and noticeable, ambient noise from the Beltway. These houses consistently sell for 5 percent to 10 percent less than the exact same house two blocks away. Purchasers have clearly expressed their valuation of noise pollution!

A multiple regression analysis is then undertaken and a coefficient is estimated for the environmental 'bad'; this coefficient is then used to value changes in environmental quality. In another version of the approach the 'priced' variables are controlled for and any residual property value is then assigned to the unpriced environmental good.

A classic example of the property-value approach is a study of the effect of air pollution on housing values in Boston (Harrison and Rubinfeld, 1978a, 1978b). One result of the study is a graph illustrating the relationship between willingness to pay for a 1pphm improvement in nitrogen oxide (NO_x) levels for households at three different income levels (Figure 11). Not surprisingly, households with higher incomes were willing (and able) to pay more for a given improvement in NO_x levels. The curves for all three income groups slope upwards, indicating that households are willing to pay more for a 1pphm improvement the higher the initial level of pollution. That is, the worse the present level of pollution, the more people are willing to pay for a unit reduction in the NO_x level.

Another example of the application of the property-value approach is the study of water quality problems in the Okoboji Lakes region of Iowa (d'Arge and Shogren, 1989a,b). The Okoboji Lakes, East and West, are connected by a small canal, are largely used for recreational purposes, and are very similar in

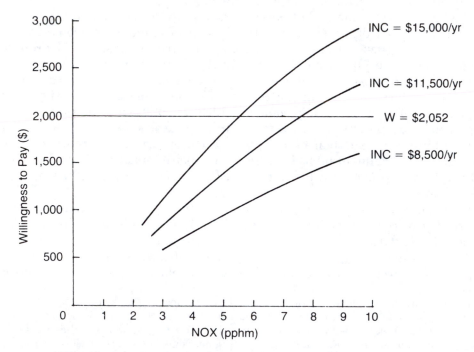

Figure 11 Willingness to Pay for 1pphm Improvement in NO_x Concentration By NO_x Level for Households at Three Income Levels (log–log version)
Source: D. Harrison and D.O. Rubinfeld, 'Hedonic Housing Prices and the Demand for Clear Air', *Journal of Environmental Economics and Management*, Vol. 5 (1978), pp. 81–102

natural attributes except for one important variable: water quality. East Okoboji is shallower and receives more wastes from agricultural and natural runoff, resulting in dense algae blooms during part of the summer recreational season, which give a lime-green tint to the water and a noticeable odour from decaying algae. West Okoboji rarely has the same problems and water quality is usually good during the important summer recreational months. The differences in water quality are reflected in the values of homes built along the lakeshore of the two lakes – homes in West Okoboji are larger (an average of 2,152 ft^2 vs. 1,415 ft^2) and are worth considerably more per square foot ($75.14 vs. $43.45) than those in the more polluted East Okoboji.

Three different valuation techniques were used to examine the differences in values between the two lakes: 1) a site valuation based on comparing property values between the two lakes; 2) a market value approach based on asking realtors and real estate agents in the area to identify reasons for the observed price differential; and 3) a contingent valuation approach asking residents their willingness-to-pay for improved water quality.

The analysts presented estimates of the importance (value) of water quality by using the data from realtors and recent sales. Three estimates were made (see Table 8): one was based on the realtors' estimate of the reasons for price differences between East and West Okoboji: the sample of realtors estimated that 46 percent of the observed difference was due to water quality (with neighbourhood and social class variables being second in importance at 24 percent); other locational variables accounted for the rest of the difference. When the 46 percent figure was applied to the $31.69 per square foot difference in assessed values of homes in the two lakes, this resulted in a price difference of $14.57 per ft^2 (.46 × $31.69) attributable to water quality, an amount equal to fully 23 percent of the value of the homes on unpolluted, West Okoboji Lake.

Second, a hedonic type of equation was estimated for West and East Okoboji Lakes separately. The dependent variable was assessed valuation in dollars and the independent variables included house area, total number of rooms, age of house, feet of lake frontage, and other number of buildings. The difference in the regression coefficients for the 'feet of lake frontage' variable was $1,009. Using the average measure of lake frontage, housing area, and the realtor estimated 'water quality factor' resulted in a difference in value attributable to water quality of $12.83 per ft^2 of house. A third estimate was made pooling the data from both lakes and putting in a dummy variable for East or West Okoboji. The value of this variable was about $84,190, a large portion of which was attributable to water quality differences. After adjustments, this approach yielded a 'clean water premium' of $13.83 per ft^2 for West Okoboji over East Okoboji.

This example illustrates an imaginative use of both expert opinion and hedonic property value approaches to identify the premium of one locale, with better water quality, over another very similar locale, with noticeable water quality problems. In this case the premium owners are willing to pay for improved water quality is substantial, averaging a bit over 20 percent of the value of the homes or up to $30,000 per house. (Since this is basically a recreational

Table 8 Comparison of Estimates of the Value of Water Quality,
West Okoboji Lake

Source of estimate	A. Difference in value per ft² of housing (1983 $)	B. Water quality as a per cent of observed average house values (West Okoboji)	C. Regression results as a per cent of realtor's estimate (Col A.)
Realtors' best estimate	$14.57	23%	–
Imputed value from regression on lake frontage	$12.83	20%	88%
Pooled regression estimate coupled with realtors' valuation	$13.58	21%	93%

Source: d'Arge and Shogren, 1989a.

community, environmental factors have, not surprisingly, a relatively greater weight.) One use of such information would be to assess the likely benefits to East Okoboji, with its poorer water quality, from investments to improve water quality. This information can then be compared to the costs of those investments in a first-cut benefit-cost analysis of the water quality improvement investment.

Obviously a great number of assumptions and considerable data are needed in order to undertake a property-value study. Some of these assumptions have been criticized by Mäler (1977). However, there may well be projects in which the approach could be used. For example, the benefits from an urban project for flood control could, in part, be estimated by examining price differences between housing units located in the flood-prone district and similar housing in less frequently flooded areas.

Similarly, the property-value approach can be used to estimate the economic benefits to households of an improved water supply system. Many water supply systems in developing countries are publicly provided. Despite the significant investment in these systems, many have failed to meet the needs of the intended beneficiaries. Information on household preferences for systems types, and particularly estimates of willingness to pay tariffs, is very useful information for systems design and tariff setting. This technique has also been applied in low income settings. North and Griffin (1993) used the property-value approach to study households' willingness to pay for water in the Bicol region of the Philippines in 1978. The model asserts that households' preferences for improved water supply systems are revealed through the differences in prices paid for housing with and without good water systems. In this case, access to a water source of a specific quality is considered as one of the total bundle of attributes of a house. It is presumed that households would be willing to pay more for a house with an 'improved' water supply than for a house with an 'unimproved' water supply, all other housing attributes being equal.

Variation in the dependent variable, imputed monthly rent, was explained by regressing it on variables that describe the characteristics of the house (such as construction, size, number of rooms, and location), and variables that describe the water source (such as type and distance from house). The coefficients of the water source variables yielded estimates of the rent premiums paid for water sources of different qualities. Households were willing to pay between $1.40 and $2.25/month in 1978 prices for access to a piped water system, representing about one-half of household imputed rent. The same households were willing to pay significantly less for deep well connections and close to zero for closer public taps.

As with any non-market valuation technique, applications of the property value approach have to be thought out carefully and all assumptions made explicit. While a precise evaluation may not be possible, an order of magnitude of the value placed on the environmental attribute may be obtained.

Other land value approaches are a variant of the property value approach, and rely on the same underlying principles. Here, rather than compare sales prices of different pieces of real estate, an observable market price (usually that of retail land prices) is used to evaluate an environmental issue. If nearby parcels of land are priced differently, for example, any differences between them will normally be due to one of two factors: the productivity of the piece of land or unpriced environmental qualities. The productivity of the land may be evaluated by measuring the change in the value of output described earlier, and the capitalized value of productivity should be reflected in the retail price of land. In addition, there may be other unpriced impacts that are also incorporated in land values. These could include such things as aesthetic values, decreased risks of flooding or of some other environmental catastrophe (although some of these should be captured in the productivity analysis), or increased attractiveness as a habitat for wildlife. By examining land prices and the capitalized value of production from that land, the residual can be determined. Part of this residual represents the 'surrogate' value of environmental or other unpriced factors.

Underground transmission lines for utilities provide an example. Domestic electricity, for instance, can be provided by power lines laid either above or below ground. Most people prefer them to be underground, but then they are more costly to install. Are the benefits worth the extra cost? In using the land-value technique the market price of similar parcels of land would be established to see if there was any difference between those with power lines above and those with power lines below ground. If such a difference were to be found, then the amount could be interpreted as representing the capitalized value of the 'benefit' from underground power lines.

In sum, the land-value approach uses real market prices for land with varying attributes as a measure for determining the value of an environmental attribute which is not normally priced. It is, of course, essential when using this method to ensure that any differences are net of the value of the direct effects on productivity (although the latter are valid measures of environmental benefits from many soil and water resources management projects).

Wage differentials

The wage differential approach is another hedonic method and is similar to property- and other land-value approaches. It uses information on differences in wages for jobs with different degrees of risk of becoming sick or dying to place values on incremental morbidity and mortality risks. The theory is that workers have to be paid a premium to undertake jobs that are inherently risky (or disagreeable) and this information can be used to estimate the implicit value individuals place on sickness or premature death.

The essence of the theory underlying this approach dates back at least to the late eighteenth century and Adam Smith's classic book, *The Wealth of Nations*. Smith recognized that if workers were relatively homogeneous in their abilities, were mobile and had accurate information about job characteristics, the demand for and supply of labour would generate wage differentials to compensate for undesirable, nonpecuniary job characteristics. The job characteristic of interest here is the above-average risk of death or serious injury inherent to some jobs (e.g. mine workers, steel workers). In other words, a higher wage would be needed to induce people to work in polluted areas or to undertake risky jobs. The wage differential is the dollar amount that would cause a worker to be indifferent between undertaking the risk to life or health inherent in the job and having a loss in income equal to that dollar amount.

The general approach for estimation of these wage differentials is to regress workers' wages on a group of explanatory variables, including personal characteristics, job characteristics, and health or death risks associated with the job. The coefficient of the job risk variable yields the wage-risk tradeoff that is used to estimate the implicit value of a statistical life[2] or the implicit value of reduced risk of morbidity.

Most applications of the wage-differential approach have been made in the United States and Great Britain (Fisher *et al* 1989). The magnitude of on-the-job risks examined by these studies are typically quite small, averaging .0001. The average value of reduction by .0001 in annual mortality risk to an individual estimated by these studies ranged between $100 and $800 (1986 US$) per year with an average value of about $300 per year. This translates into a value of $3 million per death avoided for a large population (Ostro, 1992). However, these numbers are not considered valid for use in countries other than those for which they were estimated.

---

2 The distinction between a statistical life and the life of a particular individual is discussed in Chapter 7.

Implicit in the use of this technique is an assumption regarding competitiveness of labour markets, labour mobility and the extent of information flows. This approach cannot be used if wages are set centrally or are otherwise distorted. Given the high degree of unemployment and underemployment typical in developing countries, lack of labour mobility is also a problem. Other problems similar to those encountered with use of the property- and other land-value approaches are experienced in the application of the wage differential approach. For example, it is difficult to isolate the exclusive impact of risk on wage rates, mainly because job characteristics other than risk influence wage rates and, if omitted, bias estimates. More basic problems, however, are related to the comparability across different types of risk, the likelihood of skewed risk aversion in the sample, and the effects of incomplete information.

Some critics of this technique contend that the value of different types of risk varies, and voluntary risk may not be a very good proxy for involuntary risk. This is because individuals who knowingly undertake risks are apt to be less risk averse than the general population. Problems would also arise due to virtual lack of access to information on job risks. In the absence of complete information, workers may not understand the actual risks and, if so, their subjective valuation of the risks would be a biased measure of value of actual risks.

MACROECONOMIC VARIABLES AND MODELS

Development projects often affect environmental quality and resource sustainability on a regional level, not only around the project site. Similarly, there may be macroeconomic policy decisions that have widespread, if unintended, environmental impacts. Although much of the valuation work in the past has focused on project-level impacts, there is a growing appreciation of the role of broader macroeconomic variables and their potential for both positive, and negative, environmental effects.

This last section focuses on these issues and examines three approaches. Linear programming, a formal way to model production decisions and trace out their impacts on the economy, can also be used to estimate the generation of environmental effects. Its use in this regard is somewhat limited, but the approach has considerable validity. (We have not included input-output analysis in this volume since its application to environmental issues in developing countries has been even more limited.)

A second approach is the rapidly evolving field of natural resource accounting, NRA. This is an application of the more traditional national income accounting approach widely used by countries to trace general economic conditions. Although there are a number of competing methodologies, the NRA approach commonly focuses on stocks of environmental assets – their rate of use and changes over time. Valuation of environmental goods and services plays an important role in the process of NRA.

The third approach discussed here is the broader analysis of economy-wide impacts of macroeconomic policy changes. This approach attempts to identify the environmental impacts of macro policy changes that are introduced to promote general economic growth. Although the overall benefits of macroeconomic policy reform may be very favourable, there may be unintended negative environmental impacts that then need to be addressed by more targeted policies.

Linear programming models

In complex situations which involve many choices and a large number of variables, mathematical programming models may provide suitable approaches to analysing environmental impacts. Linear programming and its extended models are mathematical programming techniques that have been widely applied to models for the optimization of environmental quality.

Linear programming is primarily concerned with the allocation of scarce resources. The model's purpose is to optimize a predetermined objective, or set of objectives, subject to a set of constraints or to other minor objectives. Decision-makers must specify in advance what weights must be attached to the variables; the implicit properties of the general linear programming model require that the functional relationships in the problem be linear and additive, divisible and deterministic.

When linear programming is applied to environmental problems, this is usually done by maximizing the economic benefits of production while at the same time preserving or enhancing environmental quality or minimizing the regional incremental capital cost of controlling emissions. The dual-primal property of every linear programming problem is one of its most useful features because it yields shadow prices for the constraints in the primal problem. The calculated values of shadow prices are especially important for sensitivity analysis.

A shadow price on a constraint indicates how much the value of the objective function changes if the constraint is altered by one unit. Shadow prices are obtained from the dual problem and allow policy-makers to see which particular constraints are exerting the greatest restriction on the attainment of primary objectives. This is particularly relevant to the management and planning of environmental quality, because shadow prices often take the place of actual market prices as guides to the evaluation of unpriced environmental services.

Environmental quality effects can be incorporated into linear programming models in several ways, depending on the nature of the objectives in environmental management, the technologies available for the reduction of pollution and the incentives offered for implementation. Where economically feasible technologies for control are unavailable, effects on the quality of the environment can be regulated by 'structural' methods. If economically feasible alternative technologies are available, then 'technical' means of reducing pollution can be implemented.

Applying linear programming to environmental issues is not an easy task. Inherent problems of linear programming such as the difficulty of incorporating joint costs and economies of scale make it difficult to model realistic situations accurately. The need to assign relative weights to economic and environmental quality may present difficulties to planners and decision-makers.

The solution to linear programming problems is affected by the constraints, since the number of variables in the problem cannot exceed the number of constraints. Insufficient basic constraints lead to oversimplicity, but the incorporation of further, arbitrary, constraints might invalidate the true restrictions on the attainment of planning objectives. Shadow prices in the dual can also be affected by this difficulty and can, therefore, lead to serious mistakes in interpretation.

Finally, like most general-equilibrium models, the technique requires much data gathering, information processing, and computing effort. The planner must take care in deciding whether or not the problem is complex enough to warrant such an elaborate model.

Natural resource accounting

The past decade has seen a major new development in thinking about how nations measure their economic growth and well-being. The traditional approach has been the United Nations' System of National Accounts (SNA). The emphasis is on GDP (Gross Domestic Product, the sum of all goods and services produced in the country, excluding intermediate goods) and on its closest derivative, NDP (Net Domestic Product, which is equal to GDP less consumption/depreciation of man-made capital), both of which are often used inappropriately as indicators of welfare. A major concern is that traditional national accounts do not measure the *sustainability* of economic activity.

GDP and NDP, in fact, do not reflect long-term sustainable growth because natural resources depletion and degradation are ignored. GDP and NDP generally fail to consider the use or depreciation of environmental assets: undesirable outputs (pollution) are usually overlooked, and environmental inputs are often implicitly valued at zero prices.

For example, many natural resources (oil or minerals in the ground, forests, or fish in the sea) are not counted as stock resources, and are only entered into the SNA when they are extracted and sold (turned from a stock resource, e.g. forested hillsides, into a flow, e.g. an annual timber harvest.) The danger in this approach, of course, is that a country can harvest potentially-renewable resources like forests, fisheries, and certain water resources in a non-renewable manner, and appear to be 'growing' rapidly, even though the resource base that is supporting this growth is being destroyed. This is equivalent to consuming 'natural resource capital', not the yearly 'income' from that capital. (For non-renewable resources like minerals and petroleum products, this problem has long been recognized and is reflected in the use of depletion premiums.) If the annual harvest of renewable resources is equal to or less than the rate of annual growth or replacement, this is not an issue – 'natural capital' is left intact and the annual harvest is a legitimate income from that resource.

In one of the first careful examinations of these problems Repetto *et al* (1989) analysed Indonesia's growth over the 1971 to 1984 period, taking into account the depletion of just three natural resources – petroleum, timber and soils. Based on this analysis, Repetto *et al.* re-estimated Indonesia's GDP growth (then labelled 'NDP') after taking into account the unsustainable use of natural resources but without considering the depreciation of man-made capital. Average GDP growth decreased by 3 percent per year, from 7.1 percent per year to only 4 percent per year (see Figure 12). The message was clear – growth that was based on the unsustainable extraction of natural resources was not sustainable, and gave a false image of the health and rate of growth of the Indonesian economy. (One should note that this type of analysis is very sensitive to both the base year chosen, and the treatment of mineral and petroleum reserves, especially the effect of new discoveries. A major contributor to the Repetto *et al* results is the discovery of new reserves in the early 1970s.)

Aside from the problem of the measurement of the stocks and flows of natural resources, another problem area with the traditional SNA is in the handling of pollution-control expenditures and the measurement of environmental damages, often from pollution. In the traditional accounts expenditures on pollution control equipment and services are counted as additions to GDP,

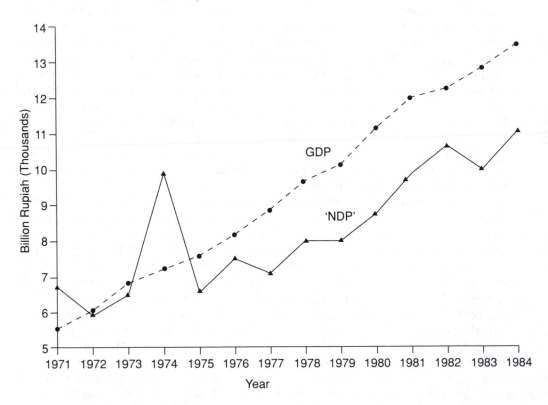

Figure 12 Indonesian GDP and 'NDP' in Constant 1973 Rupiah
Source: Repetto *et al.* (1989)

even though these so-called 'defensive expenditures' are only undertaken to counteract the harmful effects of pollution. True, any expenditure creates jobs and other economic benefits; however, defensive expenditures are basically unproductive and therefore should not be given the same importance as more traditional expenditures. Along a similar line, the health and productivity costs of pollution are ignored in the SNA, except when they result in medical treatment costs or expenditures to mitigate an impact or take preventive steps.

As quickly becomes evident, there are a number of issues involved if one wants to estimate a 'green' national account. Adjustments have to be made for the changes in stocks of resources and their values, and how to handle the various defensive expenditures and other damage costs of pollution and environmental degradation. There is no general agreement on which approach to use and a number of different approaches are now being tried.

Two basic approaches have been developed to produce measures of 'green' national income. Both can be considered as 'satellite accounts' in that they are separate from the core SNA. Their difference lies in the degree of closeness to the home planet – the core SNA.

Resource and environmental accounts usually measured in non-monetary units, accompany conventional GDP accounts and are commonly referred to as satellite accounts. They represent a compromise in that they do not change the well-established SNA, and their associated time-series, yet they do provide countries with a set of supplementary accounts and indicators for selected natural resources and the environment; there is no attempt to be all-inclusive. This form of satellite accounts typically involve physical measurement (but sometimes they may also be monetized) and have clear linkages with the standard SNA through Input/Output Accounts. These accounts measure stocks and flows of resources (extraction/harvest and discoveries), pollution emissions, and environmental protection expenditures, with the potential for sectoral disaggregation.

Integrated accounts are another form of satellite account that attempt to develop a complete system that has closer links to the core SNA. Integrated accounts attempt to monetize resource depletion and the effects of environmental pollution and are used to develop alternative national accounting aggregates, in which monetary value is assigned to environmental variables, and new measure of income, product and wealth are produced. Unresolved theoretical and methodological issues explain the existing controversy on the development of integrated accounts. Integrated accounts can produce the information needed to calculate an environmentally-adjusted net domestic product (EDP), as discussed in the following sections.

Recent Events: The 1993 SNA and Preparation of Satellite Accounts. The current system of national accounts was developed over many years; international guidelines emerged in 1954 and 1968, but by the 1980s it was evident they would have to be revised. The current revision process took nearly a decade and was completed in 1993 and recommended the preparation of satellite accounts. At the same time, in 'Agenda 21', the major policy document of the June 1992 Rio Earth Summit, 178 nations committed themselves to 'expand existing systems of national accounts in order to integrate environmental and social dimensions in the accounting framework, including at least satellite systems of natural resources in all member States.'

To help meet this need the UN Statistical Office (UNSTAT) developed the System of Integrated Environmental and Economic Accounts (SEEA) and in December 1993 it issued an SNA handbook on implementing integrated environmental and economic accounting. A number of studies have been carried out in recent years in support of that work. The World Bank has collaborated with the UNSTAT and country authorities in Mexico and Papua New Guinea to test the practicality of the new methodology and handbook (see Lutz 1993, 1994 for details on the approach and the following presentation).

Preparation of an Environmentally-adjusted net Domestic Product (EDP). Since most countries' national accounts do not calculate depreciation of man-made capital and therefore do not derive a net domestic product (NDP), the first task is usually to make such estimates. Then, two sets of environmental adjustments are made. First, resource depletion (from oil, mineral, and timber extraction, for example) is deducted from NDP, thereby obtaining EDP1. Second, the monetary value of environmental damage (air and water pollution, waste disposal, soil depletion, and groundwater use) is subtracted from EDP1, thus arriving at EDP2.

These calculations are much easier said than done, of course. Numerous judgments were required in choosing methodologies for estimating money values for both depletion and degradation, and in most instances indirect estimates were required. For example, the impact of pollution on health and future productivity should be estimated and monetized. Unfortunately, knowledge is inadequate for such calculations even in the most advanced industrial countries. Instead, an indirect measure – estimating the cost of reducing pollution to 'acceptable' levels – is used. A similar approach is employed to calculate the costs of soil erosion, but a host of conceptual challenges and methodological choices remain.

In the case of Mexico – a relatively advanced developing country with severe environmental problems – a recent study showed that Net Domestic Product (NDP) was 6 to 13 percent lower than originally estimated for 1985 if environmental degradation and damages were taken into account (van Tongeren *et al*. 1993). EDP1 was estimated as 94 percent of NDP for 1985 (the only year for which data were adequate), and EDP2 was estimated at 87 percent of NDP. Figure 13 shows the impact of adjusting Mexican investment figures for resource depletion and environmental damage to Mexico's productive base in 1985. In turn, investments in human capital formation and technological progress must then be added to see if net investment in Mexico in 1985 was positive or negative.

In Papua New Guinea – a country at a relatively early stage of development, with a large extractive industry – EDP1 was estimated at 92 to 99 percent of NDP for the 1986–90 period and EDP2 at 90 to 98 percent (Bartelmus *et al*.

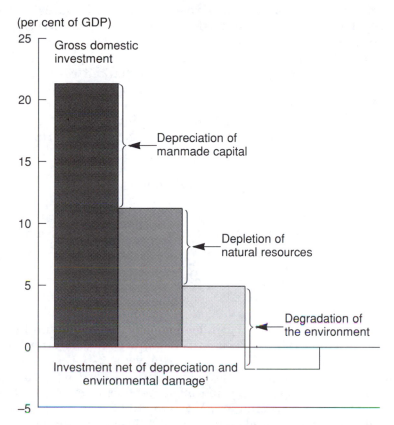

(per cent of GDP)

¹ This is not intended as an accurate representation of the change in the nation's productive capacity, since it excludes important components of human capital accumulation and technological change.

Figure 13 Mexico: Estimated Impacts of Adjustments for Depreciation of Manmade and Natural Capital, and Environmental Degradation (1985)
Source: data from van Tongeren *et al*, (1993) as reported in Steer and Lutz (1993).

1993). These figures raise awareness of the need to adjust for environmental costs but in themselves give little specific guidance to policymakers. Sectoral accounts, however, provide more insight.

In addition to the recent Mexican and PNG studies, a number of developed countries have on-going efforts on natural resource and environmental accounting. Many of these have been restricted to creating physical accounts that parallel conventional national accounts rather than to estimating the money values of resource loss and environmental damage, for adjusting the 'core' accounts themselves.

Norway, for example, the country with perhaps the longest history of interest in resource accounting, has put its efforts into refining physical stock estimates in key sectors such as oil, minerals, fish, forestry, and hydropower. The Netherlands, another country with a history of concern in this area, has endeavoured for over a decade to derive monetary measures of the loss of 'environmental functions' (so far unsuccessfully). France is trying the most ambitious system yet – 'patrimony accounting' – which is aimed at analysing and describing the natural environment in its three basic dimensions: economic, social, and ecological. However, only limited resources have been available for implementation, which has so far been limited to the physical data. US efforts in this field have been restricted to collecting data on pollution abatement expenditures, although President Clinton committed his adminis-tration to producing environmentally adjusted accounts during his term in office.

Macroeconomic and economywide policies

The focus of much of this volume has been on project-level analysis of environ-mental impacts and their valuation. Even the use of mathematical programming models tends to be sector specific. The evolving field of natural resources account-ing (NRA) discussed in the last section does examine economywide changes within an accounting framework. The NRA approach is heavily dependent on valuation methodologies to place monetary values on the resources, or impacts, that it includes. This last section, however, takes one additional step back and considers the impacts of general macroeconomic and other economy-wide policies (hereafter referred to as economywide policies) on the environment. This is a recognition that in addition to 'getting your prices right' there are also many situations where economy-wide policy reform is needed to promote general economic growth but may, in addition, have beneficial, or harmful, effects on the environment. (See Schramm and Warford, 1989, and Pearce and Warford, 1993, for additional background on economy-environment linkages.)

The impact of policy reform is an important dimension in the economic analysis of environmental impacts. Incidentally, the marginal costs of address-ing environmental problems through correcting policy failures may even be *negative*, in which case the environmental gains are essentially 'costless' to society. An example is the removal of a policy of subsidizing irrigation water for farmers (water is often provided at little or no charge to farmers). The removal (or reduction) of water subsidies has a number of beneficial effects: more efficient water use, less wastage and associated environmental problems like waterlogging and salinization, and reduced government expenditures. These types of policy reform are often referred to as 'win-win' policies – the economy gains and the environment benefits.

Governments traditionally have made decisions on economywide policies like trade regimes, foreign-exchange rates, subsidies for agriculture and industry, and sectoral development with little regard for the environment (see Munasinghe, Cruz and Warford, 1993, for a discussion of these issues). Environmental problems were handled by either an environmental impact assessment type approach for new projects, or by the use of regulations or, more recently, market-based incentives, to handle existing problems. It was thought that economywide policies were too diffuse and broad to link directly to environmental problems, and therefore Ministries of Planning or Finance rarely explicitly considered the environmental impacts of their actions.

With increased awareness of the links within the ecosystem and the economy, however, there is a growing concern that general macroeconomic policy reforms must also be evaluated for their environmental impacts if environmental damage costs are to be minimized and economic growth made more sustainable. This was a basic finding of the World Bank's 1992 *World Development Report, Development and the Environment* – economic development and environmental protection are both simultaneously possible and mutually supportive, if proper analysis is done and appropriate measures are taken. Increasingly, studies are being carried out to more fully understand the links between economywide policies and the environment, and design appropriate actions if negative environmental consequences are identified. Frequently the response to policy changes involves the substitution of certain forms of man-made capital for natural capital (e.g. fish hatcheries to replace natural spawning grounds lost as a result of wetland or coastal development).

One should note, however, that genuine uncertainty remains about the ability of society to substitute man-made capital for natural capital. Much of the history of the past 100 years has been precisely about such substitution. Whether or not this can continue indefinitely, or whether a 'cautionary principle' should apply to preserve a certain stock of natural capital, is central to the writings of Herman Daly, among others (see Daly and Cobb, 1989, for one discussion of this question). The debate about development *with or versus growth* is derived from these concerns.

Experience around the world has shown, however, that the general economic benefits from macroeconomic reforms are substantial and essential for long term economic growth and environmental protection. A major conclusion of the work done to date is that the overall benefits of improving the price system and correcting for market failures (by including some measure of the associated environmental damages caused in the price of the good or service) are by and large environmentally friendly. The removal of distortions in the pricing system (especially policy reforms that remove subsidies for energy and water) and the general process of market liberalization are important in sending the correct signals about scarcity. Scarce resources *should* cost more, and increasing prices will lead to more efficient use of such scarce resources.

In the short run, however, there may be serious environmental consequences of economywide policy reforms that must be addressed by targeted policies. It is frequently observed that when economies liberalize and reduce distortions, there may be localized or sectoral-specific environmental problems. For example, liberalizing trade, which has many economic benefits, may also encourage the harvesting of additional timber for export or an increase in fish catch to send overseas. Similarly, price reform often involves removing subsidies, which is almost always positive towards the environment. However, changes in the internal terms of trade, often to increase the artificially depressed price levels of agricultural products, may result in pressures to increase agricultural production in fragile or otherwise inappropriate areas. In spite of these problems it is usually a mistake to stop macroeconomic reform in the name of 'environmental protection.' The benefits of reform should be enough to pay the costs of targeted policies or compensation that address related environmental problems.

Two recent examples from Latin America that are part of World Bank research efforts on this topic illustrate some of these issues: fuel taxation and industrial pollution issues in Mexico City and the question of land tenure, pricing policy, and expansion of the agricultural frontier in Brazil's Amazon. Each study illustrates the links between macroeconomic policies and the environment.

In Mexico, Eskeland and Ten Kate examined the impacts of various government policies on the industrial sector and its effects in terms of pollution and energy use, and pricing policies for transport fuels in Mexico City (Eskeland, 1994a, Ten Kate 1993, Eskeland and Ten Kate, 1993). Structural changes in the composition of Mexican industry have had a major impact on the generation of pollution. Between 1950 and 1970, the pollution intensity (the production of pollution per dollar of output) of the manufacturing sector increased by 50 percent. Between 1970 and 1989, in part encouraged by government investments and subsidies in the petrochemical and fertilizer industries, the industrial pollution intensity in Mexico increased by another quarter. The entire effect observed is due to the higher-than-average growth of the more polluting sectors, since the study used fixed, sector-specific pollution output coefficients derived from US emissions data. Hence, changes are attributable to changes in the *structure or composition* of the manufacturing sector (technological changes within sectors are ignored).

At the same time, encouraged by a government policy that kept energy prices artificially low, energy intensity also increased by about 6 percent, rather than follow the world-wide trends towards *decreasing* energy intensity linked to efficiency gains in energy using devices. (During the same period industrial energy intensity *decreased* by about 35 percent in the OECD countries, in large part due to high energy prices and associated structural and technological developments.) The Mexican energy subsidies have been expensive – between 1980 to 1985 fuel and electricity subsidies absorbed 4 to 7 percent of Mexican GDP, an amount equal to $8 to $13 billion.

In his analysis of air pollution in Mexico City (an urban conglomeration of almost 20 million people) Eskeland (1994a) analysed the principal policy options the government considered to reduce transport-related air pollution. The government's two policy levers are to make cars and other vehicles less polluting, and to reduce overall travel (the number of trips). Two types of policies were considered: regulations and the use of prices. Regulations that encouraged the use of 'cleaner' vehicles had an important impact on reducing the amount of pollution per trip. These policies, however, were not effective in reducing the *number* of trips. To reduce travel overall the most effective policy was to increase energy prices, such as through gasoline taxes. An analysis of a city-wide pollution control programme showed that increasing energy prices reduced annual costs of the control programme by about $110 million, or 23 percent overall.

100

The strong interplay of economic forces is also illustrated by the estimates of elasticity for total gasoline consumption. To evaluate whether or not vehicle purchases and use are sensitive to policy instruments, econometric analysis of data from Mexico was carried out. The results for total gasoline consumption (Table 9) showed that short and long run elasticities were fairly similar, and that gasoline demand was quite responsive to gas prices. (An own price elasticity of about −0.79 means that each 10 percent increase in gas prices will result in a 7.9 percent decrease in gas demand.) However, even though consumption was quite responsive to gas prices, demand was also closely linked to incomes: as income grew, gas consumption grew equally rapidly (an income elasticity of demand of about 1.0). Clearly Mexican authorities will have a major challenge to control pollution in a rapidly growing economy. More importantly, however, the use of price policy to manage demand for polluting goods could be an important instrument in the economist's 'tool kit'.

Table 9 Elasticities for Total Gasoline Consumption, Mexico City

Elasticity with respect to:	Short run elasticity	Long run elasticity
Gasoline price	−0.785	−0.799
Car price	−0.025	−0.029
Income	0.978	1.005

Source: Eskeland, 1994a

Eskeland also considered another regulatory policy – the 'day without a car policy.' Introduced as an emergency measure to reduce pollution, this demand management policy required that drivers keep their car off the street for one day a week depending on the last digits of the license plate. The analysis indicated that the policy had a perverse result: total vehicle use was actually *higher* after an adjustment period, as families bought second cars as a legal means of circumventing the regulation. The second cars tended to be older, less efficient and more polluting, and available for additional trips throughout the week.

Schneider[3] analysed the role of government policies among the factors that influenced forest loss, agricultural expansion, and land abandonment in the Brazilian Amazon. He found that government policies were important, but that more general economic forces, including relative prices of land and important crops, interest rates, and land ownership institutions were equally important in explaining the observed pattern of deforestation and expansion of the agricultural frontier. This case is examined in more detail in Box 8.

---

3 For earlier work on the issue of government policy and land clearing in the Amazon see Binswanger (1989) and Mahar (1989).

BOX 8
PROPERTY RIGHTS AND LAND ABANDONMENT IN THE BRAZILIAN AMAZON

The deforestation and expansion of agricultural holdings in the Brazilian Amazon have received considerable attention during the past decade. Both Mahar (1989) and Binswanger (1989) discussed the role of government policy, especially subsidies and tax breaks to encourage the development of agricultural enterprises and ranches, even when real returns were negative. Land ownership and titling was often linked to clearing land (even if it wasn't cultivated), and road building allowed new settlers to flood into previously inaccessible parts of the Amazon. These policies, that promoted unsustainable development, have now largely been corrected. Still, even after removing these distortions a cycle of land opening and abandonment can be widely observed and Schneider examined this within an economic-institutional framework.

Developing a simple economic model of the opportunity cost of both time and capital to smallholder settlers, and larger business investors (capitalists), Schneider demonstrated that these two factors – the opportunity cost of the settlers and their access to capital – explained much of what was observed given the institutional development of government and property rights in the frontier. In particular, the development of effective property-right regimes (a government responsibility), and access to capital, were the two most important variables explaining the patterns of incomes, turnover, and land use.

Simply stated, settlers will move in and open up new lands depending on their opportunity cost (in effect, what they have to 'pay' themselves to undertake any action); this determines how long they are willing to wait for formal government institutions, including property rights, to evolve. Many small settlers have low human capital and hence, low opportunity costs. They also face a high cost of capital, a high interest rate. These settlers are content to survive on modest returns and await development (roads, improved markets and social services) to come to them. Capitalists, on the other hand, have better access to capital (it costs them less to borrow) but have high opportunity costs for their time. They can borrow easily but will only do so when returns to capital are reasonable. As a result they are reluctant to invest in land until the support services are available to allow them to market output and government institutions develop sufficiently to help make tenure secure.

The observed patterns of land abandonment are thus explained in part by the characteristics of the property rights regime – both its nature and the costs of defending property rights. Since occupation of land was required to enforce ownership, some observed land abandonment is explained by the abandonment of large holdings that were settled prematurely by capitalists.

Since the market and associated infrastructure were not sufficiently developed to make the holdings a going concern, and since the opportunity cost of the time of the capitalist is high, they abandoned the land.

The second type of abandonment, however, may be more important (and enforcement property rights no longer is a problem). With the development of secure property rights, capitalists can now buy out squatters, and let the land remain idle until market conditions improve sufficiently to make them an attractive investment as agricultural concerns. In this way the land owner can hold the land until the economics are such that there is a reasonable assurance of a return in the medium term. (In essence they examine the net present value of land purchase plus benefits and costs of management and decide when to begin to invest in agricultural development. Since capitalists have higher opportunity costs than settlers, they will wait longer [e.g. leave the land unproductive] to actively farm. On the other hand, since they have a lower cost of capital, they can out-bid smaller landowners for any given plot of land.)

In both cases of land abandonment the evolution of property rights (or its absence) and access to capital explain much of the observed patterns of land acquisition and abandonment by both groups. The implications for government planners are that property right regimes and security of title (matters over which they have control) are very powerful instruments. Access to capital and opportunity costs of time will also influence who settles land and when it is developed in the frontier. Finally, the two most direct ways of decreasing forest conversion are to increase the opportunity costs of marginal workers, and control the expansion of the road network in the Amazon.

Source: Robert Schneider, 1993. *Land Abandonment, Property Rights, and Agricultural Sustainability in the Amazon*, LATEN Dissemination Note #3. Washington, D.C.: the World Bank.

CHAPTER 7

The Limits to Economic Measurement of Environmental Impacts

The approaches and techniques described in the preceding chapters are designed to help those planning projects to identify, quantify, monetize and include the environmental effects of the projects they are planning into the overall analysis of the project or policy. Some of these techniques are easily applied, while others demand more in the way of data and time. Although the approaches and techniques advocated here are theoretically well founded, there are limitations to the economic measurement of sustainability and environmental effects in general, and specifically to the use of benefit-cost analysis (BCA) for this purpose.

Some of the issues, such as valuing the loss of a human life, are controversial and raise important ethical questions. Others, such as the value of genetic diversity or cultural significance, raise intractable questions of measurement. We will briefly discuss some of these issues, with short descriptions of the relevant questions and thinking concerning them.

INCOME DISTRIBUTION

Evaluating economic efficiency is the primary objective of most project analyses, but most governments and development banks are also interested in the effect of projects on income distribution. Traditional economic analysis accepts – or at least does not question – either existing income distribution or that which would prevail following the implementation of an 'efficient' project. On the assumptions that underlie BCA, a society will be economically efficient in its use of resources when net monetary social benefits – that is the difference between total monetary benefits and total monetary costs, measured in socially desirable prices – are maximized.

Efficiency is measured without regard to whom the benefits and costs accrue and irrespective of whether society considers the prevailing distribution of income to be desirable. If income distribution is of concern, as it is in most developing countries, then the distribution of costs and benefits must be considered in the BCA. Projects which will primarily benefit already wealthy individuals at the expense of poorer individuals may be undesirable on distributional grounds, even if they show high benefit/cost ratios.

Three different approaches are commonly used to address distributional effects in a project analysis: qualitative consideration, weighting, or the establishment of distributional constraints. In each of these approaches, the analyst's main task is simply to present the information to the decision-maker. It is then up to the decision-maker to determine how to use this information.

104

The simplest method of providing such information to decision-makers is to estimate net benefits by income class, group or region as applicable. Similarly, adverse impacts of the project and costs of financing must be examined to determine on which groups these burdens will fall. All this information is provided to the decision-maker, who can then evaluate the distributional implications of the project and decide whether the project is acceptable on distributional grounds.

The incidence of benefits and costs can also be very important to the ultimate success of a project. This is evident in both hydropower projects, and in activities designed to establish parks and protected areas. In both cases the group that pays the largest price are those individuals that are displaced by the project: individuals that have to be resettled from a reservoir or dam construction site, or villagers who are denied traditional use rights from newly established protected areas. If their needs are not taken into consideration, and alternative opportunities provided or compensation paid, the project may impose unacceptable (and usually unaccounted for) social costs on society. Alternatively, those displaced may directly affect the viability of the project, for example, by encroaching in a watershed or poaching animals or trees.

The controversy surrounding resettlement has been a major cause of the international concern over the Narmada dams in India and the proposed Three Gorges Dam in China. Resettlement issues are increasingly becoming the most important obstacle facing new hydropower developments. (Somewhat surprisingly, the wide-ranging environmental impacts of hydropower projects are receiving less attention as a result. See Dixon *et al.* 1989, for a discussion of the environmental impacts of major dam projects.) The success of parks and protected areas is also threatened by nearby residents whose legitimate needs for income are hurt when areas are placed 'off-limits' without adequate compensation or mitigative measures. The common result is slow encroachment and degradation of the protected area by those displaced. An active, mutually beneficial partnership between those displaced and the protected area is one solution, but not easy to implement (for discussion of some of these issues see Dixon and Sherman, 1990; Whelan, 1991; Wells and Brandon, 1992; and Barzetti, 1993). Distributional information is therefore essential to develop a complete analysis of the proposed project, and design mitigative measures to counteract any negative effects.

Another alternative is to take the distributional analysis a step further and to assign weights to the benefits received and costs borne by various groups or income classes. Normally, benefits received, or costs borne, by disadvantaged groups are given relatively more weight than those which accrue to wealthier groups. The assignment of weights is clearly a subjective decision and is the job of the decision-maker, not the project analyst. Different schemes of weighting are discussed in Ray (1984), Squire and Van der Tak (1975), and Pearce and Warford (1993).

A third approach is to set constraints on the allowable distribution of benefits among different groups. For example, targets can be established which set a minimum acceptable distribution of benefits to a designated low-income class or group. Only those projects in which at least a certain percentage of benefits accrue to that group will be given further consideration. Although the targets must be set by decision-makers, analysts may be asked how to modify projects so that their distributional aspects are improved.

INTERGENERATIONAL EQUITY

In addition to affecting income distribution (which can be viewed as intra-generational equity), development projects also affect the intergenerational endowments of resources. The primary objective of 'development' is to increase the quality of life by increasing incomes, improving health and nutrition, or in some manner making life easier for those affected by the project. However, the impacts of many projects will be felt for long periods of time, and not all future impacts will be positive. This discussion is also linked to the current 'sustainability' debate and those who take quite different views about the desirability of growth and society's responsibility to future generations. Herman Daly, for example, speaks eloquently about the need for 'development' without growth. He calls for using less, recycling more, and leaving more for future generations.[1] Laudable goals, especially for high consumption societies, but perhaps unrealistic for those poor societies that are interested in rapid development *and* growth. The debate continues and conferences on sustainability have become a major international growth industry!

The discount rate and the timing of benefits and costs are key variables. Consider a development project which replaces a tropical rainforest with grazing land for cattle. While it may be true that the tangible outputs of the rainforest are relatively small compared to the value of the cattle, there are many factors to consider. In many areas, cattle ranching will remain profitable only for a short period – the limited fertility of many altered rainforest lands will support cattle for only a few years before yields begin to decline. Often the end result is degraded, bare land which will support very little in the future. In addition, the many unpriced benefits of the rainforest are lost for ever.

On the other hand, consider a rural forestry development project in a currently degraded area. The area, which may be unused or produce little, may

---

1 A related concept is that of the 'user cost' of the use of any non-renewable resource, or, the use of any potentially renewable resources in a non-renewable manner (e.g. extracting more timber than is annually regenerated). As explained by Kellenberg and Daly (1994), user costs (defined as the opportunity cost of depleted natural capital) should be included in the cost of any input that is not derived from a sustainable, renewable resource. This additional cost component will reflect the fact that future generations are being deprived of part of their natural capital (to enhance present day consumption), and that a full benefit-cost analysis of an activity should reflect the cost of inputs both to present generations (measured by the market price) and to future generations (measured by the user cost). Although commonly used for energy or minerals (e.g. depletion premiums), user costs are rarely included for other cost items. Whether or not they should be, and how to do this, remains the focus of a heated debate.

have the potential to support a renewable source of fuelwood and other wood products indefinitely. However, a large amount of investment may be necessary, with no returns to be received for a number of years.

Both of these projects have important implications for future residents of the areas affected. In the former case (cattle grazing), future generations may have fewer resources available to them than they would have had without the project while in the latter (forestry development), both current and future generations may be enriched by the project. Even so, it is quite possible that benefit-cost analyses of the two projects may show the former to be more profitable than the latter. A great deal will depend on the discount rate used in the analysis.

As discussed in Chapter 3, discounting is used to compare costs and benefits which occur at different points in time. The choice of the discount rate to be used will greatly affect the outcome of the analysis. A high discount rate will favour projects with immediate net benefits over projects whose benefits will not be realized for a longer period. In addition, the higher the discount rate, the less the influence of negative impacts that may arise in the future. Low discount rates, on the other hand, have less restrictive effects on projects with long-term net benefits and give more weight to negative future impacts.

In effect, discounting results in less and less attention given to successive generations. To eliminate this bias of putting the welfare of the current generation above that of future generations, some people have advocated the use of a very low, or even a zero discount rate. Such suggestions, however, are ill conceived and would not result in efficient, or even equitable, use of resources. Clearly, eliminating discounting would violate two essential facts. First, people would rather be given a certain amount of money today than the same amount of money sometime in the future. Second, alternative opportunities exist in which sums of money invested today will yield larger sums of money in the future. For both these reasons, eliminating discounting would result in a net decrease, not an increase, of social welfare.

It is true that both the choice of project selected and the discount rate to be used will affect the intertemporal allocation of resources and thus have implications for intergenerational equity. However, by wisely using non-renewable resources and emphasizing projects which promote sustainable use of renewable resources, the welfare of both current and future generations can be enhanced.

A related issue concerns projects which will have irreversible effects of various kinds. These projects will also have important effects on future generations and are discussed separately later in this chapter.

RISK AND UNCERTAINTY

Many of the generally applicable valuation techniques are based on underlying damage functions. However, often there is considerable uncertainty surrounding the cause and effect relationships being evaluated. Risk is a related concept and is commonly used when we can quantify uncertainty, by assigning probabilities to various possible outcomes (e.g. the risk of one uncertain outcome, perhaps a failure of an embankment, is .0001, and is acknowledged as an 'acceptable risk'). Risk and uncertainty are commonly ignored in project analysis, even though they play a key role in predicting the likelihood of project success.

For example, in a production-oriented development project, future prices and expected yields will be subject to uncertainty. For soil-conservation projects, both the with-project and without-project rates of erosion and/or their effects on productivity may be unknown. Natural events such as drought, windstorms, hail, and plant and animal diseases may seriously affect projects.

All projects face some degree of uncertainty. The most common way of dealing with this is to use 'expected values' for prices, quantities and other variables whose precise values cannot be known in advance. Essentially, this involves transforming uncertainty (where the probabilities of different outcomes are not known) into risk (where the probabilities of various outcomes are weighted according to their likelihood of occurrence). Each potential outcome is weighted by the probability of its occurrence, and the weighted outcomes are then summed to arrive at a mean, or expected, value. These probabilities may be estimated by using past trends, subjective judgements or through a variety of appropriate techniques (see Raiffa, 1968; Pouliquen, 1970; Anderson, Dillon and Hardaker, 1977; and Anderson 1989a,b).

For example, consider a forestry project where there is some uncertainty about the yield of the project. The following might be the best estimates of annual yields available from the forester:

.4 tons/hectare 20% probability
.5 tons/hectare 40% probability
.6 tons/hectare 30% probability
.7 tons/hectare 10% probability

The expected value of the annual production would be $(.4 \times .2) + (.5 \times .4) + (.6 \times .3) + (.7 \times .1) = .53$ tons/hectare.

This 'expected-value' method of accounting for risk and uncertainty is the standard method of incorporating these variables into BCA. One problem with this technique is that it results in the use of a single number which does not indicate the degree of uncertainty or the range of values which might actually be expected. It also does not account for an individual's attitude towards risk (see Graham, 1981, for a discussion of this topic).

Another means of addressing risk and uncertainty is the use of *sensitivity analysis*. In sensitivity analysis, the project analysis is modified to examine the effects of different assumptions about key variables, and their effect on the project's overall profitability. Using optimistic and pessimistic values for different variables can indicate which variables will have the most pronounced effects on benefits and costs. Although this does not indicate a probability of occurrence of the upper or lower values, it provides information about which variables are most crucial to the project's success.

Handling risk and uncertainty is a difficult but important task in project analysis. For additional information, see Arrow and Lind (1970), Pouliquen (1970), Pearce and Nash (1981), and Haimes (1981).

IRREVERSIBILITY

Many projects entail the modification of natural habitats. Development of a major project such as a dam, a mine or an industrial facility will preclude other uses of the areas in which they are built. Since these natural lands cannot be replaced at reasonable cost, each project sited in such an area will reduce the supply of these available natural areas. In this sense, the effects of the project are irreversible. The habitat alterations may also endanger the continued existence of plants or animal species – another effect with irreversible consequences.

Projects which may have irreversible impacts must be given special attention. It is impossible accurately to foresee the future, and irreversible impacts which seem unimportant today may ultimately be of considerable importance. This uncertainty about the future implications of today's decisions mandates that extra care be taken to ensure correct decisions.

Some economists view an irreversible action as one which limits future options (Henry, 1974). Others view irreversible results as a constraint in that they limit the range of actions which can be taken subsequently (Miller and Lad, 1984). In this manner, irreversible decisions made today may reduce social welfare in the future since all future choices will be constrained by past decisions which cannot be changed.

One aspect of the value of retaining future options has been referred to as 'option value'. Krutilla and Fisher (1985) describe option value as 'the value, in addition to consumer's surplus, that arises from retaining an option to a good or service for which future demand is uncertain'. This can also be viewed as a 'risk premium', an amount people would be willing to pay to avoid the risk of not having something available which they may want in the future, over and above its expected value to them. Estimating option value is not an easy task; most attempts involve some form of contingent valuation (see Chapter 5).

Another concept related to irreversibility and uncertainty is referred to as 'quasi-option value'. This value represents the benefits of delaying a decision when one of the alternatives involves an irreversible choice and uncertainty exists about the benefits of the alternatives. Quasi-option value may be viewed as the expected value of information which could be gained by delaying a decision (Conrad, 1980). It will be positive in most cases since delaying a decision will usually reduce the uncertainty of future values, but it can also be negative if development itself leads to better information for future decisions. Current thinking now usually includes 'quasi-option value' as one part of the broader 'option-value' grouping. Nevertheless, these values can be significant, particularly when one is concerned with conservation or protection of endangered habitats or species. Brown *et al.* (1993) surveyed recent CVM studies on willingness-to-pay for preservation of many different endangered species and prized habitats (see Table 10). Annual per capita payments for individual species yielded values from $1 to $50, with a common grouping in the $8 to $10 per year range – not large, but still significant when averaged over large numbers of people. Habitat values tended to be higher: ranges of $30 to $50

Table 10 Preference Valuation for Endangered Species and Prized Habitats
(1990 US$ per person per year)

Species

Norway:	Brown bear, wolf and wolverine	15.0
USA:	Bald eagle	12.4
	Emerald shiner	4.5
	Grizzly bear	18.5
	Bighorn sheep	8.6
	Whooping crane	1.2
	Blue whale	9.3
	Bottlenose dolphin	7.0
	California sea otter	8.1
	Northern elephant seal	8.1
	Humpback whales[1]	40–48 (without information)
		49–64 (with information)

Other habitat

USA:	Grand Canyon (visibility)	27.0
	Colorado wilderness	9.3–21.2
Australia:	Nadgee Nature Reserve NSW	28.1
	Kakadu Conservation Zone, NT[2]	40.0 (minor damage)
		93.0 (major damage)
UK:	Nature reserves[3]	40.0 ('experts' only)
Norway:	Conservation of rivers against hydroelectric development	59.0–107.0

Notes: (1) respondents divided into two groups, one of which was given video informa-tion; (2) two scenarios of mining development damage were given to respondents; (3) survey of informed individuals only.

Source: *Economics and the Conservation of Global Biodiversity*, K Brown, D Pearce, C Perrings, and T Swanson. (1993). GEF Working paper No. 2, Washington, D.C. The Global Environment Facility.

per year were common (e.g. visibility in the Grand Canyon of the US, $27 per year; Kakadu Conservation Zone in Australia, $40 to $93 per year; and conser-vation of rivers against hydropower development in Norway, $59 to $107 per year).

There is no single method for accounting for irreversibility in an economic analysis. The opportunity-cost approach outlined in Chapter 4 is one possibility, since it indirectly provides information on the cost of preservation. In general, if the costs of retaining an option that would otherwise be foreclosed are relatively low, the decision-maker should weigh the possibility of retention carefully.

Another possibility is the use of the Safe Minimum Standard (SMS) criterion (Ciriacy-Wantrup, 1968, Bishop 1978). This is appropriate when dealing with resources which are renewable up to a point but are subject to irreversible damage. These include soil resources as well as genetic resources such as plants and animals, commonly referred to as biodiversity. Applying the SMS criterion involves calculating a margin of safety to prevent irreversible damage to the resource. If such a standard can be maintained without 'excessive' costs, the resource should be protected. It is up to the policy-maker, of course, to decide at what level costs become 'excessive'.

VALUE OF BIODIVERSITY

The question of biodiversity – its current state and policy options to ensure its protection – is receiving increased global attention. Wilson (1988) presents a comprehensive overview of recent thinking on the topic, and the Global Environment Facility, the GEF, is providing substantial resources to developing countries to help them to protect their endangered biological resources. One of the most difficult aspects of the debate on biodiversity is identifying a monetary value for biodiversity protection. To date, this is a topic that has presented fairly intractable analytical problems.

Brown *et al.* (1993) examine the economics of global biological diversity and present many interesting examples of people's and nations' expressed willingness-to-pay for biodiversity conservation, but no real estimates of the *value* of biodiversity. This is understandable since most of the benefits from biodiversity conservation lie to the right hand side of the Total Economic Value spectrum, especially for such items as option and existence values. Some uses of biodiversity can be marketed and measured: ecotourism and nature tourism are a rapidly growing niche of the international tourism industry (and can be measured by the use of travel-cost and various contingent-valuation experiments). Worldwide nature tourism is worth many billions of dollars per year, and demand is expected to grow rapidly as incomes increase, and as unique habitats become scarcer.

In addition to the values placed on the preservation of individual species (see Table 10) some direct measures are available of individual or national willingness-to-pay for protection of ecosystem biological diversity (or the good and services contained therein). Debt-for-nature swaps express the willingness of rich countries to help pay for protection of unique or threatened resources in poorer countries. Under these swaps, an outside group purchases an amount of the discounted national debt of one country (usually held by a private bank), with the agreement that the country then places an amount equal to the debt purchased into a special account or fund (usually in local currency) that will be used to manage protected areas or provide biodiversity benefits. To date some 15 countries have been involved in debt-for-nature swaps, but the amounts involved have tended to be small and the implicit WTP even smaller: often as little as $1 to $5 per ha.

Carbon-offsets and the purchase of set-asides to store carbon in tropical forests are another expression of some of the values placed on intact natural ecosystems. Analysis indicates that the 'value' of carbon stored (in terms of damages avoided) may range up to $5 to $10 per ton or more. With primary and secondary forests containing as much as 200 to 300 tons of C per ha, the values embodied are considerable (see Schneider [1993], Brown *et al.* [1993], and Fankhauser and Pearce [1993]).

None of these, however, are real measures of the intrinsic *value* of biodiversity or the intact ecosystems that protect it, they are merely reflections of parts of the total value. There may be valuable genetic material contained in a threatened tropical rainforest, but since we can't identify the material, or its use, we can't assign any reasonable value estimate to it. Therefore we focus on what we can identify and measure. The problem is, of course, that we just don't know whether these values represent a large share, or only a tiny fraction, of the true, total economic value of unique and endangered ecosystems.

With such uncertainty, therefore, one has to resort to the 'cautionary principle' again. Avoid irreversible losses and species extinction. Consider carefully the concept of the Safe Minimum Standard first proposed by Ciriacy-Wantrup. And always consider carefully the opportunity cost of *not* converting or losing a unique resource, for in many cases this cost might be quite low.

VALUE OF HUMAN LIFE

Chapter 4 outlined methods of evaluating projects which will affect human health. However, projects which will directly save or, alternatively, take lives cannot be evaluated in the same manner, since the ethical considerations involved transcend economic analysis.

The value of a *statistical life* should not be confused with the value of an individual life. The value of a statistical life is the value of a small change in the risks associated with an unnamed member of a large group dying. Placing a monetary value on an incremental change in risk of death, injury or illness faced by a large group is something which society must deal with routinely in such activities as the design of buildings, automobiles and other consumer products, as well as determination of the extent of pollution abatement.

One commonly used approach is to examine the extra compensation workers require to undertake risky jobs. The values for a statistical life based on these compensating wage differentials in the US vary from $100 to $800 for an annual mortality risk of 0.0001. This translates into between $1 to $8 million per statistical life (Fisher *et al.* 1989, Viscusi, 1992).

Another approach to valuing the benefits of preventing premature mortality is to ask how much it costs to save one life, and then compare various interventions. This is a form of cost-effectiveness analysis for a statistical life. For some interventions, e.g. immunization of children, or the use of oral-rehydration therapy to treat diarrhoea patients, the costs can be very small, often only a few dollars per death avoided. Other interventions may be very expensive. In a recent study on the implicit cost per life saved by various US environmental regulations, Van Houtven and Cropper (1994) estimated the costs per life saved from regulations banning various pesticide and asbestos-related products. Many of these measures were incredibly expensive: as much as $52 million for avoiding one case of cancer among pesticide applicators, and $49 million for avoiding a cancer death from some forms of asbestos exposure.[2] Information on the cost-of-death-avoided allows the decision maker to examine a 'menu' of interventions and choose those that are more cost-effective, without ever having to specify a value per life.

Placing a monetary value on the life of a *particular person*, as is attempted with the human capital approach, raises thorny moral and ethical issues. Courts of law commonly rely on the human capital and other approaches to determine compensation for premature death. The range of values one encounters from such proceedings and from some other indirect measures of willingness-to-pay to avoid premature death in the US (e.g. self-insurance and the taking of preventive steps among others) result in values in the range of many hundreds of thousands to several million dollars. (An average value of about $3 million is commonly cited.) In Great Britain comparable figures are about £750,00 to £1 million.

Obviously such measures, especially the human capital approach, are very dependent on income levels and will vary greatly across countries. As such, there is no acceptable way to compare the 'costs' of death between countries, especially when their income levels are very different. It is better in these situations to speak of the absolute numbers of deaths incurred or avoided; much as the 1993 *World Development Report* of the World Bank developed the concept of the DALY – the Disability Adjusted Life Year that combines a measure of healthy life years lost because of premature mortality, with those lost as a result of disability – to allow comparison of mortality estimates across countries. In turn, one can use cost-effectiveness analysis to discuss the cost per DALY of different interventions.

---

2 These values were estimated by comparing data on the number of potentially fatal cancer cases avoided to the costs of implementing each measure. In the case of asbestos, for example, some of the products banned included brake drum linings (fairly cost-effective at only $100,000 per cancer case avoided), through roofing felt ($4 million per case), to roof coatings at $40 million per case (Van Houtven and Cropper, 1994).

INCREMENTALISM

Incrementalism is the term used to denote problems which arise from making decisions on an individual project basis without consideration of the cumulative effect of many such decisions. For example, the removal of a few hectares of rainforest or a small portion of coral reef as part of one development project may not be highly significant in and of itself, but the cumulative effect of many such projects may have important repercussions. Often, an overall country or regional plan is needed which can be consulted to ensure that such issues are dealt with appropriately.

CULTURAL, HISTORICAL AND AESTHETIC RESOURCES

Many development projects not only entail the modification of natural habitats but may also have adverse effects on culturally or historically significant sites. Other projects will result in the loss of scenic resources. In many instances, these aspects of a project may have important implications in terms of its acceptance by local residents.

Losses of cultural or historical resources are difficult to quantify and monetize because the perception of these losses depends on cultural traditions and value systems. The contingent valuation techniques described in Chapter 5 are one way of estimating the values of these resources, but the limitations inherent in these techniques make it difficult to arrive at meaningful estimates. For example, attempts to determine local residents' willingness to accept compensation for the loss of an important cultural site may show that they are unwilling to accept any level of compensation, no matter how high. Though their willingness to pay to keep the site may be constrained by income, the amount needed to compensate them for such a loss may be extremely high, or even infinite.

Aesthetic resources represent similar measurement problems, though the values involved are likely to be much smaller. In these cases, either the property-value approach or the contingent valuation methods can be applied to obtain estimates.

When such issues threaten to have significant impacts on project acceptance, compromises may be necessary. These may involve moving the site of the project, moving the cultural or historical relic to a nearby site, or some other form of mitigation measure to reduce the losses involved. The relocation of Abu Simbel and other historic treasures in Egypt when they were threatened by the rising waters of the Aswan High Dam is one notable example.

SUMMARY

Despite the limitations to economic analysis of the environmental impacts of development projects, it is important that such impacts be included in the analyses. In many cases the techniques described in the preceding chapters can be extremely useful in providing more accurate estimates of the value of the impacts of development on the environment and, therefore, in generating more accurate and balanced appraisals of the proposed projects. Where environmental assessment with economic valuation fails completely to capture certain impacts on the environment, these impacts may at least be included qualitatively in the project analysis.

The candid discussion in this chapter of some problem areas in the evaluation of environmental impacts should not be taken to mean that the techniques for valuation are ineffectual. Many developmental impacts on the environment may be valued and included in economic analyses by using the techniques described in this book. The challenge is twofold – the identification of major impacts on the environment from development projects, and the valuation and incorporation of these impacts into project analysis.

PART II

CASE
STUDIES

Introduction

The nine case studies presented in this section have been selected to illustrate some of the generally applicable and selectively applicable valuation techniques introduced in the text (Chapters 4 and 5, respectively). In addition to demonstrating the valuation techniques themselves, these cases also highlight some of the finer points of the overall analysis, such as the with- and without-project format, and coping with uncertainty through sensitivity analysis.

The first case uses changes in the values of milk, fertilizer and firewood production to assess a watershed management and forest development project in Nepal. The second evaluates selected mangrove management schemes for Bintuni Bay, Indonesia, on the basis of changes in productivity of mangrove-based activities, including forestry, fisheries, hunting, gathering and agriculture, as well as benefits of erosion control and biodiversity. The use of the cost-of-illness approach to estimate the health costs of air pollution in Jakarta, Indonesia, is illustrated in the third case. The fourth case uses a combination of preventive expenditures, replacement costs and opportunity costs to estimate the benefits of a soil conservation project in the Loess Plateau area of the Yellow River basin, China.

The fifth compares the cost-effectiveness of several waste-water disposal methods for a proposed geothermal plant in the Philippines. The travel-cost method and the use of CVM in a developing country are illustrated in the sixth case, which examines the values to local residents and foreign tourists associated with establishing a new national park in Madagascar. The seventh case study examines the tradeoffs between the ecological and economic functions of a marine park in the Caribbean and provides a simple demonstration of contingent valuation. The eighth case study examines the use of data from water vendors and a survey instrument to estimate willingness to pay for improved water supply in Nigeria. The last case study focuses on the process of setting priorities for investment in pollution control measures in Central and Eastern Europe.

1

Nepal Hill Forest Development Project

This case study, based on an Asian Development Bank project appraisal report and on reports of a similar project by Fleming (1983) (also found in Hufschmidt *et al.*, 1983), is a description of the benefit valuation for a benefit-cost analysis of a management programme for two watersheds in Nepal. It is an example of the use of change-in-productivity techniques in which actual market prices are used as a measure for valuing the benefits of environmental improvements. In this example, physical changes in production brought about by the project are valued using market or, where appropriate, shadow prices for inputs and for outputs. The productivity effects of both introducing the project and of not doing so (with- and without-project analysis) are evaluated. Both on-site and off-site effects are included in the analysis.

INTRODUCTION TO THE PROJECT

The forests of Nepal are continually being degraded by overcutting and over-grazing; the results are inadequate and polluted water supplies, shortages of fuelwood and leaf fodder, and increasing soil erosion.

The major causes of the overexploitation of the forests around Kathmandu and Pokhara are the need of the rural population for greater income and the shortage of fuelwood in the urban settlements. Most of the forests in the middle hills, where 52 percent of the population live, have been converted into shrubland. Trees are being cut down or lopped heavily and the forest floor is overgrazed. The shrubland is being exploited for fodder and stripped of fuelwood. As a result, the water-retaining capacity of natural vegetation in the hill forests has been reduced and runoff has increased in both quantity and speed. Each year an estimated 240 million cubic meters (m³) of eroded soil is transported downstream by the country's major rivers and their tributaries, causing major damage.

The introduction of systematic hill-forest management was proposed to help meet the fuelwood and fodder requirements of rural and urban communities and to reduce the effects of downstream siltation. The project area is 38,500 hectares, of which 10,000 hectares are used for agriculture and 1,500 for pasture. The management component of the project is concerned only with the remaining 27,000 hectares of forested and grazing land: 22,000 of these hectares are made up of three forest ranges in the Kathmandu Forest Division (KFD) and the other 5,000 are two forest beats in the Pokhara Forest Division (PFD). These two forest divisions are major catchment areas of the Bagmati and Seti rivers and serve the urban centers of Kathmandu and Pokhara.

Among the elements of the project are:

- management planning for the entire area which includes forest inventory, preparation of working plans and the delineation of land-use compartments in the forest;
- shrubland and timber-stand improvement which includes the tending of 16,000 hectares of shrubland, the improvement of 7,000 hectares of timber stand and additional fencing within the total 27,000 hectares of forest; and
- afforestation of 4,000 hectares of grasslands within the total forest area with species for both fuelwood and fodder as well as for fencing materials.

Subsistence agriculture is the main economic activity in the area. The principal crops are rice, maize, millet, wheat, potatoes and other vegetables. The average holding is half a hectare. Buffalo and cattle are kept for milk, manure and ploughing. Feed for livestock is made up of agricultural residues (about 50 percent) and fodder from the forests. The forests also provide fuelwood and timber.

LAND USE WITHOUT THE PROJECT: PROJECTIONS

Population growth, accentuated by urbanization, is reducing state forests around Kathmandu and Pokhara. The three main demands that this produces on the forest are for fuelwood – both for home and industrial use – fodder and grazing for livestock, and land for agriculture. With the average consumption of fuelwood at around one cubic meter per capita per year, the total demand is estimated at around 8–9 million cubic meters per year. An estimate of fuelwood production in the forests around Kathmandu and Pokhara puts the annual sustained production at well below the amount required. The deficit is met by importing wood from the Terai, the illegal removal of wood from the surrounding forests, or by using cattle dung as a substitute. The illegal removal and sale of firewood and leaf fodder from government forests is a major source of income for the local population of the area of the proposed project and is the main reason why the forests are being denuded. The use of cattle dung as fuel diminishes the already scarce supply of fertilizer for agricultural production.

Given that the population is growing at the rate of 2.6 percent per annum and that there is no foreseeable increase in agricultural productivity, the pressure to convert forest to agricultural land will continue. There is also a considerable pressure to convert forests into grazing land to support the growing numbers of livestock.

Projections show that the present rates of use, together with increased pressure from a growing population, will, within fourteen years, destroy the entire forested area of the Nepalese hills, some 2.5 million hectares. Without the project, therefore, as a consequence of the indiscriminate removal of the vegetation, the water-retaining capacity of the area would continue to decline, water runoff would increase both in velocity and volume, and even greater siltation problems would emerge below the hills.

Land-use projections, both with and without the project, are given in Table 11.

Table 11 Projected Land Use With and Without Project, Five-Year Intervals
1983–2022 (in hectares; after Fleming, 1983)

Land Use without Project	1983	1988	1993	1998	2022
Agriculture	10,000	13,730	15,769	18,424	26,848
Grazing	4,000	4,520	5,107	5,771	7,475
Pasture	1,500	1,500	1,500	1,500	1,500
Scrubland	16,000	13,830	13,555	12,805	2,677
Forest	7,000	4,920	2,569	0	0
Land Use with Project[a]	1983	1988	1993	1998	2022
Agriculture	10,000	10,000	10,000	10,000	10,000
Grazing	4,000	0	0	0	0
Pasture	1,500	1,500	1,500	1,500	1,500
Scrubland[b]	16,000	16,000	16,000	16,000	16,000
Forest[b]	7,000	7,000	7,000	7,000	7,000
Plantations[b]	0	4,000	4,000	4,000	4,000

[a] Assumes existence of a separate agricultural management plan that eliminates the need to convert land to agriculture.
[b] See Table 15 for project production projections.

Note: Actual data were not available; data shown are synthetic.

PROJECTED LAND USE WITH THE PROJECT

It is assumed that a separate agricultural programme would increase productivity on existing cultivated lands at rates equal to, or greater than, the rate of population increase and that the amount of agricultural land would remain constant at 10,000 hectares. No grazing, pasture, scrubland or forest would be converted into terraces.

The project will contribute significantly to the control of erosion, landslides and flash floods. Establishing vegetative cover on barren hill slopes will improve the water regime by increasing the recharge of aquifers. However, these types of benefit are not easily quantifiable.

The project will also help to alleviate shortages in fuelwood and livestock fodder in the Kathmandu and Pokhara valleys. Further, it will reduce the incidence of the destructive and illegal removal of forest products by soliciting community cooperation in forest protection. It will also help to improve overall agricultural productivity in the area once livestock dung, currently used as fuel because of wood shortages, is applied as fertilizer.

122

VALUATION OF BENEFITS

The project is planned to reduce soil erosion, to increase the productivity of the different land uses within the watershed and to provide a sustainable flow of resources which would include fuelwood and fodder. Benefit-cost analysis, based on estimates of the economic values of the products from differing uses of land, can be used to assess the project. The benefits of the programme may be considered to be equal to the land values (the economic value of the products) achieved with the project, minus the land values without the project. These benefits and costs can then be used to calculate the EIRR in the usual manner. The main problem is in valuing the differing outputs from the various uses of land, a problem considered in the following pages. The calculations are based on the values in Tables 12 and 13.

Table 12 Per Hectare Production of Various Products (Without Project)

	Grazing Land	Pasture Land	Unmanaged Scrubland	Unmanaged Forest
Grass (kg/ha/yr)	1,200	6,000	500	–
Tree foliage (kg/ha/yr)	–	–	700	1,400
Wood (m³/ha/yr)	–	–	1	2.2

Table 13 Production and Value of Animal Products (Without Project)

	Fertilizer Production per Animal per year (kg)	1983 Value (Rs/kg)		Milk Production per 1,000 kg feed (l)	1983 Value (Rs/l)
Nitrogen (N)	15	6	Grass feed	60	1.5
Phosphorous (P)	2	18	Foliage feed	120	1.5

l = litre

DETERMINATION OF LAND-USE VALUES

Grazing Land. Grazing animals produce milk and fertilizer. Given the values in Tables 12 and 13 and assuming a fodder consumption rate of 14,000 kilograms per animal per year, the annual value of fertilizer production is calculated to be 126 rupees per animal per year or 11 rupees per hectare per year, Rs/ha/yr. This figure is found by determining the value of the fertilizer produced per animal from Table 13 and multiplying this amount by the carrying capacity of one hectare of land. In the case of grazing land, the carrying capacity is .0857 based on grass production on grazing land, 1,200kg, divided by the annual feed requirement per animal, 14,000kg. Similarly, the annual value of milk production per hectare of grazing land can be calculated to be 108 Rs/ha/yr. The total annual productive value of grazing land would, therefore, be the total of the values of milk and fertilizer production or 119 Rs/ha/yr.

Since market prices are used to establish fertilizer and milk values per hectare of grazing land, it is important to confirm that these prices reflect the true opportunity cost or marginal willingness to pay. Any input-price subsidies should be added to the price and, if milk prices are controlled by the government, alternative prices which more accurately reflect marginal willingness to pay should be obtained.

Pasture. Since fodder production from pasture is estimated to be five times that of grazing land, the annual value from pasture would be 595 Rs/ha/yr.

Unmanaged Scrubland. The production data for scrubland (degraded forest land) are given in Table 12. From these data it was calculated that the annual value of fertilizer produced from scrubland grass was 5 Rs/ha/yr and that the annual value of the milk was 45 Rs/ha/yr.

Assuming that the average grazing animal consumes about 7,100 kilograms of tree foliage per year, the value of the fertilizer so produced on scrubland was calculated at 12 Rs/ha/yr and the milk production at 126 Rs/ha/yr. Taking production from both grass and tree foliage together, each hectare of unmanaged scrubland could, therefore, produce Rs17 worth of fertilizer and Rs171 worth of milk each year.

Fuelwood is produced on both scrub and forest lands. Three methods were presented in order to estimate fuelwood values.

Direct Market-Value Approach
In 1983 the economic price for fuelwood (the market price minus the cost of bringing wood to the market) in Pokhara and Kathmandu, the principal marketplaces, was 560 Rs per metric ton (mt). Assuming an average wood density of 500 kg/m^3, fuelwood would be worth 280 Rs/m^3, (500 kg/m^3 × 0.001 mt/kg × 560 Rs/mt). At present, the Fuelwood Corporation of Nepal (FCN) is supplying only 2 percent and 8 percent, respectively, of the total fuelwood for all of Nepal and Kathmandu valleys. Unless the FCN finds an alternative source of supply, market prices for fuelwood are expected to rise. The project's production would represent approximately 20 percent of the current fuelwood consumption in Kathmandu. Because the fuelwood markets are small and isolated, the market price may not represent the value of fuelwood outside the market. Therefore two other indirect measures of fuelwood value were made.

Indirect Substitute Approach

Fuelwood can also be valued in terms of the value of alternative uses of its closest substitute (for example, cattle dung which can be dried and burned when wood is unavailable). The opportunity cost of using cattle dung as fuel rather than fertilizer can be estimated in terms of the losses in foodgrain production. This would be based on the following assumptions:

- 1 m³ of wood is the energy equivalent of 0.6 ton of dried cattle dung or 2.4 tons of fresh manure;
- an average family uses 6 tons per year of fresh manure on 0.5 ha of culti-vated land;
- the increase in maize yields expected as a result of using dung as fertilizer would be 15 percent, which gives an opportunity cost of Rs27 per ton of fresh manure, assuming that the increase in maize yields is from 1.53 mt/ha to 1.8 mt/ha and that the price of maize equals 1,200 Rs/mt. The value of fuelwood would thus be Rs65 per m³.

Indirect Opportunity-Cost Approach

The third method is an opportunity-cost approach based on the time families spend carrying fuelwood from the forest, and assumes that fuelwood is a common property resource. This method is based on the following assumptions:

- 30kg of fuelwood are collected daily by each family;
- each family spends an average of 132 workdays per year collecting fuelwood. Assuming an average wood density of 500 kg/m³, each family gathers 7.92 m³ of fuelwood per year (132 person days × 0.06 m³ per day). At a daily gathering wage of Rs5 (the opportunity cost of labour based on other employ-ment), the estimated value is calculated to be 83 Rs/m³. The value of fuelwood as estimated in the three approaches is therefore as follows:

Method	*Value* (Rs/m³)
Direct-Market Value	280
Indirect-Substitute	65
Indirect-Opportunity Cost	83

The most conservative estimate (the lowest) was chosen for the analysis. Therefore, the annual fuelwood value per hectare of unmanaged scrubland would be 65 Rs/ha/yr (based on production of 1 m³/ha/yr, Table 12). The *total* annual value of scrubland was estimated to be the value of the milk, fertilizer and fuelwood, or a total of 253 Rs/ha/yr.

Unmanaged Forest. This land is open to restricted grazing and harvesting of fuelwood and fodder. The annual value of the fertilizer was estimated to be 25 Rs/ha/yr and the annual value of milk 252 Rs/ha/yr. Using the indirect-substitute method, the annual value of fuelwood was estimated to be 143 Rs/ha/yr. The total annual value of unmanaged forest would therefore be 420 Rs/ha/yr. The per hectare values for grazing, pasture, unmanaged scrub and unmanaged forest land are summarized in Table 14.

125

Table 14 Per Hectare Values of Various Products (Without Project) (Rs/ha/yr)

Land Use	Milk	Fertilizer	Fuelwood	Total
Grazing	108	11	—	119
Pasture	540	55	—	595
Unmanaged Scrub	171	17	65	253
Unmanaged Forest	252	25	143	420

LAND VALUES WITH THE PROJECT

Based on calculations similar to those used when considering land use without the project, the per hectare physical yields on land affected by the project are given in Table 15. Physical yields were translated into economic values based on the values of the fuelwood, fertilizer and milk produced. These results are summarized in Table 16.

ANALYSIS

The total land values under each management alternative can be calculated by multiplying the number of hectares of each type of land by their values. The types of land are shown in Table 11, the values without the project are given in Table 14 and those with the project in Table 16. The per hectare values of grazing and pasture land are assumed to be the same in both cases. Total land values for unmanaged lands (without the project) are given in Table 17. Table 18 gives the with-project, managed-lands figures.

The contribution of the project to the control of soil erosion, landslides and flooding is not accurately quantifiable and is therefore not included in this analysis. The incremental benefits of the management programme are assumed to be the difference between the values of products from the unmanaged land (that is, without the proposed scheme) and the values of products if the management scheme is adopted. In each case the value of agricultural production is assumed to be constant. The incremental benefits of the project, minus its costs, result in a stream of net benefits which yield an EIRR of 8.5 percent (see Table 19).

This case illustrates the use of valuation techniques to place monetary values on a change in pasture and scrubland/forest productivity brought about by a project. A with-and-without-project framework was used to determine the scale of productivity changes. Both direct and indirect methods were used to estimate prices for the fertilizer, milk and fuelwood produced.

Table 15 Projected Yields (With Project) (tons/ha)

Operational Year	Plantations	Managed Scrubland	Managed Forest
Fuelwood			
1	0	1.2	5.5
2	0	0	0
3	0	2.5	0
4	0	0	0
5	0	2.0	0
6	20.0	0	22.5
7–9	0	0	0
10	0	5.2	0
11	8.0	0	25.0
12–15	8.0	0	0
16	8.0	0	27.5
17–19	8.0	0	0
20	8.0	20.0	0
21	8.0	0	27.5
22–25	8.0	0	0
26	8.0	0	27.5
27–29	8.0	0	0
30	8.0	35.0	0
31	8.0	0	27.5
32–34	8.0	0	0
35	8.0	35.0	0
36–40	8.0	0	36.2
Fodder			
1–5	2.0	0.7	1.4
6–10	5.6	0.9	1.6
11–15	5.6	1.3	3.0
16–20	5.6	1.7	3.3
21–25	5.6	2.1	3.3
26–40	5.6	2.7	3.3

Note: (tons/ha × 2 = m3/ha; tons/ha × 1000 = kg/ha).
Source: Asian Development Bank, *Appraisal of the Hill Forest Development Projects in the Kingdom of Nepal* (1983).

Table 16 Per Hectare Values of Various Products (With Project) (Rs/ha/yr)

Operational Year	Plantations	Managed Scrubland	Managed Forest
Fuelwood			
1	0	156	715
2	0	0	0
3	0	325	0
4	0	0	0
5	0	260	0
6	2,600	0	2,925
7–9	0	0	0
10	0	676	0
11	1,040	0	3,250
12–15	1,040	0	0
16	1,040	0	3,575
17–19	1,040	0	0
20	1,040	2,600	0
21	1,040	0	3,575
22–25	1,040	0	0
26	1,040	0	3,575
27–29	1,040	0	0
30	1,040	4,550	0
31	1,040	0	3,575
32–34	1,040	0	0
35	1,040	4,550	0
36	1,040	0	4,706
37–40	1,040	0	0
Milk			
1–5	360	126	252
6–10	1,008	162	288
11–15	1,008	234	540
16–20	1,008	306	594
21–25	1,008	378	594
26–40	1,008	486	594
Fertilizer			
1–5	35	12	25
6–10	99	16	28
11–15	99	23	53
16–20	99	30	59
21–25	99	37	59
26–40	99	48	59

Table 17 Total Value for Unmanaged Lands (Rs)

	Grazing			Scrubland			Forest			Total Value
Yr	ha	Rs/ha	Rs	ha	Rs/ha	Rs	ha	Rs/ha	Rs	
1	4,000	119	476,000	16,000	253	4,048,000	7,000	420	2,940,000	7,464,000
2	4,104	119	488,376	15,566	253	3,938,198	6,584	420	2,765,280	7,191,854
3	4,208	119	500,752	15,132	253	3,828,396	6,168	420	2,590,560	6,919,708
4	4,312	119	513,128	14,698	253	3,718,594	5,752	420	2,415,840	6,647,562
5	4,416	119	525,504	14,264	253	3,608,792	5,336	420	2,241,120	6,375,416
6	4,520	119	537,880	13,830	253	3,498,990	4,920	420	2,066,400	6,103,270
7	4,638	119	551,922	13,775	253	3,485,075	4,450	420	1,869,000	5,905,997
8	4,755	119	565,845	13,720	253	3,471,160	3,980	420	1,671,600	5,708,605
9	4,872	119	579,768	13,665	253	3,457,245	3,510	420	1,474,200	5,511,213
10	4,990	119	593,810	13,610	253	3,443,330	3,040	420	1,276,800	5,313,940
11	5,107	119	607,733	13,555	253	3,429,415	2,569	420	1,078,980	5,116,128
12	5,240	119	623,560	13,405	253	3,391,465	2,056	420	863,520	4,878,545
13	5,373	119	639,387	13,255	253	3,353,515	1,542	420	647,640	4,640,542
14	5,506	119	655,214	13,105	253	3,315,565	1,028	420	431,760	4,402,539
15	5,639	119	671,041	12,955	253	3,277,615	514	420	215,880	4,164,536
16	5,771	119	686,749	12,805	253	3,239,665	0	420	0	3,926,414
17	5,842	119	695,198	12,383	253	3,132,899				3,828,097
18	5,913	119	703,647	11,961	253	3,026,133				3,729,780
19	5,984	119	712,096	11,539	253	2,919,367				3,631,463
20	6,055	119	720,545	11,117	253	2,812,601				3,533,146
21	6,126	119	728,994	10,695	253	2,705,835				3,434,829
22	6,197	119	737,443	10,273	253	2,599,069				3,336,512
23	6,268	119	745,892	9,851	253	2,492,303				3,238,195
24	6,339	119	754,341	9,429	253	2,385,537				3,139,878
25	6,410	119	762,790	9,007	253	2,278,771				3,041,561
26	6,481	119	771,239	8,585	253	2,172,005				2,943,244
27	6,552	119	779,688	8,163	206	2,065,239				2,844,927
28	6,623	119	788,137	7,741	253	1,958,473				2,746,610
29	6,694	119	796,586	7,319	253	1,851,707				2,648,293
30	6,765	119	805,035	6,897	253	1,744,941				2,549,976
31	6,836	119	813,484	6,475	253	1,638,175				2,451,659
32	6,907	119	821,933	6,053	253	1,531,409				2,353,342
33	6,978	119	830,382	5,631	253	1,424,643				2,255,025
34	7,049	119	838,831	5,209	253	1,317,877				2,156,708
35	7,120	119	847,280	4,787	253	1,211,111				2,058,391
36	7,191	119	855,729	4,365	253	1,104,345				1,960,074
37	7,262	119	864,178	3,943	253	997,579				1,861,757
38	7,333	119	872,627	3,521	253	890,813				1,763,440
39	7,404	119	881,076	3,099	253	784,047				1,665,213
40	7,475	119	889,525	2,677	253	677,281				1,566,806

Table 18 Total Value for Managed Lands (Rs)

Yr	Plantations			Scrubland			Forest			Grazing			Total Value
	Rs/ha	ha	Rs	Rs/ha	ha	Rs	Rs/ha	ha	Rs	Rs/ha	ha	Rs	Rs
1	395	1,000	395,000	294	16,000	4,704,000	992	7,000	69,444,000	119	4,000	476,000	12,519,000
2	395	2,000	790,000	138	16,000	2,208,000	277	7,000	1,939,000	119	3,000	357,000	5,294,000
3	395	3,000	1,185,000	463	16,000	7,408,000	277	7,000	1,939,000	119	2,000	238,000	10,770,000
4	395	4,000	1,580,000	138	16,000	2,208,000	277	7,000	1,939,000	119	1,000	119,000	5,846,000
5	395	4,000	1,580,000	398	16,000	6,368,000	277	7,000	1,939,000	119			9,887,000
6	3,707	4,000	14,828,000	178	16,000	2,848,000	3,241	7,000	22,687,000				40,363,000
7	1,107	4,000	4,428,000	178	16,000	2,848,000	316	7,000	2,212,000				9,488,000
8	1,107	4,000	4,428,000	178	16,000	2,848,000	316	7,000	2,212,000				9,488,000
9	1,107	4,000	4,428,000	178	16,000	2,848,000	316	7,000	2,212,000				9,488,000
10	1,107	4,000	4,428,000	854	16,000	13,664,000	316	7,000	2,212,000				20,304,000
11	2,147	4,000	8,588,000	257	16,000	4,112,000	3,843	7,000	26,901,000				39,601,000
12	2,147	4,000	8,588,000	257	16,000	4,112,000	593	7,000	4,151,000				16,851,000
13	2,147	4,000	8,588,000	257	16,000	4,112,000	593	7,000	4,151,000				16,851,000
14	2,147	4,000	8,588,000	257	16,000	4,112,000	593	7,000	4,151,000				16,851,000
15	2,147	4,000	8,588,000	257	16,000	5,376,000	593	7,000	4,151,000				16,851,000
16	2,147	4,000	8,588,000	336	16,000	5,376,000	4,228	7,000	29,596,000				4,356,000
17	2,147	4,000	8,588,000	336	16,000	5,376,000	653	7,000	4,571,000				1,853,500
18	2,147	4,000	8,588,000	336	16,000	5,376,000	653	7,000	4,571,000				1,853,500

19	2,147	4,000	8,588,000	336	16,000	5,376,000	653	7,000	4,571,000	1,853,500
20	2,147	4,000	8,588,000	2,936	16,000	46,976,000	653	7,000	4,571,000	60,135,000
21	2,147	4,000	8,588,000	415	16,000	6,640,000	4,228	7,000	29,596,000	44,824,000
22	2,147	4,000	8,588,000	415	16,000	6,640,000	653	7,000	4,571,000	19,799,000
23	2,147	4,000	8,588,000	415	16,000	6,640,000	653	7,000	4,571,000	19,799,000
24	2,147	4,000	8,588,000	415	16,000	6,640,000	653	7,000	4,571,000	19,799,000
25	2,147	4,000	8,588,000	415	16,000	6,640,000	653	7,000	4,571,000	19,799,000
26	2,147	4,000	8,588,000	534	16,000	8,544,000	4,228	7,000	29,596,000	46,728,000
27	2,147	4,000	8,588,000	534	16,000	8,544,000	653	7,000	4,571,000	21,703,000
28	2,147	4,000	8,588,000	534	16,000	8,544,000	653	7,000	4,571,000	21,703,000
29	2,147	4,000	8,588,000	534	16,000	8,544,000	653	7,000	4,571,000	21,703,000
30	2,147	4,000	8,588,000	5,084	16,000	81,344,000	653	7,000	4,571,000	94,503,000
31	2,147	4,000	8,588,000	534	16,000	8,544,000	4,228	7,000	29,596,000	46,728,000
32	2,147	4,000	8,588,000	534	16,000	8,544,000	653	7,000	4,571,000	21,703,000
33	2,147	4,000	8,588,000	534	16,000	8,544,000	653	7,000	4,571,000	21,703,000
34	2,147	4,000	8,588,000	534	16,000	8,544,000	653	7,000	4,571,000	21,703,000
35	2,147	4,000	8,588,000	5,084	16,000	81,344,000	653	7,000	4,571,000	94,503,000
36	2,147	4,000	8,588,000	534	16,000	8,544,000	1,228	7,000	29,596,000	46,728,000
37	2,147	4,000	8,588,000	534	16,000	8,544,000	653	7,000	4,571,000	21,703,000
38	2,147	4,000	8,588,000	534	16,000	8,544,000	653	7,000	4,571,000	21,703,000
39	2,147	4,000	8,588,000	534	16,000	8,544,000	653	7,000	4,571,000	21,703,000
40	2,147	4,000	8,588,000	534	16,000	8,544,000	653	7,000	4,571,000	21,703,000

Table 19 Economic Evaluation: Benefit-Cost Streams (Rs '000)

Year	Cost [a]	Incremental Benefits	Net Benefits
1	22,597	5,055	−17,542
2	27,128	−1,898	−29,026
3	28,648	3,850	−24,798
4	27,646	−802	−28,448
5	32,246	3,512	−28,734
6	34,604	34,260	−344
7	8,996	3,582	−5,414
8	9,183	3,779	−5,404
9	5,278	3,977	−1,301
10	5,763	14,990	9,227
11	3,309	34,485	31,176
12	3,215	12,448	8,757
13	3,120	12,210	9,090
14	3,215	12,448	9,233
15	3,309	12,686	9,377
16	3,403	14,805	36,231
17	3,498	14,707	11,209
18	3,402	14,805	11,402
19	3,309	14,904	11,595
20	3,215	56,602	53,387
21	3,120	41,389	38,269
22	3,215	16,462	13,247
23	3,309	16,561	13,252
24	3,403	16,659	13,256
25	3,498	16,757	13,259
26	3,403	43,785	40,382
27	3,309	18,858	15,549
28	3,215	18,956	15,741
29	3,120	19,055	15,935
30	3,215	91,953	88,738
31	3,309	44,276	40,967
32	3,403	19,350	15,947
33	3,498	19,448	15,950
34	3,403	19,546	16,143
35	3,309	92,445	89,136
36	3,215	44,768	41,553
37	3,120	19,841	16,721
38	3,215	19,940	16,725
39	3,309	20,038	16,729
40	3,403	20,136	16,733

[a] Project costs are given in ADB, *Appraisal of the Hill Forest Development Project* (1983) and represent the initial project costs and continuing management expenses for the project.

Note: Economic internal rate of return (EIRR) = 8.5 percent.

Mangrove Valuation in Bintuni Bay, Irian Jaya, Indonesia

This case study is an example of an application of the change-in-productivity method. Ruitenbeek (1992, 1994) performs an extended benefit cost analysis of six management strategies for approximately 300,000 ha of mangroves in the Bintuni Bay area of Irian Jaya, Indonesia (Figure 14). Considerable uncertainty surrounds the underlying damage functions relating loss of mangrove area to changes in productivity of other resource assets. Sensitivity analysis is used to test the effect of changes in assumed linkages between the rate and extent of mangrove cuttings and the production of other goods and services, as well as to evaluate the effect of changes in discount rates.

Bintuni Bay supports a lucrative commercial capture fishery for shrimp, and coastal areas support 3,000 households in a mixed economy dependent on farming, wage labour, and traditional mangrove uses. Commercial sago production has also been established in the area recently. In addition, many other goods and services derived from mangroves, while not traded, bring considerable benefits to local residents. A recent development is the introduction of a commercial mangrove woodchipping operation. Continued productivity of the fishery, as well as other beneficial uses of the mangrove area, may be threatened by the rapid growth of mangrove woodchip exports. Recent interest in the problems of the area have led to the proposal to establish the Bintuni Bay Nature Reserve that would include some 267,000 ha of the local ecosystem, including 60,000 ha of the Bay itself.

This study estimates the benefits and costs of various management alternatives. In addition to direct costs and benefits of different management plans for mangrove harvesting for woodchip production, the analysis considers the impacts of the harvest activities on other beneficial goods and services, both traded and untraded, which are derived from or dependent on the mangrove ecosystem. These include the following:

- local uses including traditional fishing, hunting, gathering and manufacturing;
- control of coastal erosion;
- commercial fisheries;
- sago production; and
- 'capturable biodiversity'.

Since many of the goods and services derived by local residents are non-traded, observable market transactions are not an adequate basis for valuation. A survey of 101 households was carried out to analyse the composition of total household production, especially the proportion of non-traded goods and services coming from the mangroves.

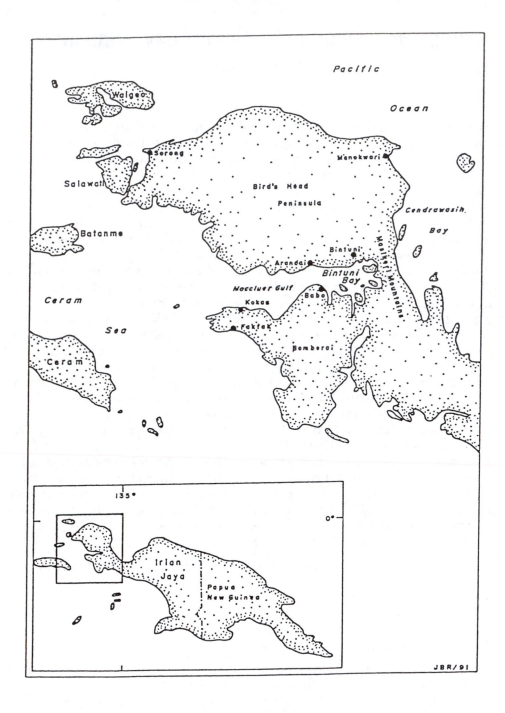

Figure 14 Location of Bintuni Bay, Irian Jaya, Indonesia
Source: Ruitenbeek, 1992.

134

A change-in-productivity approach to valuation (based on physical changes in production and observed or estimated prices) is used for all these categories except 'capturable biodiversity', which is defined as the potential benefit which Indonesia might be able to obtain from the international community in exchange for maintaining its biodiversity base. A value of $1,500 per square kilometer of contiguous areas of mangrove left intact is assigned to 'capturable biodiversity' based on another study that evaluated transfers between developed and developing countries related to conservation initiatives.

The change-in-productivity approach requires that the cause and effect relationships be known. Unfortunately, the relationships between loss of mangrove and direct reduction of productivity of fisheries, or indirect reduction of agriculture production through erosion, is highly speculative, especially with regard to the magnitude and timing of impacts. Therefore, the study tested the significance of various possible linkages between mangrove loss and other economic activities in the area. These linkages were specified by two parameters – an impact intensity parameter (a), and an impact delay parameter (T). The relationship between these parameters and the year of initial harvest (t) is as follows:

$$(P_t/P_{t=0}) = (M_{t-T}/M_{t=0})^a$$

where   P = productivity of the resource in question
             M = mangrove area.

For example, an impact intensity parameter of a=1 for the fishery would mean that there is a 1 to 1 linear relationship between loss of mangrove area and decline in fishery production. Similarly, a value of a<1 implies a less than proportional change, and a>1 implies a more than proportional change in productivity. A zero impact intensity parameter, a=0, would mean that there is no linkage between mangrove removal and loss in fishery productivity. The linkage scenario assumptions used in the analysis are summarized in Table 20.

The delay parameter, T, recognizes that impacts might not be immediate, and the timing of the impacts will influence the streams of costs and benefits of various management strategies, thereby affecting the NPV of the activity. T is measured in years, with the delayed impacts represented by values of 0, 5 or 10 years for T.

Based on the survey of local households, estimates were made of the present values of many traditional economic activities that formed a very substantial part of household income. For *local, traditional uses*, such as traditional fishing, hunting, gathering and manufacturing, three steps were taken in the valuation. First, total income from all traded goods was estimated from the household survey; this value was approximately Rp1.4 million (ca $700) annually per household. Second, this estimate was adjusted upwards to account for the share that non-traded goods and services played in the household economy; this resulted in a total of Rp5.1 million (ca $2,550) annually per household. Finally, distortions in local prices were corrected to reflect free market prices. The

Table 20 Linkage Scenario Assumptions

	Local Uses; Erosion; Fisheries		Commercial Sago		Capturable Biodiversity	
Linkage Scenario	a	T	a	T	a	T
A None	0.0	–	0.0	–	0.0	–
B Weak	0.5	10	0.0	–	1.0	0
C Moderate	0.5	5	0.5	10	1.0	0
D Strong	1.0	5	1.0	10	1.0	–100b
E Very Strong	1.0	0	1.0	5	1.0	–100b

Note: a = Impact intensity parameter; b= Negative values imply that benefits which can be captured in any year are based on expectations of future undisturbed mangrove area; T = Impact delay parameter.

Source: Ruitenbeek, 1992.

corrections were based on prices in the nearest large market net of transportation costs. At imputed shadow prices, the total value of local production was estimated at Rp9.0 million (ca $4,500) per household per year, a surprisingly large figure (of which the traded portion amounted to only about 15 percent of the total value). The survey also found that traditional mangrove uses contributed proportionately more to low income households.

For *erosion control*, the imputed benefit is based on the value of agricultural output from local production, estimated at Rp 1.9 million (ca $800) per household per year, which it is assumed would be'lost if coastal areas were seriously eroded.

For *commercial fisheries* it is assumed that sustainable yields for the commercial shrimp fishery are approximately 5,500 tons per year; with an average value of about $6.25/kg this represents about $35 million per year. There is also another potentially important fishery component: the 'bycatch' that is caught with the shrimp and represents up to 90 percent of the trawl catch by weight. These fish are little used and are either thrown back into the Bay or, less frequently, eaten by the crew or sold to local communities. The bycatch has a potential value of as much as $10 million per year (assuming a very low value of $0.15/kg) if commercial processing for fish meal and fertilizer are developed.

A total of 15,000 ha has been allotted to *commercial sago production* in the Bintuni Bay area since 1990. It is assumed that the area dedicated to sago will remain the same and production will reach a sustainable level of 225,000 tons per year by 2001. Production characteristics and input requirements for processing virgin sago palm into starch are based on available literature. It is assumed that sago prices remain constant at Rp300 per kilo ($0.15/kg) over the 90-year period covered by the analysis.

It is assumed that real *woodchip* export prices remain constant at $40 m^3 over the period covered by the analysis. Production costs were based on investment costs provided by companies, and on operating costs estimated from typical operations. Transfer payments such as royalties, taxes and compensation payment were excluded from the analysis.

Six different mangrove cutting options are evaluated, ranging from a complete cutting ban on one extreme to complete clear cutting on the other (Table 21). Related assumptions on the area and volumes involved are given in Table 22. The benefit-cost analysis was conducted over a period of 90 years with 1991 as the base year, and assuming different linkage scenarios for each option. The scenarios, therefore, included both the benefits and costs of woodchip production but also the impacts on other goods and services dependent on the mangrove.

Table 21 Mangrove Cutting Options Evaluated

Option		Description
I	Cutting Ban	Total mangrove area (304,000 ha) is maintained in virgin state.
II	20-year clear cut	Total harvestable area (240,000 ha) is cut over once only.
III	30-year clear cut	Total harvestable area (240,000 ha) is cut over once only.
IV	30-year rotation 80% selective cut	80% of total harvestable area (192,000 ha) is cut in perpetuity on a 30-year rotation.
V	30-year rotation 40% selective cut	40% of total harvestable area (96,000 ha) is cut in perpetuity on a 30-year rotation. This is equivalent to 100% of total harvestable area outside of proposed nature reserve.
VI	30-year rotation 25% selective cut	25% of total harvestable area (60,000 ha) is cut in perpetuity on a 30-year rotation. This is equivalent to 62% of total harvestable area outside proposed nature reserve. It is also equivalent to operating current woodchip plant at 80% capacity for 20 years.

Source: Ruitenbeek, 1992.

137

Table 22 Mangrove Area and Related Assumptions

Total Management Area = 364,000 ha.

Total Mangrove Area	304,000 ha.
Total Harvestable Area	240,000 ha.
Within Proposed Nature Reserve	143,000 ha.
Outside Proposed Nature Reserve	97,000 ha.
Total Unharvestable Area	64,000 ha.
Total Area in Bintuni Bay to 10 m Depth	60,000 ha.
Proposed Nature Reserve	267,000 ha.

Chipwood Plant Requirements:

Mangrove Stock Rate = 80m^3/ha
Chipwood Plant = 300,000 m^3/year
Current Concession Length = 20 years

Stock Requirement for 20-year Life at 100% Capacity	6,000,000m^3
Stock Requirement for 20-year Life at 80% Capacity	4,800,000m^3
Area Requirement for 20-year Life at 100% Capacity	75,000 ha
Area Requirement for 20-year Life at 80% Capacity	60,000 ha

Source: Ruitenbeek, 1992.

The base case involves 'no linkages', where each resource component is assumed to function independently. This is the implicit assumption used when resources are managed separately and interdependence of production among sectors is not recognized. It is not surprising, therefore, that of the evaluated options under the 'no linkage' assumption, the 'clear cut' case is the optimal cutting strategy, because the discount rate is greater than the growth rate of the mangroves. Under this strategy, however, important economic costs would be imposed on other users of the Bay's resources if the 'no linkage' assumption is inaccurate. As seen in Table 23, the total NPV for each option is composed of six different sources of income, three of which (local uses, erosion control, and biodiversity) are usually ignored in project analysis.

Net present values (NPV) of 26 different management options were calculated (the cutting ban and five different linkage scenarios for each of the other five management options) at a base discount rate of 7.5 percent. Table 23 gives a summary of several of these options. There are no linkages in the case of a cutting ban. Several results from the benefit-cost analysis are presented in Table 23; these include three options for clear cutting (with the presence of none, moderate and strong linkages), and the moderate linkage scenarios for 80 percent and 25 percent selective cutting options. Table 24 presents the

Table 23 Summary of Benefit-Cost Analysis Results (Billion of Rp in 1991 constant prices; discounted at 7.5%)

Case	Scenario	Linkage	NPV Local Uses	NPV Erosion Control	NPV Wood Cut	NPV Fish	NPV Sago	NPV Biodiversity	NPV Total
I	Cutting ban		399	145	0	1,016	546	131	2,237
IIA	Clear cut (20 years)	None	399	145	756	1,016	546	131	2,994
IIC	Clear cut (20 years)	Moderate	295	102	756	824	440	74	2,491
IID	Clear cut (20 years)	Strong	237	79	756	710	378	27	2,189
IVC	Select cut (80%)	Moderate	339	119	532	908	487	95	2,481
VIC	Select cut (25%)	Moderate	383	138	166	986	530	120	2,321

Source: Ruitenbeek, 1992.

Table 24 Marginal Change from Base 'Cutting Ban' Scenario

Case	Scenario	Linkage	NPV Local Uses	NPV Erosion Control	NPV Wood Cut	NPV Fish	NPV Sago	NPV Biodiversity	NPV Total
I	Cutting ban		399	145	0	1016	546	131	2237
IIA	Clear cut (20 years)	None	0	0	+756	0	0	0	757
IIC	Clear cut (20 years)	Moderate	−104	−43	+756	−192	−106	−54	254
IID	Clear cut (20 years)	Strong	−162	−66	+756	−306	−168	104	−48
IVC	Select cut (80%)	Moderate	0	−26	+532	−108	−59	−36	244
VIC	Select cut (25%)	Moderate	−16	−7	+166	−30	−16	−11	84

Source: Ruitenbeek, 1992.

Table 25 Impact of a Change in Discount Rate on NPV of Management Alternatives (Billion of Rp in 1991 Constant Prices)

Scenario	Linkage	7.5% per year	5% per year	10% per year
Cutting ban		2,237	3,498	1,625
Clear cut (20 years)	Moderate	2,491	3,364	1,988
Select cut (80%)	Moderate	2,481	3,640	1,877
Select cut (25%)	Moderate	2,321	3,563	1,707

Source: Ruitenbeek, 1992.

same options and illustrates the marginal change from the cutting ban scenario. One notes that the increased 'wood cut' benefits offset losses from other uses in all but one case (clear cutting over 20 years with strong linkages). In general, the stronger the linkages between mangrove harvesting and other non-wood-chip benefits, the more attractive the 'cutting ban' scenario becomes. Conversely, the higher the discount rate, the more attractive are the options that permit some harvesting.

The optimal cutting strategy changes, therefore, when the effect of linkages is considered. Under the 'very strong linkages' scenario (linear and immediate impacts), the 'clear cut' option is the worst alternative and the 'cutting ban' option the best. If 'weak linkages' exist, selective cutting options are optimal, and these options are also competitive under the assumption of 'moderate linkages'. For example, under a scenario with linear but delayed linkages of five years (the strong linkage scenario), selective cutting of 25 percent of the mangrove has a present value of $35 million greater than the 30-year clear cutting option, and only $1.5 million greater than the cutting ban option.

Sensitivity analyses were carried out at 5 percent and 10 percent discount rates; constant prices were assumed. As seen in Table 25, at lower discount rates the cutting ban is more attractive than options of clear cut or selective cut assuming moderate linkages. At higher discount rates, however, the alternative management options are consistently more attractive than a cutting ban.

The expanded analysis allows the decision maker to choose a mangrove management plan that recognizes and protects the importance of the mangrove to the continuing production of a wide range of economic goods and services.

Sources:
Ruitenbeek, H. Jack. 1992 *Mangrove Management: An Economic Analysis of Management Options with a Focus on Bintuni Bay, Irian Jaya*. Environmental Management Development in Indonesia Project, Dalhousie University, Halifax.
Ruitenbeek, H, Jack. 1994. 'Modelling ecology-wide linkages in mangroves: Economic evidence for promoting conservation in Bintuni Bay, Indonesia.' *Ecological Economics*, vol 10, no. 3, pp. 233–47.

3

Estimating the Health Impact of Air Pollution: Methodology and an Application to Jakarta

Countries around the world are investing increasingly large amounts of money to combat air and water pollution. A major analytical problem is to identify the benefits of those investments to determine if the benefits are likely to exceed the costs. This information is also an aid in prioritizing interventions, both among different control options and between air and water pollution. Air pollution is a growing urban problem affecting hundreds of millions of people. This case study presents an illustration of the use of one increasingly accepted methodology – the damage function approach using dose-response relationships – to estimate the health impacts of air pollution reduction. Additional information can then be used to place monetary values on these health effects – by either using the cost-of-illness approach to estimate monetary values of reduced illness (morbidity) or, in the case of death, estimates usually based on willingness-to-pay to reduce premature mortality.

Dose-response relationships are functions mostly based on data from the US, Canada, and the United Kingdom that relate information on changes in ambient air quality for different pollutants to different health outcomes. The principle is that changes in ambient air pollution levels for certain pollutants can be statistically related to observed changes in morbidity (sickness) and mortality (death) in a population. Through regression analysis, coefficients are estimated that are then multiplied by changes in ambient pollution concentrations and the population exposed. Most of this work has previously been done in Europe and the US and this case study shows an application of the approach to Jakarta (Ostro, 1994).

The estimated health impact can be estimated by the following relationship:

$$dH_i = b_i * POP_i * dA$$

where:

dH_i = change in population risk of health effect i;
b_i = slope from the dose-response curve for health impact i;
POP_i = population at risk of health effect i;
dA = change in ambient air pollutant under consideration.

AN APPLICATION TO JAKARTA

Jakarta, the capital of Indonesia, is located in the tropics just south of the equator. The population is between 8.2 to 9 million, and the city covers some

650 km². Air and water pollution are both major environmental problems. The results presented here focus on air pollution, particularly suspended particulate matter, often referred to as TSP (total suspended particulates) and the finer, more damaging, portion called PM10, or particles smaller than 10 microns in size. Pollution exposure is measured in various ways, often in terms of micrograms of TSP or PM10 per m³ of air. (One can convert directly from TSP to PM10: PM10 is about 55 percent of the total TSP; that is, a level of TSP of 100 micrograms/m³ is equal to a PM10 measurement of 55 micrograms/m³).

This study uses dose-response functions estimated in developed countries since none were available for local conditions in Jakarta. It is implicitly assumed, therefore, that the relationship between the levels of air pollution and subsequent health effects in the developed countries can be extrapolated to estimate the health impacts in Jakarta. It is recognized that there are significant differences between developed country and Indonesian populations in baseline health status, access to health care, demographics, and occupational exposures, among other factors. It is therefore likely that the model will underestimate the health effects for Indonesia.

In the study, dose-response functions have been identified and adapted from the available literature (see Ostro, 1994, for details on the background studies). Since there are variations in the coefficients estimated by the various studies, three alternative assumptions about health effects are presented, with the central estimate being given the most weight. High (low) end estimates are calculated by increasing (decreasing) the coefficient by one estimated standard deviation.

Available epidemiological studies relate concentrations of ambient particulate matter and several adverse health outcomes including mortality, respiratory hospital admissions, emergency room visits, restricted activity days for adults, respiratory illness for children, asthma attacks and chronic disease. TSP is the measure of particulates most commonly used in Indonesia. Therefore all dose response functions were adapted to be used with TSP concentrations.

Estimates were made of the benefits of reducing TSP levels from present levels in Jakarta (ranging from less than 100 to over 350mg/m³ in certain parts of the city; see Figure 15) to both the Indonesian standard (90 mg/m³) and the midpoint of the WHO guidelines (75 mg/m³). In each case the estimates were based on information on population exposed to different levels of pollution. (This information is based on census data on population density and the results of citywide information on emissions and air quality monitoring and the use of a dispersion model.)

MORTALITY

Premature mortality is a major problem associated with high levels of particulates. Based on a survey of the literature, a central estimate of the change in 'all-cause mortality' associated with a change in PM10 can be expressed as follows:

Figure 15 Isopleths of Annual Average TSP Concentrations in Jakarta
Source: Ostro, 1994.

Central percentage change in mortality = 0.096 * change in PM10

with upper and lower estimates having coefficients of 0.130 and 0.062, respectively. The central estimate of the number of cases of premature mortality can then be expressed as:

Change in mortality = 0.096 * change in PM10 * 1/100 * crude mortality rate * population exposed.

Assuming the crude mortality rate in Jakarta is 0.007, the range in changes in mortality (per person) is:

143

Upper estimate of change in mortality   = $9.10 * 10^{-6} *$ change in PM10

Central estimate of change in mortality = $6.72 * 10^{-6} *$ change in PM10

Lower estimate of change in mortality   = $4.47 * 10^{-6} *$ change in PM10

For example, if average PM10 levels decreased by 10 micrograms per m³ for Jakarta, and if 5 million people were exposed to this reduction, the estimated health benefit would be 335 fewer cases of premature mortality per year:

$6.72 * 10^{-6}$ (DRR coefficient) $* 10$ (change in PM10) $*$ 5,000,000 (population) = 335.

MORBIDITY

A similar approach was also used to estimate the effects of changes in air quality on air pollution-related illnesses. In each case a dose-response relationship was identified and was linked to a discrete health outcome:

Respiratory Hospital Admissions (RHA). Based on Canadian and US studies, there is a statistically significant relationship between the incidence of hospital admissions due to respiratory diseases (RHA) and ambient sulphate and TSP levels. The following functions are suggested per 100,000 population:

Upper change in RHA per 100,000   = 1.56 * change in PM10

Central change in RHA per 100,000 = 1.20 * change in PM10

Lower change in RHA per 100,000   = 0.657 * change in PM10

Emergency Room Visits (ERV). The relationship between emergency room visits (ERV) and TSP exposure based on US studies was adjusted by plus or minus one standard deviation from the central coefficient to generate high and low estimates for Jakarta:

Upper change in ERV per 100,000   = 34.25 * annual change in PM10

Central change in ERV per 100,000 = 23.54 * annual change in PM10

Lower change in ERV per 100,000   = 12.83 * annual change in PM10

Restricted Activity Days (RAD). Restricted activity days (RAD) include days spent in bed, days missed from work, and other days when normal activities are restricted due to illness, even if medical attention is not required. Studies from the US suggest a statistically significant relationship between particulates of various sizes and RAD. After standardizing on PM10 the relationship

144

between RAD and PM10 is estimated as follows (these estimates are applied to all adults):

Upper change in RAD per person per year = 0.0903 * change in PM10

Central change in RAD per person per year = 0.0575 * change in PM10

Lower change in RAD per person per year = 0.0404 * change in PM10

Lower Respiratory Illness in Children (LRI). US studies suggest the following relationship between the occurrence of chronic coughs, annual change in bronchitis and other respiratory diseases in children and PM10, adjusted for a number of variables including the incidence of bronchitis in children:

Upper change in annual bronchitis = 0.00238 * change in PM10

Central change in annual bronchitis = 0.00169 * change in PM10

Lower change in annual bronchitis = 0.0008 * change in PM10

This relationship is applied to the 34.7 percent of the population below the age of 18 in Jakarta.

Other estimates. Estimates were also made for a number of other air pollution-related illnesses. These included asthma attacks, respiratory symptoms, and chronic bronchitis. Table 26 summarizes the dose-response estimates of the morbidity outcomes of changes in PM10 levels for all of these possible health outcomes, and presents the central estimate and the high-side estimate. Note that some of the effects are estimated per 100,000 people in the general population, while others are person or group specific (e.g. RAD per person, or asthma attacks per asthmatic).

Table 26 Morbidity Effects of 10 microgram/m^3 Change in PM10

Type of Morbidity	Central Estimate	High Estimate
RHA/100,000	12.0	15.6
ERV/100,000	235.4	342.5
RAD/person	0.575	0.903
LRI/child/per asthmatic	0.0169	0.0238
Asthma attacks/ per asthmatic[a]	0.326	2.73
Respiratory symptoms/ person	1.83	2.74
Chronic bronchitis/ 100,000	61.2	91.8

[a] Applies to the 8.25% of the Indonesian population that is assumed asthmatic. High estimates are obtained by increasing the coefficient by one estimated standard deviation.

An Application of the Approach to Jakarta. When the coefficients listed in Table 26 were applied to Jakarta, Ostro was able to estimate health impacts associated with decreasing particulate levels to both the Indonesian standards (90 micrograms/m^3) and WHO standards (about 75 micrograms/m^3). Figure 15 shows annual average TSP measurements for Jakarta in 1989; many parts of the city had levels between 100 and 200, and 'hot spots' with readings of 300 or 350 were common. Table 27 presents the health benefits of reducing particulate matter to the Indonesian standard (90 micrograms per m^3). (Meeting the more stringent WHO standards would produce even larger benefits, of course, but would cost more to achieve.)

The numbers of lives saved and illnesses avoided are impressive. Using the central or medium estimate of the dose-response relationships, Ostro estimated that each year in Jakarta the benefits from reducing particulates to Indonesian standards include 1,200 premature deaths avoided, 2,000 fewer hospital admissions, 40,600 saved emergency room visits, and over 6 million fewer restricted activity days, among other benefits for the population of 8.2 million.

Achieving Indonesian TSP standards will not be easy, however, and would involve major investments. To estimate which investments and control options should be undertaken, the policymaker would ideally like to compare the benefits to the costs. The benefits are largely due to health costs that are avoided, and a decrease in premature deaths. Placing monetary values on premature death or small changes in risks of mortality is very difficult, although estimating the costs of illness is easier (for a discussion of this, see the Box at the end of the case study). In this case monetary values were not placed on the health outcomes. Still, presenting the impacts of TSP pollution in physical terms, as is done in Table 27, can still be a powerful message prompting government action. At a minimum, a cost-effective approach can be applied to identify those policy interventions that produce the largest health benefit per dollar invested.

Table 27 Health Benefits of Reducing Particulates in Jakarta to Indonesian Standards

Health effect	Medium estimate
Premature mortality	1,200
Hospital admissions	2,000
Emergency room visits (ERV)	40,600
Restricted activity days (RAD)	6,330,000
Lower respiratory illness (LRI)	104,000
Asthma attacks	464,000
Respiratory symptoms	31,000,000
Chronic bronchitis	9,600

BOX 9: ANNEX
ECONOMIC VALUATION OF HEALTH EFFECTS

Ideally, valuation of health impacts should include both the out-of-pocket costs of illness such as medical costs, lost income and averting expenditures, and the less tangible effects of illness on well-being such as pain, discomfort and restriction in non-work activities. Health impacts valued by willingness-to-pay (WTP) incorporate all of these impacts, whereas a cost of illness (COI) approach only includes out-of-pocket expenses such as medical costs and lost income.

Ostro did not estimate the economic costs of mortality and morbidity in Jakarta, although estimates can be made fairly easily in the case of illness (morbidity). There is a sizeable literature on the cost of ill-health in the US.

WTP estimates to prevent or accept small changes in the risks of death are based on empirical evidence gathered in the US and Great Britain of people making actual tradeoffs between the risks of death and some benefit, such as income. In addition, some contingent valuation studies have been conducted in which respondents are asked directly what they would be willing to pay to reduce risks associated with, for example, work or traffic accidents. As discussed in Chapter 7, considerable controversy exists over the 'value of life.' One commonly used value in the US is $300 for a .0001 reduction in risk. Thus, for a large population, the reduction in risk translates to $3 million per death avoided.

Economic costs for changes in morbidity are, of course, very country-specific. In the high cost, US medical care sector, some estimates of the costs of illness include the following (Ostro, 1992):

Respiratory Hospital Admission, RHA:
    average stay – 10.13 days
    average cost of stay – $26,898
    lost day wage rate – $125
    So, each RHA is assumed to cost $28,164.

Emergency Room Visit, ERV:
    lost day wage rate – $125
    average stay – 1 day
    average cost of stay – $133
    So, each ERV is assumed to cost $258

Restricted Activity Day, RAD:
    20 percent of RAD result in lost work days, and the remaining 80 percent of RAD valued at one-third of the average wage rate.
    lost day wage rate – $125
    So, each RAD is assumed to cost $58

Lower Respiratory Illness in children (LRI):
   2 weeks of illness per episode valued at $15 per day
   two RAD per parent for care per episode
   So, total per episode of BC is assumed to cost $326

These costs are for the US. To estimate the costs of ill-health in Jakarta, separate Indonesian-specific cost estimates are needed. These will be lower than US costs and may vary by type of illness, depending on relative differences between the US and Indonesia for labour and capital.

Sources:
Ostro, Bart. 1992. 'Estimating the Health and Economic Effects of Particulate Matter in Jakarta: A Preliminary Assessment,' paper presented at the Fourth Annual Meeting of the International Society for Environmental Epidemiology, 26–29 August. Cuernavaca, Mexico.
Ostro, Bart. 1994. *Estimating Health Effects of Air Pollutants: A Methodology with an Application to Jakarta*. Policy Research Working Paper 1301. Washington, D.C: the World Bank.

4

Benefits and Costs of Soil Conservation in the Loess Plateau of China

Soil conservation measures are usually undertaken to improve agricultural production in the project area. It is also realized that there may be important off-site, downstream benefits from reducing soil erosion. This case illustrates the use of several different approaches to place 'order-of-magnitude' estimates on offsite benefits in the lower reaches of the Yellow River basin from erosion control and sediment reduction in the Loess Plateau area of China (Magrath, 1992). The project consists of a number of measures undertaken in the upstream Loess Plateau area:

*   construction of structures that physically trap sediment (gully plugs, check dams and warping dams);
*   modification of land form (terracing of steeply sloping lands); and
*   modification of land use (introduction of improved land use practices such as afforestation and grassland development).

Sediment delivery to the lower reaches of the Yellow River averages 1.6 billion tons per year. About 1.1 billion tons flows into the Bohai Bay of the Yellow Sea (requiring about 20 to 24 billion m^3 of river water for flushing); approximately 300 to 400 million tons of sediment are deposited along the lower reaches of the river, and about 100 to 200 million tons are left in the irrigation systems located in this area (Figure 16).

DOWNSTREAM IMPACTS OF SEDIMENTATION

There are three categories of impacts associated with the deposition of sediment in the lower reaches of the Yellow River: flooding, damage to irrigation systems, and inefficient use of scarce water supply. The deposition of large amounts of sediment increases the danger of *flooding* by raising the level of the river bed on average about 8 to 10 cm per year, and decreasing the capacity of its channel. To counter this danger, major dikes have been built over the centuries to contain the river. The net result is that large sections of the river are 'suspended' above the surrounding plain. On average the river is now 3 to 5 m above its surrounding floodplain. A breach of this system would impose enormous costs in terms of loss of property and life. Given the continuing sedimentation, periodically recurring preventive expenditures are needed to incrementally raise the dikes to reduce the likelihood of a breach; this has been done three times since 1950. (It is estimated that the next increment will cost RMB Yuan 4 billion.)

149

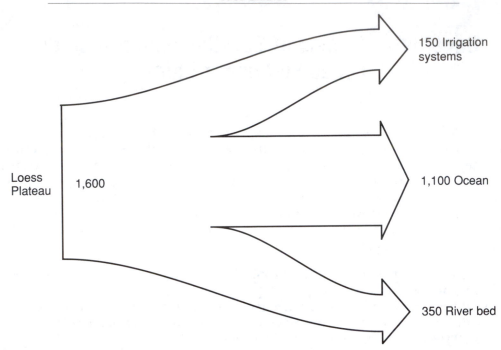

Figure 16 Downstream Deposition of Sediment Flows from the Loess Plateau
(millions of tons per year)

An average of approximately 150 million tons of sediment reaches the area's *irrigation systems* each year. Of this amount, approximately 67 million tons is removed by dredging and other means.

The *opportunity cost of water supply* is high relative to its value in flushing sediment. Another benefit, therefore, of reduced sediment in the Yellow River is releasing additional amounts of water for other uses.

DOWNSTREAM ECONOMIC BENEFITS OF THE PROJECT

In addition to the upstream benefits from the various land-forming and agricultural measures sponsored by the project, the economic analysis considered each of the downstream impacts and estimated the potential benefit from reducing sediment delivery to the downstream area. These benefits are correctly measured by the flood and other damages avoided, including release of water to uses other than sediment flushing. However, since flood control benefits are hard to measure (a break in the dikes would create a major catastrophe), if the preventive expenditures of dike raising are assumed to be economically justified, the flood prevention benefits can be thought of as at least equal to these avoided expenditures. The total benefits of the project can be thought of as all costs avoided – preventive expenditures for raising dikes, restoration costs to desilt irrigation systems, and opportunity costs of water now used for flushing sediment.

The three benefits are estimated using three separate valuation approaches – the preventive expenditure approach, mitigative expenditures, and the opportunity cost approach.

The project is evaluated over a 30-year period. It is calculated that the annual reduction in sediment due to the project will be about 41 million tons, or about 1.2 billion tons over this period. This represents an annual reduction of about 2.6 percent in the sediment load of the Yellow River. The cumulative and annual reduction in sediment loads due to each of the treatments in the project area is outlined in Table 28. To calculate these values one starts with pre-project estimates of sediment production per hectare; these values are then adjusted by sediment reduction indices for each of the major project interventions. For example, conservation tillage is expected to reduce sediment production per hectare by 60 percent in three of the provinces included in the project. These coefficients vary for each treatment and by province. The coefficients used are given in Table 29.[1]

ESTIMATING THE ECONOMIC VALUE OF REDUCED SEDIMENTATION

Magrath estimated three benefits from reduced sediment delivery in the lower reaches of the Yellow River: savings from delayed dike raising, reduced irrigation system dredging costs, and the release of water to other uses.

To estimate the *benefits of delayed dike raising*, information on the Xiaolongdi Dam was used. This dam will trap sediment in its reservoir for its first 20 years of operation. The total amount of sediment to be trapped is about 7.55 billion tons, and this has been estimated to generate savings in dike raising costs of RMB Yuan 319 million per year. Adjusted for timing, this translates into a savings of roughly RMB Yuan 0.77 per ton of sediment trapped in the reservoir. However, as seen in Figure 16, only 350 million tons per year of the total sediment production of 1,600 million tons is actually deposited in the stream bed. The value of RMB Yuan 0.77 is therefore adjusted by the fraction 350/1600, or 22 percent, to represent the benefit in terms of delayed dike raising from each ton of sediment captured in the Loess Plateau. Thus, the value of delayed dike raising per ton of sediment retained in the Loess Plateau is RMB Yuan 0.17 (RMB Yuan 0.77 × 22 percent).

The value of sediment reductions in terms of *reduced irrigation system maintenance* was also estimated. In the late 1980s it cost around RMB Yuan 100 million per year to remove 30 million tons of sediment, a cost equal to about RMB Yuan 3.33 per ton of sediment. In a similar manner to the analysis above, since only about 10 percent of the sediment that starts in the Loess Plateau is actually

---

1 Those interventions that result in changes in land form or cropping pattern can, in theory, yield benefits indefinitely. Physical structures such as check dams, however, have finite useful lives before they are filled with sediment. The useful lives of the various physical structures were also calculated, but this information is not presented here.

Table 28 Cumulative and Average Annual Sediment Reduction Benefit by
Treatment and Province (million tons)

Treatment	Shaanxi	Shanxi	Inner Mongolia	Gansu	Total
Structures	40	11	24	20	95
Terraces	71	48	3	57	179
Afforestation	129	131	116	154	530
Grassland Rehabilitation	167	18	130	45	360
Other	25	23	7	13	68
Total	432	231	280	289	1,232
Annual Average	14	8	9	10	41

Table 29 Percentage Reduction in Sediment Yields

Treatment/land use	Shaanxi	Shanxi	Inner Mongolia	Gansu[a]
Conservation Tillage	60%	60%	60%	5–15%
Irrigation	5%	40%	40%	17–57%
Terracing	20%	66%	80%	20–60%
Forestry	40%	75%	70%	2–13%
Grass	50%	80%	50%	1%
Orchard	20%	75%	20%	–

[a] Range based on land type (i.e. plateau, hill slope, gully area, gully ridge, and flat land)

deposited in the lower irrigation systems (about 150 million tons out of a total of 1.6 billion tons), and only one-fifth is removed, this value is reduced to RMB Yuan 0.07 per ton.

The last benefit is the value of *additional water* that is now available for other uses since it is no longer needed for flushing sediment. Estimates of the value of the additional water that is released as a result of reduced sediment in the river vary widely. The estimates range from 0 to as much as RMB Yuan 14.5 per ton of sediment, based on the opportunity cost of water that would be released by not flushing sediment. These values are highly dependent on the timing of the additional water and whether or not flows could be diverted to agricultural or industrial uses.

If only downstream benefits from avoided costs of dike construction (RMB Yuan 0.17) and irrigation maintenance (RMB Yuan 0.07) are considered, the value of sediment reduction is RMB Yuan 0.24 per ton. If the more speculative opportunity cost of additional water is also included, the total benefits could range as high as RMB Yuan 14.74 per ton. Table 30 presents these results.

Table 30 Annual Benefits per Ton from Sediment
Reduction (RMB Yuan)

Source of Benefit	RMB Yuan per ton
Delayed dike raising	0.17
Decreased irrigation system sedimentation	0.07
Release of water to other uses	0.0 – 14.5
Total	0.24 – 14.74

Given this wide range in downstream benefits from reduced sediment deposition, a base value of RMB Yuan 1 per ton was selected. The present value of sediment reduction over the life of the project due to all treatments is RMB Yuan 95.9 million, of which 21 percent is attributable to physical structures, 37 percent to afforestation, and the rest to other agricultural measures such as horticultural development, pasture improvement, and conservation tillage.

Although these numbers are substantial, they had only a marginal impact on the project's internal rate of return (IRR), increasing it from about 19 percent to about 22 percent. The off-site, downstream benefits were not necessary to justify the project. The information could be helpful, however, in determining what share of the project costs should be paid by the upstream and downstream provinces, and what share by the central government.

Source:
Magrath, W.B., 1992. *Loess Plateau Soil Conservation Project, Sediment Reduction Benefit Analysis*. Manuscript, Agriculture and Natural Resources Department. Washington, D.C.: The World Bank.

5

Tongonan Geothermal Power Plant, Leyte, Philippines

The complete case study, of which this is a part, was adapted by Somluckrat Grandstaff from materials prepared by Beta Balagot, and may be found in Dixon and Hufschmidt (1986). It presents the analysis of the cost-effectiveness of various options for disposing of waste water from a geothermal power plant built on the island of Leyte in the Philippines. The decision to build the power plant and to tap the local geothermal energy had already been made; it was necessary to decide which means of waste-water disposal from the plant would protect the environment in the most cost-effective manner. The cost-effectiveness approach is discussed in Chapter 4.

Seven ways of disposing of waste water are considered in the full case study; the costs of building and operating each are different and each has a different effect on the environment. The analysis examines each option in turn, determining its monetary values and, where possible, its environmental effect.

Not all of the effects on the environment can be quantified and monetized, but those which cannot be quantified should not be ignored in the analysis. These effects are listed in a qualitative manner and taken into consideration when the final decision is made. In this way the decision-maker or project designer is presented with a range of information on the actual costs of construction and operation of each option as well as the various effects of each upon the environment.

While each option is subjected to a complete benefit-cost analysis, a more complete presentation would include a benefit-cost analysis of the entire project including the differing options for design of the power plant as a whole as well as those for disposing of waste water. In this way the economic worth of the entire project, not just one part of it, could have been explored and then compared with other ways of producing electricity.

BACKGROUND INFORMATION

In the past the Philippines has been highly dependent on imported crude oil to meet its energy requirements and so has adopted an energy policy which will promote various forms of domestic energy production. These include nuclear energy, hydroelectric power, coal, petroleum, natural gas and geothermal energy. This last is derived from the natural heat of the earth. With existing technology only geothermal reservoirs associated with recent hot intrusive rocks and with vulcanism can be harnessed for the generation of electrical power. High-temperature geothermal energy is found in two forms: dry-steam fields, as seen in the geysers of the United States, and hot-water (wet) fields, as seen at Wairakei and Broadland in New Zealand. At present the Philippines is exploiting only the wet fields which produce a mix of steam and water.

Exploration at Tongonan in Leyte started in 1973, and in 1978 a potential productive capacity of 3,000 MW of geothermal electricity was confirmed. This case study considers Phase I of the Tongonan Geothermal Power Plant (TGPP) which has a capacity of 112.5 MW (see Figure 17). This power station relies on a wet-steam geothermal resource and produces residual liquids and gases. These have chemical and thermal characteristics that may affect the environment adversely; the degree to which they might do so depends on the rate and frequency of discharge and the method of disposal.

ENVIRONMENTAL DIMENSIONS

An Environmental Impact Report prepared by Kingston, Reynolds, Thom and Allardice Limited (KRTA), consultants to the Ministry of Energy and the Philippine National Oil Corporation, indicated that the major adverse effects on the environment would be caused by the disposal of the geothermal waste fluids. The fluids from the Tongonan wells contain more dissolved solids than those from most other geothermal fields; these include chloride, silica, arsenic, boron and lithium. Arsenic, boron, lithium and mercury all have known toxic effects on plants, animals and people, and the full case study examines these effects. The indiscriminate disposal of geothermal waste water would have severe effects on health and productivity and, to minimize these, the government has set limits to its discharge. Concentrations of arsenic, boron and lithium in water from the Tongonan wells were found to exceed the limits recommended by the National Pollution Control Commission.

Although the full case study examined the costs and benefits of all seven methods of disposing of the waste water, our abbreviated version will outline the analysis of only four of them; the analysis of the remainder may be found in Dixon and Hufschmidt (1986).

THE DATA

Seven options for disposal for the waste water of the plant were proposed:

(1) Reinjection.
(2) Discharge into the Mahiao River without treatment.
(3) Discharge into the Mahiao River after treatment for the removal of arsenic.
(4) Discharge into the Bao River without treatment.
(5) Discharge into the Bao River after treatment for the removal of arsenic.
(6) Discharge at sea without treatment through an outfall at Lao Point.
(7) Discharge at sea without treatment through an outfall at Biasong Point.

In the first option, geothermal fluids from separator stations would be piped to reinjection wells within the field. At full capacity the 112.5 MW power plant

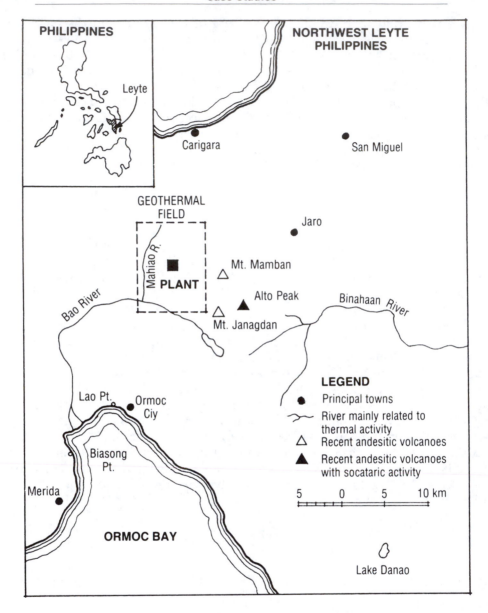

Figure 17 Location of Tongonan Geothermal Field, Leyte
Source: East-West Center

would need seven such wells. A standby disposal system consisting of thermal ponds and other contingency structures would also be needed. They would be used while the reinjection system was temporarily shut down either for maintenance or for some limited emergency. When the system is shut down for longer periods the stand-by scheme would permit the discharge of chemically treated waste fluids into the river.

The second and third options involve the direct discharge of waste fluids into the Mahiao River (see Figure 17). Before being discharged, the fluids would be retained for a few days in a thermal pond where they may be treated with chemicals to remove arsenic.

In Options (4) and (5) waste fluids would be discharged into the Bao River through a pipeline. A thermal pond would also be required for cooling the fluids before releasing them into the river. Option (5) would entail treatment of the fluids in the pond in order to precipitate the arsenic.

Options (6) and (7) involve the selection of an outfall at sea throuh which to discharge the wastes. Two possible sites have been studied: Lao Point and the Biasong Point. An outfall at the former would involve 22 kilometers of pipeline and at the latter 32 kilometers.

COSTS AND ENVIRONMENTAL EFFECTS OF THE OPTIONS

Each of the seven options has different capital and operations, maintenance and replacement (OM&R) costs as well as different effects on the environment. These are briefly described here, and 1980 prices are used in the analysis.

(1) Reinjection

The construction of seven reinjection wells and the stand-by waste-disposal system will take two years. Each well will cost P10 million, or P70 million in all. The construction of a system of pipelines from the separator stations to the reinjection wells will cost P20 million. The stand-by waste-disposal system will involve another P17 million. The annual operation and maintenance costs will total P10.4 million.

Although reinjection is seen as the most ecologically sound method of disposal, it is not yet a well-established technology. In areas where water supplies are drawn from underground aquifers, as in the site of this project, it is important to know the local groundwater hydrology and to monitor carefully any effects of injecting geothermal waste water.

Reinjection may also lower the temperature and hence the potential energy of the sub-surface geothermal water. In addition the geothermal liquids at Tongonan contain large amounts of dissolved solids like silica, which may clog the reinjection pipes. Such problems could be dealt with by adding chemicals to keep the solids in solution, but the effect of these chemicals may be to create other environmental problems.

(2) Discharge into the Mahiao River without treatment

The construction of a thermal pond would take one year and cost P7 million. Operation and maintenance costs are estimated at P43,300 per year (P0.0433 million).

High levels of arsenic and boron in the untreated waste fluids discharged into the river would affect adversely the productivity of 4,000 hectares of rice fields served by the Bao River Irrigation System.

If the irrigation waters are heavily polluted, farmers will probably not irrigate their crops; the consequence is a severe reduction in productivity. Irrigated rice fields yield an average of 61 cavans (1 cavan = 50kg) per hectare against a yield of 37.9 cavans from unirrigated fields (NIA Region 8 Office, 1980). Production would also be reduced to one crop a year. However, since the rice produced in the Bao River Irrigation System is only a small part of the regional total, it can safely be assumed that these changes in production will not affect local rice prices.

Based on the cost of production data for the area over the 1975–78 period, the net return per hectare for irrigated rice was estimated at P346 and, for unirrigated rice, P324. If irrigation water were made unusable for the entire 4,000 hectares, the economic loss would be as follows:

$$4,000 \text{ ha} \times \text{P346 per ha} \times 2 \text{ crops} = \text{P2,768,000}$$

One crop of unirrigated rice could be grown, yielding the following net return:

$$4,000 \text{ ha} \times \text{P324} = \text{P1,296,000}$$

The annual loss, therefore, would be the difference, P1.47 million.

An added environmental cost of discharging untreated waste water into the river system is the risk to human health and livestock. To evaluate this, the cost of a water-purification system that will render the river water safe for domestic use and for drinking was also estimated. The construction of such a system would cost P50 million and cost P15 million annually to operate and maintain.

Estimating the costs to the freshwater ecosystem is more difficult, since there are no data on the economic value of the fishing along the river. However, another environmental cost which can be estimated will be the pollution of the delta, which will affect the marine fisheries of the area. The delta or mangrove area of Ormoc Bay plays an important role in sustaining productivity in the adjoining fishing grounds because it is the feeding and spawning ground of several species of fish.

Fishing is an important industry in the Ormoc Bay–Camotes Sea area. Based on 1978 figures, the net return from fishing was estimated at 29 percent of the gross return from the catch. Although the annual value of the fish catch varied from year to year depending on the actual size of the catch and on market prices, a gross value of P39.4 million was taken as representative. If this fishery was lost as a consequence of heavy-metal contamination, the annual economic loss would be about P11.4 million (P39.4 × 0.29). It is assumed that the capital equipment could be sold or shifted to other areas, but that the lost catch would not be replaced by additional fish catches elsewhere.

(3) Discharge to Mahiao River After Treatment
A thermal pond will be constructed at a cost of P7 million and completed in one year. In addition to the regular operation and maintenance costs of the pond itself, there will be further costs for the treatment of arsenic. These will amount to P4 million per year for each of the fifteen producing wells.

There are no scientific studies of the interactive effects of boron and arsenic on a rice field; hence there is no basis at this point for determining whether or not the effects on productivity will be less severe if the arsenic is removed. There may also be some residual effects on the aquatic ecosystems, but these are not identifiable.

Capital costs for a water-purification system are estimated at P26 million and annual operating and maintenance costs at P7.5 million.

(4) Discharge of Untreated Effluent into the Bao River

A thermal pond will cost P7 million. A pipeline some six or seven kilometers long would take two years to build at a cost of P13 million. Operation and maintenance costs will be P6.2 million a year.

Since the point of discharge will be downstream from the diversion for irrigation, the area of the Bao River Irrigation System will not be affected by the waste fluids.

A water-purification system will be needed to serve the residents along the reaches of the Bao River below the point of discharge. Its construction will take two years at a cost of P15 million. Annual operation and maintenance costs are estimated at P4.5 million.

The information on fishery productivity used in Option (2) will be used in this option to estimate the costs to the marine environment.

(5) Discharge of Treated Effluent into the Bao River

The capital costs will be the same as in Option (4). However, the operation and maintenance costs will be higher. The annual cost of treating the waste fluids for arsenic is estimated at P4 million per producing well.

The cost of establishing a water-purification system will be lower when the fluids are treated for arsenic. The capital cost is estimated at P7.5 million, but the time needed for construction remains the same. Operation and maintenance costs of P2 million are expected.

(6) Discharge at Sea with an Outfall at Lao Point

This scheme will need a 22-kilometer pipeline which will take two years to build at a cost of P45 million. Its annual operating and maintenance cost will be P41.8 million.

The disposal of waste water at sea may affect the productivity of coastal fishing as well as the commercial fishing in Ormoc Bay and the Camotes Sea. Not enough information is available, however, to quantify these effects.

(7) Disposal at Sea with an Outfall at Biasong Point

For this option a 32-kilometer pipeline would be constructed. This would take two years and would cost P65 million. Operation and maintenance costs would come to P60.8 million per year.

The productivity of marine fishing may be affected. In estimating the effects of Options (6) and (7) on marine productivity, hydrological and dispersal patterns in Ormoc Bay and the Camotes Sea should be taken into account.

ANALYSIS OF THE OPTIONS

There is enough information available to carry out an analysis of some of the major environmental effects of the various options. While the overall approach is that of cost-effectiveness analysis, individual effects are usually valued using direct productivity changes based on market prices.

The assumption is therefore made that market prices can be used to value agricultural and fishery production – that is, that there are no major distortions requiring the use of shadow prices This may or may not be correct for the Philippines, but in this example no price adjustments are made. A similar assumption is made in the case of imported capital equipment used in the disposal systems and for petroleum products used to power the pumps and other equipment involved. Again, if major distortions like subsidies, foreign exchange controls, or capital rationing exist, then shadow prices would be needed.

The present value of the direct costs and the associated environmental costs for each of the proposed waste-water disposal schemes are calculated with a discount rate of 15 percent and an estimated project life for the geothermal power plant of thirty years. Table 31 presents the calculations of direct capital, OM and R costs for Options (1), (2), (3) and (6). Table 32 presents the calculation of environmental resource costs for the same options.

The results of these calculations for all seven options are summarized in Table 33. Without including the values of environmental costs, Option (4), in which untreated waste fluids are discharged into the Bao River, would have been chosen because it entailed the lowest direct cost. Once the environmental effects are valued and added to the direct cost, the total direct and indirect measurable costs are obtained.

Options (3), (5), (6) and (7) can be rejected because they are all relatively costly compared to Options (1), (2) and (4), among which the choice would now seem to lie. If the decision is based strictly on measurable costs, then Option (4) is the cheapest scheme. However, both Options (4) and (2) may seriously contaminate the marine ecosystem with unknown and unquantifiable results. Option (2), which calls for the discharge of untreated waste into the Mahiao River, is rejected because not only does it pollute, like Option (4), but it is also more expensive. In contrast, the main non-quantifiable effect of Option (1) is the possible loss of energy from the lowering of the steam temperature. Hence reinjection becomes the most desirable method, although its total measured costs are slightly higher than for Option (4). In this case a slightly larger measured cost in Option (1) is preferred over the greater environmental uncertainty inherent in Option (4), the least-cost alternative.

Table 31 Calculation of Direct Capital, OM and R Costs of Alternative Waste-water Disposal Options (in Pesos)

Option (1)	*Reinjection*	*Million P*

1. Construction (2 years)
   a. reinjection wells   70
   b. pipeline   20
   c. stand-by system   17

        107
   construction cost per year   = 107.2
        = 53.50

2. Operation and maintenance per year   10.4
   Cash flow:

year	1	2	3	. . .	30
million P	53.5	53.5	10.4		10.4

   Present value at 15 percent discount rate

year	1	$= 53.5 \times 0.8696$	=	46.5
year	2	$= 53.5 \times 0.7561$	=	40.4
years	3-30	$= 10.4 \times 4.9405$	=	51.4

   Present value of total direct cost   138.30

Option (2)	*Discharge to Mahiao river without Treatment*	*Million P*

1. Construction
   a. thermal pond (1 year)   7
   b. water supply system (2 years)   50

2. Operation and maintenance per year
   a. thermal pond   0.0433
   b. water supply system   15.0
   Cash flow:

year	1	2	3	. . .	30
million P	25	25	15		15.0
		7	0.0433		0.0433
cost/year	25	32	15.0433		15.0433

   Present value 15 percent discount rate

year	1	$= 25 \times 0.8696$	=	21.74
year	2	$= 32 \times 0.7561$	=	24.20
years	3-30	$= 15.0433 \times 4.9405$	=	74.32

   Present value of total direct cost   120.26

Option (3)	*Discharge to Mahiao River with Treatment*	*Million P*

1. Construction
   a. thermal pond (1 year) — 7
   b. water supply system (2 years) — 25

2. Operation and maintenance per year
   a. thermal pond — 0.0433
   b. arsenic removal for 15 steam-
      producing wells (at 4 million
      each) — 60
   c. water supply system — 7.5

Cash flow:

year	1	2	3	. . .	30
million P	12.5	12.5	0.0433		0.0433
		7	60		60
			7.5		7.5
cost/year	12.5	19.5	67.5433		67.5433

Present value at 15 percent discount rate

	10.87	14.74	(—333.7—)

Present value of total direct cost = 10.87
14.74
333.7
———
359.3

Option (6) *Disposal at Sea with an Outfall at Lao Point*	*Million P*

1. Construction
   a. pipeline (2 years) — 45

2. Operation and maintenance per year — 41.8

Cash flow:

year	1	2	3	. . .	30
million P	22.5	22.5	41.8		41.8

Present
value 19.57 17.01 (—206.51—)

Present value of total direct cost = 243.09

162

Table 32 Calculation of Environmental and Resource Costs of Alternative
Waste-water Disposal Options (in Pesos)

Option (1)   Reinjection

The environmental cost cannot be estimated although it involves: (i) possible loss of
potential energy; (ii) treatment cost for dissolved solids in reinjection pipes; and (iii)
additional environmental problems from chemicals used to keep the reinjection pipe
from being clogged.

Option (2)   Discharge to Mahiao River without Treatment

The environmental effects in this case include both the quantifiable and the non-
quantifiable consequences, namely:

1. rice productivity: 4,000 ha per season serviced by BRIS;
2. river fishery: no data;
3. stock health;
4. laundry, bathing and human health; and
5. sea ecosystems.

Quantifiable Effects:
Value of rice production loss:
Total rice area = 4,000 ha
Return/ha for irrigated rice
    (average 1975-8) = 1,838 − 1,492 = P346
    Return/ha for non-irrigated rice = 1,082 − 758 = P324
    Annual loss if irrigation water cannot be used due to heavy contamination
$$= 4,000 \times 346 \times 2 - [4,000 \times 324]$$
$$= 2,768,000 - 1,296,000$$
$$= \text{P1.47 million}$$

Present value of rice loss at 15 percent discount rate (years 3–30)
1.47 × 4.9405   = P7.26 million
Value of fishery product loss:
Assuming total loss of product currently obtained
From data on average costs and return profile of fishing operation in Leyte, the net
    return
$$= 6,914 - 4,918$$
$$= 1,996$$
or   = 29 percent of gross return

Total value of fishery product in the Camotes Sea and Ormoc Bay in 1980
                              = P39.4 million
Annual loss of fishery product   = 39.4 × 0.29 gross return
                              = P11.4 million
Present value of fishery loss at 15 percent discount rate (years 3–30)
11.4 × 4.9405   = P56.3 million

163

Non-quantifiable Effects:
River fishery, stock health, human health, loss of water use for laundry and bathing, effects on the marine ecosystems, plus possible family dislocation.

Option (3)   Discharge to Mahiao River with Treatment

Environmental Effects:
1. rice productivity: unknown;
2. river fishery: no data;
3. stock health, laundry, bathing and human health: non-quantifiable but less than Alternative 2; and
4. marine ecosystems: unknown.

Option (6)   Disposal at Sea

Environmental Effects: unknown effects on marine ecosystems.

Table 33 Costs of Waste Disposal under Alternative Schemes
(in million Pesos)

Alternative	Direct Cost	Environment Cost	Total Measured Costs	Non-quantifiable or Non-Measured Costs
1. Reinjection	138.3	Unknown	138.3	Energy loss
2. Untreated Mahiao Discharge	120.2	Rice 7.3 Fishery 56.5	184.0	Freshwater fishery, stock health, laundry, bathing uses, human health, sea ecosystems
3. Treated Mahiao Discharge	359.3		359.3	Rice production and a lower loss on items in Alternative 2 with the exception of sea ecosystems
4. Untreated Bao Discharge	81.1	Fishery 56.5	137.6	Freshwater fishery, stock health, domestic use, human health, sea ecosystems
5. Treated Bao Discharge	359.1		359.1	Less than Alternative 4
6. Lao Point	243.1	Unknown	243.1	Non-quantifiable but high
7. Biasong Point	353.2	Unknown	353.2	Non-quantifiable but high

Source: Dixon and Hufschmidt (eds) (1986).

The Benefits and Costs of Establishing a National Park in Madagascar

This case study presents the application of the opportunity cost, contingent valuation, and travel cost methods to estimate some of the benefits and costs associated with the creation of a National Park in Madagascar. This study is innovative because it is one of the first applications of contingent valuation to measure the economic impacts of a park on local villagers. An additional strong point of the study is that it uses more than two different valuation techniques to estimate each benefit or cost and compares the estimated results. The study is derived from the work of Kramer, Munasinghe, Sharma, *et al.* (1993, 1994), and Kramer (1993).

Madagascar's high rates of endemism make it one of the ecologically richest countries in the world. It is also one of the economically poorest countries in the world, with a per capita annual income of only $190. This combination of factors has put great stress on Madagascar's biodiversity, while also making the country a prime target for investment in conservation. One action the government is undertaking to protect biodiversity is the creation of a system of parks and reserves, one of which is the subject of this study: the Mantadia National Park.

This study estimates both the costs to nearby villages of establishing the park, and the benefits to foreign visitors of the park as an international tourism destination. These estimates are useful in making a rational decision about whether or not to protect the park, estimating the size of consumer's surplus enjoyed by visitors, and assessing the compensation required by local villagers in order for them to forgo access to the park.

COSTS TO LOCAL VILLAGERS

Establishment of the park will pose an economic cost on the local population in terms of their losing access to the park and the resources it contains. The villagers have traditionally depended on the forest in and around the park for forest products and agricultural land for swidden (shifting) cultivation of rice. Commonly harvested forest products include fuelwood, fish and animals, grasses, and medicines. The traditional form of shifting cultivation practised by the villagers is also the primary cause of deforestation in the park. If the park is established, the villagers will lose those products harvested or grown in the park lands. In the study, the costs imposed on the villagers were measured using both the opportunity cost approach and the contingent valuation method.

The *opportunity costs* associated with traditional activities were measured using a survey of 351 households in 17 villages surrounding the park. The survey contained questions related to socio-economic variables, land use, time allocation among economic activities, and household production. Price data on forest products and time spent gathering them were obtained from shop owners, household and village leaders, and published reports. This information was used to estimate total value of forest products collected by the villagers (Table 34). These estimates were then combined with information on land use and resource extraction in the park to determine the share of total household income coming from the park that would be potentially lost each year. The mean value of losses to villagers of establishing the Mantadia National Park was thus estimated at $91 per household per year. The village survey also

Table 34 Value of Forest Products Collected by Villagers

Forest Products	Number of Observations	Total Annual Value of all Villages ($US)	Mean Annual Value per Household (US$)
Rice	351	44,928	128.0
Fuelwood	316	13,289	42.0
Crayfish	19	220	11.6
Crab	110	402	3.7
Tenreck	21	125	6.0
Frog	11	71	6.5

Source: Kramer *et al.*, 1994.

contained *contingent valuation questions*. These questions were phrased in terms of compensation which would make the household as well off with the park as they would have been if they continued to have access to the forests in the park. The numeraire used to elicit willingness-to-accept bids was units of rice, because rice is the main crop in this region and transactions in rice are well known to the local people. The results of the contingent valuation survey indicate that the average household requires $108 worth of rice per year as compensation to forgo use of the park.

BENEFITS TO INTERNATIONAL TOURISTS

The second part of the study focused on the benefits from the establishment of the park. Travel cost and contingent valuation are used to estimate the economic value of international nature tourism. Estimating demand by international tourists requires reformulation of traditional travel cost models, because individuals that travel to a country like Madagascar engage in a variety of activities. The visit to the proposed national park would be only one of a number of activities visitors engage in.

166

Questionnaires based on this model were prepared and administered to visitors to the small Perinet Forest Reserve adjacent to the proposed Mantadia National Park. Table 35 presents selected summary statistics from these questionnaires for the sample of international visitors. The average visitor tended to be well-off and well-educated: they had an annual income of $59,156, 15 years of education, and stayed in Madagascar for 27 days. Political unrest in the country cut short the survey process at 94 interviews, however, and required the data to be supplemented with data from an expert survey of US and European tour operators who specialize in nature tourism. Using combined data from the two surveys, an econometric analysis was conducted to apply the travel-cost approach. The model was then used to predict the project benefits to tourists assuming that the Mantadia National Park will result in a 10 percent increase in the quality of local guides, educational materials, and facilities for interpreting natural areas in Madagascar. The travel cost method produced an average increase in willingness to pay per trip of $24 per tourist. Based on the conservative assumption that 3,900 foreign tourists would visit the new park (the same number as currently visit the Perinet Reserve), this is equivalent to an annual 'benefit' to foreign tourists of $93,600.

Table 35 Summary Statistics for International Visitors

Variable	Number of Observations	Range	Mean
Annual Income	71	$3,040 to $296,400	$59,156
Education	86	10 to 18 years	15 years
Age	87	16 to 71 years	38.5 years
Number of Days in Madagascar	83	3 to 100 days	26.6 days
Number of Days in Perinet	80	1 to 8 days	2 days
Total Cost of Trip to Madagascar	78	$355 to $6,363	$2,874

Source: Kramer *et al.*, 1993

The *contingent valuation method* was also used to directly estimate the value of the park for foreign tourists. Visitors to the Perinet Forest Reserve were provided with information about the new park and, using a discrete choice format, they were asked how much more they would have been willing to pay for their trip to Madagascar to visit the new national park if they saw twice as many lemurs, or if they saw the same number of lemurs as on their current visit. Since most of these visitors are only expected to visit Madagascar once, their response represents a one-time, lump sum payment they are willing to make in order to preserve the park. Mean willingness-to-pay for the park (conditional on seeing the same number of lemurs) was $65. Assuming current visitation patterns, the total annual willingness-to-pay for the park would be $253,500.

COMPARISON OF RESULTS

For the village component, the welfare estimates, which are based on the two quite different valuation methods of opportunity cost and contingent valuation, are remarkably similar ($91 and $108 per household per year). Based on esimated household incomes for this area, this amount is equivalent to about 35 percent of present household income, a very significant amount for a poor population.

For the international visitor benefits, travel cost and contingent valuation produced somewhat more disparate estimates ($24 and $65 per trip). The contingent valuation estimate may be higher because it includes some non-use values, whereas the travel cost estimate contains only direct use values. As seen from Table 35, these estimates represent a virtually insignificant amount of the average visitor's annual income.

Table 36 provides a summary of the economic analysis of Mantadia National Park in terms of the opportunity cost to nearby villagers and the consumer's surplus enjoyed by international visitors. The analysis reveals that villagers will require approximately $500,000 to $700,000 of compensation to forgo the use of the park and international tourists are willing to pay an additional $800,000 to $2,160,000 to visit the park. The establishment of the park potentially produces many benefits, including local income from tourism, protection

Table 36 Summary Economic Analysis of Mantadia National Park

Estimates of Welfare Losses to Local Villagers from Establishment of the Park

Method Used	Annual Mean Value per Household ($)	Aggregate Present Value[a] ($)
Opportunity Cost	$91	$566,070
Contingent Valuation	$108	$673,078

Estimates of Welfare Gains to Foreign Tourists from Establishment of the Park

Method Used	Annual Mean Value per Trip ($)	Aggregate Present Value[a] ($)
Travel Cost	$24	$796,870
Contingent Valuation	$65	$2,160,000

[a] Aggregated over 20 years at a 10% discount rate.

Source: Kramer, 1993; Kramer, *et al.*, 1993.

of biodiversity, watershed protection and climate regulation. The existence of substantial consumer's surplus on the part of international visitors can be used to help devise a compensation scheme for local villagers who will be losing part of their economic base. The actual form in which compensation is made – direct compensation, creation of alternative income producing opportunities, other methods – still has to be determined. What is clear, however, is that the creation of Mantadia National Park will impose costs on nearby villagers but the Park also creates benefits that can be used to meet those costs.

Sources:
Kramer, R.A. 1993. 'Tropical Forest Protection in Madagascar'. Paper prepared for Northeast Universities Development Consortium. Williams College.
Kramer, R.A., M. Munasinghe, N. Sharma, E. Mercer, and P. Shyamsundar, 'Valuation of Biophysical Resources in Madagascar' in M. Munasinghe, *Environmental Economics and Sustainable Development*, World Bank Environment Paper Number 3. Washington, D.C.: The World Bank, 1993.
Kramer, R.A., N. Sharma, P. Shyamsundar, and M. Munasinghe, 'Cost and Compensation Issues in Protecting Tropical Rainforests: Case Study of Madagascar', Environment Working Paper No. 62, Washington, D.C.: The World Bank, January 1994.

7

An Economic and Ecological Analysis of the Bonaire Marine Park

This case study of the Bonaire Marine Park (BMP) in the Caribbean is a combined ecological and economic analysis. It has become increasingly obvious that, rather than selecting the extremes of strict preservation or unmanaged development, balanced use of marine resources for both economic and ecological functions is central to their sustainable management. This study estimates the benefits and costs associated with dive tourism, as well as the willingness-to-pay for park protection. The BMP study explicitly considers the link between the production of ecological and economic benefits, and identifies the limits to increasing use. (For details see Scura and van't Hof, 1993, and Dixon, Scura and van't Hof, 1993, 1994).

THE PHYSICAL AND SOCIO-ECONOMIC SETTING OF BONAIRE

Bonaire, a crescent shaped island with an area of 288 square km, is located in the Caribbean Sea approximately 100 km north of the coast of Venezuela (Figure 18). The resident population of Bonaire was estimated at 10,800 in 1990. The waters of the Caribbean Sea surrounding Bonaire – from the shoreline to a depth of 60 meters – are officially protected as the Bonaire Marine Park (BMP).

The economy of Bonaire is strikingly undiversified: the economic mainstay for Bonaire is tourism, particularly that related to SCUBA diving; almost 17,000 SCUBA divers visited Bonaire in 1991. Supporting activities include hotels, a modest number of restaurants and shops, and a few casinos and night-clubs, ground tour operators, rental cars agencies and transport services. Based on tourism statistics, the annual rate of growth of diver visitation to Bonaire is approximately 9 to 10 percent per year.

In the early 1980s the BMP was established with aid from the Dutch Government and other sources. The failure to introduce a visitor fee system in 1981 created serious financial difficulties for the Park. Eventually, with no staff or funding, the Park became a 'paper park' – established on paper but without any actual management presence. Early in 1990, however, after serious concerns about the lack of formal management of the BMP, an increase in diver activity, and the consequences of coastal development in general, the Island Government of Bonaire commissioned an evaluation of the situation which resulted in the following major recommendations:

- Introduce a visitor fee system;
- Introduce a licensing system for commercial watersports operators; and
- Create a new institutional structure for the BMP, including representation from the tourism industry.

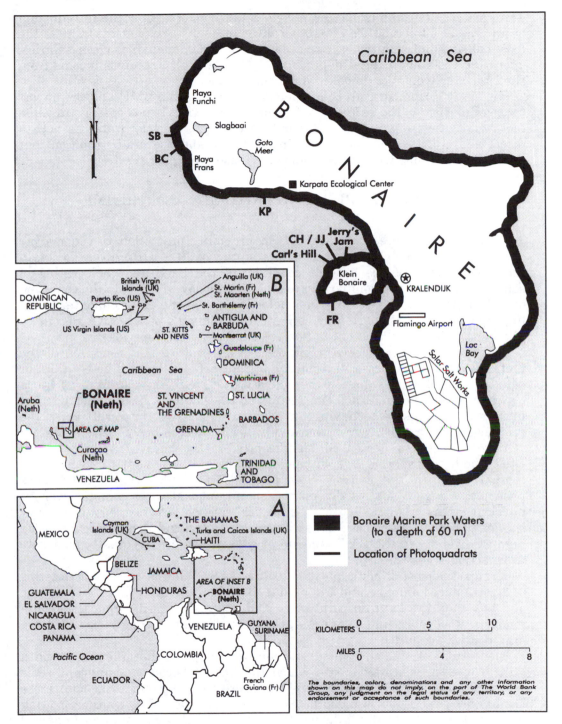

Figure 18 Bonaire, Netherlands Antilles

The Park was re-established and revenues were generated by the introduction of an annual admission fee of $10 per diver to help pay expenses. In 1992 the fees (called 'admission tickets') raised over $170,000, enough to cover salaries, operating costs and capital depreciation. The Park also receives income from the sale of souvenirs and books, and from donations.

The study estimated both the impact of tourism on the BMP, and the importance of tourism to the economy of Bonaire. Although it is not possible to value biodiversity *per se*, one can consider biodiversity and clear water as both a direct and a derived demand from dive tourism, and use information on that demand to examine willingness-to-pay for these ecological services.

ECOLOGICAL BENEFITS AND COSTS OF THE BMP

To evaluate the success of the BMP in providing protection to the marine ecosystem, van't Hof conducted a visitors' survey of 79 SCUBA divers to obtain their perceptions of the present condition of the Park and their rating of selected parameters in comparison to other Caribbean areas or to the condition of BMP in the past. These questions helped to assess the environmental carrying capacity of the Bonaire Marine Park from a diver's perspective. Second, a photoanalysis was carried out to analyse coral cover and species diversity.

The majority of the divers interviewed rated the present condition of the reefs as high and the overall condition of the reefs in Bonaire better than or equal to any other destination they have visited, with the exception of Little Cayman and Cayman Brac. The results of the photoanalysis indicated that increased diver use was having an adverse impact on the coral reefs. The comparison of coral, both over time and between sites, indicated that the *extent of coral cover* has decreased significantly at the most frequently dived sites. The higher species *diversity* indices at the most frequently dived sites in comparison with the control sites confirm the intermediate disturbance principle: a higher species diversity is maintained at intermediate levels of physical stress or disturbance as ecological 'niches' are opened up for new species to occupy. As stress increases, however, species diversity declines. The highest diversity in the BMP is found at sites which are exposed to moderate wave action and swell.

Perhaps the most difficult question to address is: 'What is acceptable in terms of diver-induced damage and what isn't?' Based on the interviews with divers, and based on the data on coral cover and species diversity from the photo-analysis, it appears that visitation at certain sites had already exceeded the local carrying capacity.

The results of the photoquadratic analysis suggest that there may be a critical level of visitation above which the impact becomes significant. This relationship is illustrated in Figure 19, where the apparent threshold stress level is between 4,000 to 6,000 dives per year per site. (The average visiting diver makes 10 or 11 dives during the course of his or her stay on Bonaire.) Based on the number of available dive sites, it was possible to estimate a

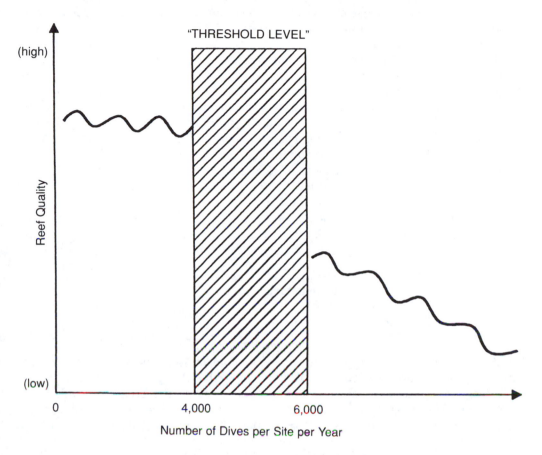

Figure 19 Diving Intensity and Threshold Stress Level
Source: Dixon, Scura, and van't Hof, 1993.

conservative 'annual carrying capacity' of 190,000 to 200,000 dives per year. Annual use was already more than 180,000 in 1992, so this level will be reached in the next few years. If this capacity is exceeded, fairly rapid loss of reef biodiversity is expected.

QUANTIFICATION OF ECONOMIC BENEFITS AND COSTS ASSOCIATED WITH THE BMP

The working hypothesis in Scura and van't Hof (1993) is that Bonaire is attractive because its unique resources are protected. Aided by its protected status, a significant privately operated sector is successfully marketing Bonaire as a tourist destination. However, if protection of the marine ecosystem is not maintained, much of Bonaire's attraction would be lost, and along with it part of the associated revenues currently accruing to the private and public sectors.

It was not possible to estimate the true 'economic' benefits of the BMP since resource constraints prohibited carrying out either a travel cost or a survey-based contingent valuation study (CVM) analysis of park users. Estimating other economic benefits from protection, including both ecosystem services and biodiversity benefits, is difficult. In the analysis, therefore, Scura focused on the generation of gross financial revenues due to the existence of world-class diving in Bonaire. Since there are few other attractions on the island, a decrease in the level of protection and degradation of the marine resource would result in loss of both ecological and economic benefits: any loss of reef and water quality and reduction in the fish population would result in divers shifting their demand to other islands competing for the same market. The loss of this market would be very difficult to replace with other visitors.

To analyse this dimension, Scura examined the benefits and costs associated with the dive tourism business on Bonaire. The main categories of benefits included in the financial analysis are gross revenues to the private sector and BMP user fees. The primary uses of the waters contained in the Park are:

- dive-based tourism;
- small-scale and recreational fisheries;
- yachting and other water sports;
- cruise tourism; and
- ocean transport.

Land-based activities supporting dive-tourism include hotels, restaurants, souvenir sales, and car rental. Table 37 lists the main revenues and costs, including divers' fees, associated with dive tourism and the BMP. In 1992, diver (the 'admission tickets') and other user fees , the one source of 'direct' revenues from use of BMP, totalled about $190,000. This amount is very small in comparison to other park-related gross revenues.

Total *gross revenue generated* through dive-based tourism was estimated at $23.2 million in 1991. Data on revenues were obtained through interviews with hotels and dive operators. Of the total revenues generated, $10.4 million is attributable to hotels (including hotel restaurant sales), $4.8 million to dive operations (including retail sales in dive shops), an estimated $4.7 million attributable to other expenditures including non-hotel restaurants, souvenirs and car rentals, and $3.3 million for air transport of diving tourists on the local airline.

Employment should not strictly be considered a benefit. In an economic sense employment is a cost of generating total gross revenue. Nevertheless, employment, particularly of locals, is probably the most long lasting 'benefit' to the local economy of the activities in the BMP, especially since alternative employment opportunities are very limited. Employment in activities associated with the BMP is estimated to be as much as 755 local workers and up to 238 foreign workers.

The financial returns from Park-based recreation contribute to *tax revenues* for the Island Government and generate employment. The Island Government of Bonaire collects several direct and indirect taxes; it is estimated that for 1991

Table 37 Revenues and Costs Associated with the Bonaire Marine Park
(1991 Summary Table US$)

Revenues	US $ (millions)
Direct Revenue	
Diver fees (1992 est.)	0.19
Indirect (private sector) Revenues (gross)	
Hotels (rooms/meals)	10.4
Dive operation (including retail sales)	4.8
Restaurants, souvenirs, car rentals, misc. services	4.7
Local air transport	3.3
Subtotal	23.2

Costs	US $ (millions)
Costs of Protection	
Direct costs – establishment, initial operation,	
rehabilitation	0.52
annual recurring costs	0.15
Indirect costs	?
Opportunity costs	?

Source: Dixon, Scura and van't Hof, 1993.

total government revenue from *indirect taxes* (e.g. income, land, and business profit taxes) was approximately $8.4 million. Even if the portion of this revenue attributable to dive-based tourism could be easily calculated, these revenues represent transfer payments rather than additional benefits generated by use of the park. Taxes levied by the Island Government directly on tourists include room tax, casino tax and departure tax. Room tax is calculated at $2.25 per room night. Casino tax and departure tax are calculated on a per visitor basis at $1.12 and $9.83, respectively. The total government revenue generated in 1991 through these taxes levied directly on visiting divers is estimated at $340,000. Revenues from these taxes may be considered as additional revenue generated for the Island Government through use of the BMP.

Retention of Economic Benefits in Bonaire
There are, however, several factors which combine to limit the amount of revenues which remain in the local economy. First of all, sales in the tourism sector are dominated by offshore sales of packages commonly referred to as voucher sales. The tourist pays the agent in the United States or Europe for

the complete package, including the goods and services to be provided in Bonaire, and in return receives a voucher to be presented to the hotel and/or dive operation representative upon arrival in Bonaire. As a consequence of this only a small portion of gross revenues generated by dive tourism effectively remains in Bonaire. This surplus, however, is a clearer measure of the true economic benefits to Bonaire of the BMP.

Costs of Protection
The costs of the establishment and protection of BMP include direct costs, indirect costs and opportunity costs. Based on data provided by the BMP management, the direct costs associated with the establishment, subsequent rehabilitation and initial operation of the BMP were estimated to be approximately $518,000; annual recurring costs are approximately $150,000. (The $10 user fee generated revenues of over $170,000 in 1992, its first year, enough to cover operating costs and contingencies.) The opportunity costs of a park or protected area are the benefits that are lost as a result of the establishment and operation of the park. These include the value of forgone output from prohibited uses of resources in the protected area or, the forgone value of conversion of the site to an alternative use. Since BMP is managed as a multiple use area where few uses are strictly prohibited, opportunity costs are minimal.

Willingness-to-pay for BMP
Given the controversy surrounding the institution of a user fee system, a contingent valuation survey was conducted in late 1991 to get an inference of visitors' general perception of and willingness to pay user fees for the BMP. An overwhelming 92 percent agreed that the user fee system is reasonable and would be willing to pay the proposed rate of $10/diver/year.

Approximately 80 percent of those surveyed said that they would be willing to pay at least $20/diver/year, 48 percent would be willing to pay at least $30/diver/year, and 16 percent would be willing to pay $50/diver/year, yielding an average value for WTP of $27.40 (excluding the 8 percent who were not willing to pay a fee). One could only capture this average value if one were a perfectly discriminating price setter and charged each visiting diver their entire WTP for park use. Of course, one cannot do this, so an admission fee is set that captures part of the WTP.

Clearly the average willingness-to-pay exceeded the relatively modest $10 fee instituted in 1992 (although this amount would cut off some use as you moved up the demand curve). The difference between what people would be willing to pay for a good or service and what they actually pay is known as consumers' surplus (CS). This value is not observed in market transactions and, in the case of BMP, is not captured by dive operators or hotels. However, it is a very important economic value, as it represents that portion of the value of the diving experience that is above what is paid for it in the market (including transport and ground costs). At the current rate of dive visitation (an estimated 18,700 divers in 1992) admission fees and estimated CS total $512,000 per year, of which $325,000 is CS. Figure 20 presents the information from the WTP survey, and indicates the area of remaining CS.

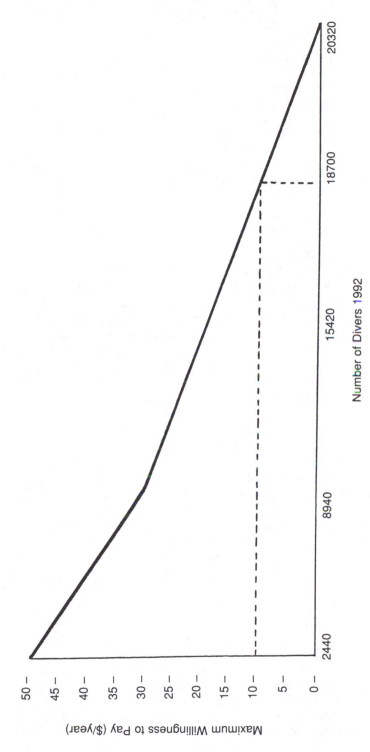

Figure 20 Willingness-to-Pay for Park Management, Bonaire Marine Park
Source: Dixon, Scura and van't Hof, 1994.

CONCLUSIONS

The ecological studies carried out on the marine ecosystem found measurable degradation around the dive-boat moorings. The data suggest that there may be a critical level of diver use of about 4,500 dives per year at individual sites, after which reef degradation becomes apparent. (In this case information on actual diver use was compared to observed degradation [a physical indicator] to develop an estimate of the threshold stress level.)

The economic analysis illustrates the dependence of Bonaire on dive tourism. Its small size, modest resource endowment, dry climate and relatively remote location combine to limit the potential for other forms of economic development. There is scope for both increasing diver-based revenues (e.g. attract more visiting divers) and increasing retention of diver-related income in Bonaire; the latter will require changes in the type and style of tourism development.

Assessing the tradeoffs

Are continued expansion of dive tourism (with its associated economic benefits) and ecosystem protection compatible? The data presented from Bonaire indicate that it may rapidly be approaching a point whereby increased dive tourism results in measurable degradation of the marine environment. The physical stress constraint, however, may be changeable. Figure 21 presents a simple schematic relating an apparent stress threshold on the marine eco-system on the vertical axis to the intensity of diver use on the horizontal axis. Level A represents the level of stress (either from divers or on-shore activities) at which reef degradation becomes noticeable. Below this level there is no, or minimal, impact. Above this level there is a loss of coral cover, reduction in species diversity, decreased visibility and other impacts.

It may be possible to raise the apparent stress threshold to level B by improved management – rotating dive sites, spacing out divers, regulation of underwater photography (e.g. ban tripods, promote better buoyancy control), controlling land-based pollution, and monitoring and supervision of park users. (These management measures do not *increase* the tolerance of the marine ecosystem to stress, rather they help to reduce the amount of stress per dive and to distribute the burden more evenly across the ecosystem. Such measures require both money and legal authority.)

The horizontal axis maps the most important direct determinant of reef stress – diver activity. Line ON represents the impact of diver use of the park, measured in the number of single tank dives per year. At point S1 diver use is such that ecosystem degradation begins to be noticeable. If there is improved park management, this 'stress point' is shifted to point S2. However, not all divers are equal and the level of stress per dive varies with the skill of the diver. In general, an experienced diver has better buoyancy control and 'reef etiquette' and imposes less stress on the reef ecosystem than the novice diver. Consequently, diver education can shift out line ON to ON' by reducing the average stress per dive, thereby expanding permissible use of the park's waters, and leading to increased economic benefits.

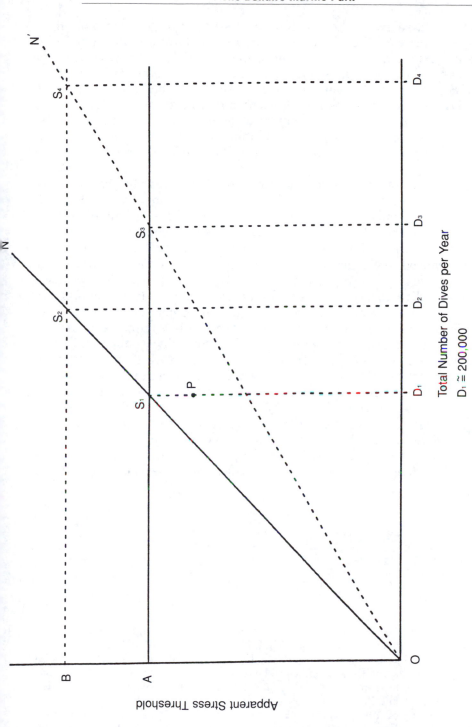

Figure 21 Park Management, Diver Education, and Apparent Stress Threshold
Source: Dixon, Scura and van't Hof, 1993.

Total Number of Dives per Year

$D_1 \cong 200,000$

$D_4 \cong 400,000$

179

The result of these two factors – improved park management and diver education – is to increase the effective carrying capacity of any given site and the park as a whole. Improved diver education can shift the carrying capacity to point S3, while improved park management and diver education can shift the point to S4. Since more divers mean more revenue, the increase in dives from D1 to D4 represents an estimate of the potential economic gain to the economy of Bonaire from these management measures. Based on study results, the increased spending associated with a doubling of the number of dives (and divers) could mean increasing gross revenues in Bonaire by $20 million or more per year.

At present Bonaire Marine Park, with some 200,000 dives per year, already receives many experienced divers who have good 'reef etiquette', and actual diver impact thereby falls on a line between ON and ON'. The management of the park, both by the BMP authorities and the dive operators themselves, has also helped to raise the effective damage threshold level and there is only limited, localized reef degradation. The current situation is represented by point P. Nevertheless, Bonaire is approaching the limit where the two uses – protection and dive tourism – are still compatible. It may be possible to expand from the estimated present level of 200,000 dives per year to as much as 300,000 to 400,000 dives or even more. Whether this in fact happens is directly dependent on both improved management and improved diver education.

It is somewhat ironic that the BMP has faced such severe financial restrictions in the past. As the BMP study has shown, dive tourism and the existence of BMP are intimately linked and form the cornerstone of the local economy – without world class diving, Bonaire would receive many fewer visitors. The study illustrated the use of different approaches to estimate both the contribution of dive tourism to a local economy, the role of a marine protected area in providing these ecological services, diver willingness-to-pay for improved park management, and the identification of ecologically-defined limits on park use.

Sources:
Dixon, J.A., L.F. Scura and T. van't Hof. 1993. 'Meeting Ecological and Economic Goals: Marine Parks in the Caribbean.' AMBIO, vol. XXII, Nos. 2–3, pp. 117–125.
Dixon, J.A., L.F. Scura and T. van't Hof. 1994. 'Ecology and Microeconomics as "Joint Products": the Bonaire Marine Park in the Caribbean' in C. Perrings, K.G. Maler, C. Folke, C.S. Hollings and B.O.Jansson, eds. *Biodiversity Conservation: Problems and Policies*, Dordrecht: Kluwer Academic Press.
Scura, L.F. and T. van't Hof. 1993. 'Economic Feasibility and Ecological Sustainability of the Bonaire Marine Park.' Environment Department Divisional Working Paper 1993-44. Washington, D.C.: The World Bank.

8

Willingness to Pay for Improved Water Supplies in Onitsha, Nigeria

This is a case study of water vending and willingness to pay (WTP) for water in Onitsha, Nigeria (Whittington, Lauria and Mu, 1991). The study illustrates the use of two approaches to estimate WTP for domestic water supplies. Information on water purchases is used to define the private distribution system and revealed demand for potable water. In addition, a contingent valuation survey is used in a relatively simple, rapid manner to estimate household water demand behaviour. The data collected in both surveys provides policy-relevant information to water utility managers and can be used to help local water authorities make more informed decisions about how much to charge their customers.

Onitsha is a rapidly growing city of about 100,000 households located in Southern Nigeria. It is an important market town, and much of the population is engaged in trading. Annual average household income is probably N7,000, or about US$ 1,630,[1] and average household size is 6–7 persons. One-third to one-half of the population of Onitsha lives in squatter settlements in one- and two-room tenements, without piped water or indoor toilets. At the time of this study, only about 8,000 households had functioning water connections to the public water supply system. In Onitsha, piped water is a public service that the local water authority provides free or for a nominal fee. Since water supply is so heavily subsidized, the water authority does not have sufficient resources to expand water service to more households.

WATER VENDING SURVEY

As a result of the inadequate coverage by the public water company, Onitsha has a highly developed and well functioning water vending system which has been created and is operated by the private sector. The vending system consists of private boreholes, tanker trunks, small retail vendors, and distributing vendors. Households can purchase water from several points in the system. If they live in an area accessible to tanker trucks, they can purchase a storage tank and buy water directly from a tanker truck. If they are willing to haul water by the bucket to their homes, they can buy it from a private borehole or from a small retail vendor. If the value they place on their time is high, they can have water delivered directly to their door by a distributing vendor.

Four categories of people were interviewed for the study: 12 borehole managers, 31 tanker truck drivers, 34 distributing vendors, and 235 households. Also, enumerators were placed on tanker trucks and rode with the driver all day,

---

1 In August 1987, US$ 1.00 = N4.3.

recording in a log book the time required to fill the truck at the borehole, the number of sales, the prices charged for different quantities of water, the status of each customer (resident or business), and the number of customers who would resell the water. Because of the uncertainty introduced by the lack of a well-defined sample frame, the interviews were designed to include as many cross-checks on the data as possible.

Table 38 summarizes the prices charged by water vendors at different stages of the vending distribution system. A household which purchases its water from a distributing vendor pays about eight times more per gallon than a household which buys large volumes from a tanker truck. In turn, both are much more expensive than the water provided by the public utility, the Anambra State Water Corporation, ASWC. Water vending transactions for Onitsha during the dry season are summarized in Figure 22. In the dry season households are paying on average a total of about N120,000 per day to the private water vending industry. In the rainy season the distribution system is similar, with the addition of 2.3 MGD from rain water and major increases in public supplies; as a result households purchase much less water from private vendors and only spend about N51,000 per day for water. During both seasons the public utility only manages to collect about N5,000 per day.

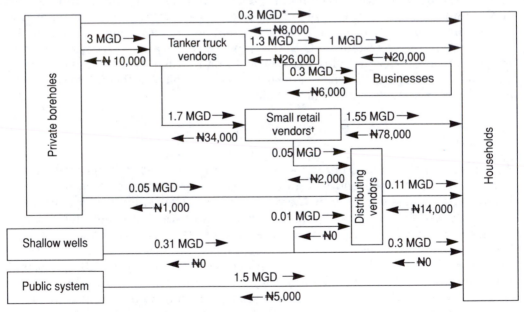

*MGD = Millions of gallons of water per day.
†Water input is not equal to water output because a small amount of water is consumed by small retail vendors themselves.

Figure 22 Money and Water Transaction in Onitsha, Nigeria (per day) – dry season
Source: Whittington, D., D. Lauria and X. Mu, 'A Study of Water Vending and Willingness to Pay for Water in Onitsha, Nigeria.' *World Development*, Vol. 19, No. 2/3, pp 179–198, 1991.

Table 38 Average Prices Charged by Vendors in Onitsha, Nigeria
(naira per gallon)

Prices charged by:	*Rainy season*	*Dry Season*
Private boreholes		
a. to tanker trucks	0.003	0.004
b. to individuals	0.01	0.02
Tanker trucks, to		
individuals / businesses		
a. per 1,000 gallons	0.014	0.018
b. per drum	0.04	0.04
Small retail vendors		
a. to individuals	0.04	0.05
Distributing vendors		
a. to individuals	0.12	0.13

Source: Whittington, D., D. Lauria and X. Mu, 'A Study of Water Vending and Willingness to Pay for Water in Onitsha, Nigeria.' *World Development*, Vol. 19, No. 2/3, pp 179–198, 1991.

CONTINGENT VALUATION, WILLINGNESS-TO-PAY SURVEY

Following interviews with water vendors, the enumerators completed 235 in-depth household interviews throughout the city. The household interviews included questions about socioeconomic characteristics, water-use practices, willingness to pay for water, housing characteristics and household assets, and occupation and monthly cash income. The focus of the questionnaire was on the estimation of the households' willingness to pay for improved water supplies. The enumerator read each respondent a carefully worded statement that was designed to set the scene for a 'bidding game' in which respondents would tell whether they would be willing to pay certain specified amounts for water under certain circumstances. The bidding game consisted of asking each respondent whether he or she would like to be connected to the New Onitsha Water Scheme and have a meter if the price of water were N1 per drum.[2] If the respondent answered 'yes' to a price of N1 per drum, then the enumerator raised the price to N2 per drum, and again asked whether the respondent would like to have the metered connection. If the respondent answered 'no' to a price of N2 per drum, the enumerator lowered the price to N1.5 per drum and again asked the respondent whether he would like to have a metered connection. After this question was answered, the enumerator stopped the bidding game.

Figure 23 presents a frequency distribution of the households' willingness-to-pay bids. The price of water charged by the vendors was effectively an upper

2 45 gallons

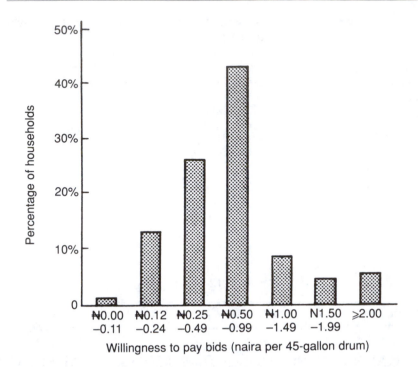

Figure 23 Frequency Distribution of Willingness-to-pay Bids (Onitsha, Nigeria)
Source: Whittington, D., D. Lauria and X. Mu, 'A Study of Water Vending and Willingness to Pay for Water in Onitsha, Nigeria.' *World Development*, Vol. 19, No. 2/3, pp 179–198, 1991.

bound on the amount respondents would bid for water; respondents were not willing to pay more than the price of water charged by vendors because the water provided by the vendors was perceived to be of good quality and readily available. The bidding game revealed that respondents would pay substantial amounts for water from a piped distribution system. This confirmed survey results on current water use practices; in addition, the study of water vending indicated households were paying significant amounts for water. In the dry season 49 percent of the sample households report spending 5 percent or more of their income on water. In the rainy season 25 percent of the households still spent 5 percent or more of their income for water.

The poor pay a larger relative portion of their income for water in Onitsha. Households making less than N500 per month (58 percent of the total sample) are estimated to pay 18 percent of their income on water during the dry season. These results are consistent with those from the water vending study. For example, if the average family of six purchased all of its water from a small retail vendor, this would entail a monthly expenditure on water of N72. If this household had two wage earners making N200 per month each, the monthly expenditure on water of N72 would represent 18 percent of monthly household income.

CONCLUSIONS

In the answers to the questions in the bidding game, each respondent expressed his or her preferences as to whether to connect to the piped distribution system as specified prices. From Figure 23, one can calculate the percentage of sample households which would choose to connect at different prices of water. At a price of N3 per 1000 gallons (WTP bids of ₦0.00–0.11 in Figure 23), 99 percent of respondents indicated that their households would choose to connect to the system, while at a price of N6 per 1000 gallons, 86 percent of the respondents reported that their households would connect. Based on the relationship between the price of water and the percentage of households that would connect to the system, it is possible to calculate the annual revenues associated with different water prices.[3] This information can be used to illustrate the tradeoff that the water authority faces between financial and social objectives (Figure 24). Moving from point A to point D, both revenue and the percentage of households desiring connections increase. The 'north-east' portion of the curve (between points D and F) characterizes the tradeoffs between the water authority's financial and social objectives, and presents the management of the water authority with a hard set of financial choices.

The calculations of the relationships between the price of water, the percentage of households desiring connections, and annual revenues should only be considered indicative of the general magnitude of the tradeoffs facing the water authority, and it is important to emphasize their limitations. All of the relationships depend on the accuracy and validity of WTP bids. Also, these calculations assume that the frequency distribution of WTP bids of the sample respondent are representative of the entire population of Onitsha.

The data collected from the contingent valuation survey seem consistent with the data from the water vending surveys, and the results appear sufficiently accurate to be useful for decision making. Prices on the order of N8–10 per 1,000 gallons would be affordable by most households in Onitsha, and would result in a substantial increase in the water authority's revenues. This price would still be much less than the per gallon prices charged by private vendors (although consumption per household would definitely increase with the availability of piped water).[4]

---

3 It is possible, of course, that respondents may have failed to give reliable, truthful answers to the willingness-to-pay questions. For example, respondents may have bid low in the hope of influencing the water authority to set a low price for water, or they may have bid high, thinking that a high bid might convince the water authority to extend service into their neighbourhood sooner.

4 In order to increase its market share, the water authority must not only offer a lower-priced product than vendors, but also provide a better product in terms of both water quality and reliable service. This is because the household surveys indicate that people perceive the water from tanker trucks and small retail vendors to be of better quality than the water from the old public system.

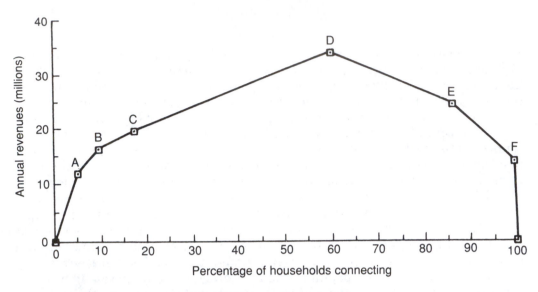

*Assumes average water use of 20 gallons per capita per day

Figure 24 Percentage of Households Connecting to Piped Water System vs. Annual Revenues of Water Utility (millions of naira). Onitsha, Nigeria.
Source: Whittington, D., D. Lauria and X. Mu, 'A Study of Water Vending and Willingness to Pay for Water in Onitsha, Nigeria.' *World Development*, Vol. 19, No. 2/3, pp 179–198, 1991.

This study demonstrates that the willingness for households to pay for improved water services in Onitsha is surprisingly high. On an annual basis, households in Onitsha pay water vendors over twice the operation and maintenance costs of a piped distribution system. This indicates that households can afford to pay for a connection to a piped water system which charges full economic costs of water. Because they will receive more water at a lower price, these households will be better off as a result of connecting to the system than they would be buying water from vendors.

Source:
Whittington, D., D. Lauria and X. Mu, 'A Study of Water Vending and Willingness to Pay for Water in Onitsha, Nigeria.' *World Development*, Vol. 19, No. 2/3, pp 179–198, 1991.

9

Setting Priorities in Central and Eastern Europe

Setting priorities among environmental problems is a difficult task because the range of factors that must be taken into account is large and the quality of the data is often highly suspect. This case study focuses on using an economic framework to set priorities among different types of pollution in Central and Eastern Europe (CEE). Given the wide range of environmental problems facing the economies in transition, and the limited resources available to tackle them, priority setting is essential to maximize the benefits from environmental investments. Since many environmental problems cannot be addressed in the first phase, the choice of interventions is crucial to improving environmental conditions.

Many of the valuation approaches presented in this volume can be used in this priority setting process, for both the 'brown' and 'green' agenda. The material for this study was developed from the 'How to Set Priorities' chapter in the Environmental Action Programme for Central and Eastern Europe (World Bank and OECD, 1993).

Setting priorities is a three-step process that requires defining criteria for assessing environmental problems, determining the most serious environmental problems, and identifying the most efficient ways to achieve environmental goals. Valuation has an important role to play in determining the economic costs of pollution, and the expected benefits from pollution reduction. A good example of this is Case Study 3, which illustrates how valuation is used to estimate the cost of air pollution in terms of human health effects.

DEFINING CRITERIA

Criteria for assessing the economic and social costs of environmental damage should be dependent on what people care about. In the CEE Action Programme, these criteria are divided into three broad categories: health costs, productivity costs, and loss of environmental quality or amenity costs.

Health costs
Most CEE governments give the highest priority to dealing with those aspects of environmental damage which will affect human health. Since there are relatively few reliable local studies, assessing the consequences of environmental damage in the CEE means relying mainly upon epidemiological studies from OECD countries. Health damage is the primary cost of environmental pollution in some of the wealthiest OECD countries, therefore it is also probably the largest component of environmental damage in the CEE.

Productivity costs
Environmental degradation reduces the productivity of natural resources and physical capital. The costs of reduced productivity are very unevenly distributed in the CEE. For example, discharges of saline water from mines are a problem in Poland and a small part of the Czech Republic. Soil contamination, salinization and acidification all cause considerable loss of agricultural productivity and damage to forests and lakes in some places.

Loss of environmental quality
Examples of improved environmental quality are a clear view or a pristine lake. People are willing to forgo expenditure on other goods and services in order to enjoy the benefits of better environmental quality. This aspect of environmental quality is particularly hard to quantify and very little is known about the amenity value of a better environment in CEE.

DETERMINING THE MOST SERIOUS PROBLEMS

The most important single environmental problem in the CEE is thought to be damage to human health caused by air pollution, especially from exposure to high levels of particulates. The next most important problems are high levels of water salinity (caused by discharges from coal mines) and high levels of nitrate runoff into the country's principal rivers, which have high productivity costs. Poor air quality in urban areas also imposes some amenity costs.

The CEE Action Programme uses existing data on the location of major industrial plants in selected pollution 'hot-spots' to tentatively identify locations where people are exposed to specific health risks from particular kinds of pollution. It was found that the most common health problems are the result of exposures to a fairly narrow range of pollutants, the most important of which are: lead in air and soil, which can affect the mental development of children; airborne dust, which may cause acute and chronic respiratory conditions; and sulphur dioxide and other gases, which cause respiratory problems and contribute to acid rain.

There is a large and growing body of scientific evidence that fine particle air pollution causes serious health damage and significantly raises the risk of death. The most recent study, which followed 8,111 adults for 14–16 years and which adjusted for age, sex, smoking, education level, and occupational health risks, concludes that mortality is most strongly associated with fine particles (Dockery *et al.* 1993). These particles, usually referred to as PM10, are less than 10 microns in size. Air pollution is potentially the most serious short- to medium-term environmental problem for human health. Polluted air is more difficult to avoid than polluted water, and its pervasive effects damage human health, buildings, and nature.

The principle cause of air pollution in CEE countries is the heavy reliance of households and small enterprises upon poor quality brown coal, which has a higher content of ash (the source of particulates) and sulphur (the source of SO_2)

than the coal commonly used in the West. Table 39 compares the minimum damage costs from pollution emitted by high and low stacks in Poland. The emissions of particulates from low stacks are 12 times more damaging than from high stacks. Low stacks are a more concentrated, direct source of human exposure to particulates than high stacks. Therefore pollution from low stacks is significantly more harmful to human health.

Table 39 Minimum Damage Costs from Pollution Emitted by High and Low Stacks (US$ per ton)

Source	Sulphur Dioxide	Particulate Matter	Nitrogen Oxides
High Stacks	265	60	180
Low Stacks	650	720	460

Source: Environmental Assessment of the Gas Development Plan for Poland (World Bank).

IDENTIFYING THE MOST EFFICIENT WAYS TO ACHIEVE ENVIRONMENTAL OBJECTIVES

In identifying the most efficient way to achieve environmental objectives it is necessary to balance the costs of a policy against its likely benefits. Such an approach provides a simple basis for ranking alternative courses of action. A minimum estimate of the benefits of a policy is equivalent to the amount of environmental damage that would occur if the policy were not implemented.

In principle, benefit-cost analysis should be used to rank priorities so that each incremental unit of resources spent will have the greatest impact in bringing about environmental improvement. In practice, this approach is complicated by the presence of many possible projects with similar benefit-to-cost ratios. Therefore, it is necessary to identify interventions that are urgent versus those that are not so urgent.

Guiding principles proposed in the CEE Action Programme to help identify the best interventions include:

Clearly defining environmental problems
This will largely determine the solution and the way it is implemented. In the Action Programme, the problem is particulate air pollution caused by the burning of coal by home heating and small industries. In addressing this problem there is a risk that investments are made which later on turn out not to have solved the real problem. For example, money may be spent to reduce the pollution from a large power plant, when in fact most of the serious pollution is caused by home heating and small industries.

Looking for measures that solve several problems simultaneously
As several environmental problems are sometimes related to the same cause
(like the use of coal), some measures will reduce several kinds of pollution at
the same time. In the CEE, a reduction in the use of coal diminishes the risks
to health from particulates, and it simultaneously reduces SO_2, acid rain, and
greenhouse gases.

Concentration on prevention
Prevention always costs less than cleaning up or mitigating problems after they
have occurred. Therefore, improving the efficiency of coal extraction and
handling – in order to reduce losses – will yield significantly more net benefits
than will cleaning up lead in soil.

Look at economic policies first
Some economic policies – such as market reforms, higher energy prices and
improvements in industrial efficiency, are 'win-win' policies, because the costs
associated with achieving the environmental benefits are extremely low. In
CEE, the removal of energy subsidies will have two effects on air pollution. The
first is that it will promote energy conservation, and the second is that it will
also shift the composition of fuel use away from coal.

Remembering that it is the incremental benefit-to-cost ratios that matter
The basis of comparison for investments must be how much environmental
improvement can be obtained by spending an additional unit of investment on
one problem rather than on another.

Knowledge of the relative importance of the health impacts of particulates
and gases does not give a basis on which one can set environmental action
priorities which would target one type of pollution and not the other. However,
even if the health impacts of dusts and gases is similar, the costs of controlling
particulates is typically much lower. The figures in Table 40 represent the
typical costs of controlling particulate and gas emissions in the power and
district heating sectors. The figures indicate that the costs of controlling
particulates are significantly less ($10–90 per ton) than the costs of controlling
either SO_2 or NO_x ($400 to 45,000 per ton). Therefore, priority should be
given to fitting particulate control devices to plants that currently have no such
facilities installed, and to repairing or upgrading existing facilities that are
currently not working to design capacity.

Source:
The World Bank and the Organization for Economic Co-operation and Development,
Environmental Action Programme for Central and Eastern Europe: Setting Priorities.
Document of the Ministerial Conference, Lucerne, Switzerland, April 1993.
D.W. Dockery *et al.*, 'An Association between Air Pollution and Mortality in six U.S. Cities',
New England Journal of Medicine 1993; 329: 1753–9. This article also refers to 18 earlier
studies.

Table 40 Typical Costs of Controlling Emission from the Power and District Heating Sectors

Pollutant	Abatement technology	Removal efficiency (%)	Abatement cost ($ per annual tonne emission avoided)
Particulates	a. ESP[a]	97–98	15–65
	b. High efficiency ESP	99–99.9	20–90
	c. Baghouse	99–99.9	15–65
	d. Mechanical collector	50–90	10–70
SO_2	a. Dry Sorbet	50–80	400–3,500
	b. Semi-dry FGD[b]	80–95	600–4,000
	c. Wet FGD	96–98	800–5,000
NOx	a. Low-NOx burners	30–70	750–7,000
	b. SCR[c]	80–90	5,000–45,000

[a] Electrostatic percipitator
[b] Flue Gas Desulphurization
[c] Selective Catalytic Reduction
Source: The World Bank and Organization for Economic Co-operation and Development, *Environmental Action Plan for Central and Eastern Europe*, 1993.

References

Ahmad, Y.J., S. El Serafy and E. Lutz (eds.) (1989) *Environmental Accounting for Sustainable Development. A UNEP-World Bank Symposium*. Washington, D.C: The World Bank.

Anderson, J.R. (1989a) 'Reconsiderations on Risk Deductions in Public Project Appraisal'. *Australian Journal of Agricultural Economics* 33(2), pp. 136–40.

—— (1989b) *Forecasting, Uncertainty and Public Project Appraisal*, International Economics Department WPS 154. Washington, D.C: The World Bank, pp. 52.

Anderson, J.R., J.L. Dillon and J.B. Hardaker (1977). *Agricultural Decision Analysis*. Ames: Iowa State University Press.

Arrow, K.J. and R.C. Lind (1970) 'Uncertainty and the Evaluation of Public Investment Decisions'. *American Economic Review* 60, pp. 364–78.

Asian Development Bank (1975) *Appraisal of the Fisheries Development Project in Thailand*. Manila: Asian Development Bank.

—— (1983) *Appraisal of the Hill Forest Development Project in the Kingdom of Nepal*. Manila: Asian Development Bank.

—— (1984) *Project Performance Audit Report on Fisheries Development Project in the Kingdom of Thailand*. Manila: Asian Development Bank.

—— (1986) *Environmental Planning and Management*. Manila: Asian Development Bank.

—— (1987) *Environmental Planning and Management and the Project Cycle*. ADB Environment Paper No. 1. Manila: Asian Development Bank.

Attaviroj, P. (1986) *Soil Erosion and Degradation, Northern Thai Uplands: An Economic Study*. Paper presented to the International Conference on the Economics of Dryland Degradation and Rehabilitation, 10–14 March 1986. Canberra, Australia.

Barbier, E.B., J.C. Burgess, T.M. Swanson and D.W. Pearce (1990) *Elephants, Economics and Ivory*. London: Earthscan Publications Limited.

Barde, J. and D.W. Pearce (eds.) (1991) *Valuing the Environment: Six Case Studies*. London: Earthscan Publications Limited.

Bartelmus, P., E. Lutz and S. Schweinfest. (1993) 'Integrated Environmental and Economic Accounting: A Case Study for Papua New Guinea', in *Toward Improved Accounting for the Environment*, ed. E. Lutz. A UNSTAT-World Bank Symposium. Washington, D.C: The World Bank.

Barzetti, V. (ed.) (1993) *Parks and Progress*. IV World Congress on National Parks and Protected Areas, Caracas, Venezuela. Washington, D.C: Inter-American Development Bank and IUCN.

Baumol, W.J. (1968) 'On the Social Rate of Discount'. *American Economic Review* 58, pp. 788–802.

Becker, G. (1960) 'An Economic Analysis of Fertility', in *Demographic and*

References

Economic Changes in Developed Countries. Princeton: Princeton University Press, pp. 209–31.

Berry, J.B. (1994) 'What's a Life Worth to EPA Regulators? Try $49 Million'. *The Washington Post*. April 3.

Binswanger, H. (1989) 'Brazilian Policies That Encourage Deforestation in the Amazon'. World Bank Environment Department. Working Paper 16. Washington, D.C: The World Bank.

Bishop, R.C. (1978) 'Endangered Species and Uncertainty: The Economics of a Safe Minimum Standard', *American Journal of Agricultural Economics* 60, pp. 10–18.

Bojö, J. (1991) *The Economics of Land Degradation: Theory and Applications to Lesotho*. Stockholm: Stockholm School of Economics.

Bojö, J., K. Mäler and L. Unemo (1990) *Environment and Development: An Economic Approach*. Dordrecht, Netherlands: Kluwer Academic Publishers.

Brown, G., Jr. and W. Henry (1989) *The Economic Value of Elephants*. London Environmental Economics Centre, Discussion Paper 89–12.

Brown, K., D. Pearce, C. Perrings and T. Swanson (1993) *Economics and the Conservation of Global Biological Diversity*. Global Environment Facility Working Paper No. 2. Washington, D.C: UNDP/UNEP/The World Bank.

Carpenter, R.A. (ed.) (1983) *Natural Systems for Development: What Planners Need to Know*. New York: Macmillan.

Carpenter, R.A. and J.E. Maragos (eds./authors) (1989) *How to Assess Environmental Impacts on Tropical Islands and Coastal Areas*. South Pacific Regional Environment Programme Training Manual. Sponsored by Asian Development Bank. Prepared by Environment and Policy Institute East–West Center. Honolulu, Hawaii.

Carson, R.T. and R.C. Mitchell (1984) *Non-Sampling Errors in Contingent Valuation Surveys*. Discussion paper No. D-120. Washington, D.C: Resources For the Future.

Cernea, M.M. (1993) *The Urban Environment and Population Relocation*. World Bank Discussion Paper No. 152. Washington, D.C: The World Bank.

—— (1988) *Involuntary Resettlement in Development Projects: Policy Guidelines in World Bank-Financed Projects*. World Bank Technical Paper No. 80. Washington, D.C: The World Bank.

Chua, T., and L.F. Scura (eds.) (1992) *Integrative Framework and Methods for Coastal Area Management*. Proceedings of the Regional Workshop on Coastal Zone Planning and Management in ASEAN: Lessons Learned. Manila, Philippines.

Ciriacy-Wantrup, S.V. (1968) *Resource Conservation* (2nd edn). Berkeley: University of California Press.

Clawson, M. (1959) *Methods of Measuring Demand for and Value of Outdoor Recreation*. RFF Reprint No. 10. Washington, DC: Resources for the Future.

Clawson, M. and J.L. Knetsch (1966) *Economics of Outdoor Recreation*. Baltimore: Johns Hopkins University Press for Resources for the Future.

Conrad, J. (1980) 'Quasi-Option Value and the Expected Value of Information' *Quarterly Journal of Economics* 92, pp. 813–19.

References

Costanza, R. (ed.) (1991) *Ecological Economics: The Science and Management of Sustainability*. New York: Columbia University Press.

Cummings, R., D. Brookshire and W. Schulze (1986) *Valuing Environmental Goods: A State of the Art Assessment of the Contingent Valuation Method*. Totowa, NJ: Rowan & Allenheld.

d'Arge, R.C. and J.F. Shogren (1989,a) 'Non-Market Asset Prices: A Comparison of Three Valuation Approaches', in *Valuation Methods and Policy Making in Environmental Economics*, eds. H. Folmer and E. van Ireland. Amsterdam: Elsevier Science Publishers.

—— (1989,b) 'Okoboji Experiment: Comparing Non-Market Valuation Techniques in Unusually Well-Defined Market for Water Quality', *Ecological Economics* 1: 3, pp. 251–259.

Daly, H.E. and J.B. Cobb, Jr (1989) *For the Common Good: Redirecting the Economy Toward Community, the Environment, and a Sustainable Future*. Boston: Beacon Press.

Dixon, J.A. and M.M. Hufschmidt (eds) (1986) *Economic Valuation Techniques for the Environment: A Case Study Workbook*. Baltimore: Johns Hopkins University Press.

Dixon, J.A., D.E. James and P.B. Sherman (eds) (1990) *Dryland Management: Economic Case Studies*, London, Earthscan.

Dixon, J.A. and P. Lal (1994) 'The Management of Coastal Wetlands: Economic Analysis of Combined Ecological-Economic Systems', in *The Environment and Emerging Development Issues*, eds. P. Dasgupta and K.G. Mäler. Oxford: Clarendon Press (forthcoming).

Dixon, J.A., L. Fallon Scura and T. van't Hof (1993). Meeting Ecological and Economic Goals: Marine Parks in the Carribean. *Ambio* 22 (2–3), pp. 117–125.

Dixon, J.A., L. Fallon Scura and T. van't Hof (1994). 'Ecology and Micro-economics as "Joint Products": The Bonaire Marine Park in the Carribean' in C. Perrings, K.G. Maler, C. Folke, C.S. Hollings and B.O. Jansson, eds. *Biodiversity Conservation: Problems and Policies*, Dordrecht: Kluwer Academic Press.

Dixon, J.A., and P.B. Sherman (1990) *Economics of Protected Areas: A New Look at Benefits and Costs*. Washington, D.C: Island Press.

Dixon, J.A. and L.A. Fallon (1989) 'The Concept of Sustainability: Origins, Extensions, and Usefulness for Policy'. *Society and Natural Resources* 2, pp. 73–84.

Dixon, J.A., L.M. Talbot and G.J-M. LeMoigne (1989) *Dams and the Environment: Considerations in World Bank Projects*. World Bank Technical Paper No. 110. Washington, D.C: The World Bank.

Dixon, J.A., R.A. Carpenter, L.A. Fallon, P.B. Sherman and S. Manopimoke (1988) *Economic Analysis of the Environmental Impacts of Development Projects*. London: Earthscan Publications Limited in association with The Asian Development Bank.

Dockery, D.W. et al. (1993). An Association Between Air Pollution and Mortality in Six U.S. Cities, *New England Journal of Medicine*, Vol 329, pp. 1753–1759.

References

Eskeland, G.S. (1992) 'Attacking Air Pollution in Mexico City'. *Finance and Development*, 29:4, pp. 28–30.

Eskeland, Gunnar S. (1994a). 'A Presumptive Pigovian Tax: Complementing Regulation to Mimic an Emission Fee'. *World Bank Economic Review*, Vol. 8, No. 3, September, Washington, D.C., pp. 373–94.

Eskeland, Gunnar S. and Tarhan Feyzioglu (1994b). 'Is Demand for Polluting Goods Manageable? An Econometric Model of Car Ownership and Use in Mexico'. Working Paper No 1309, June. Policy Research Department, World Bank, Washington, D.C., U.S.A.

Eskeland, Gunnar S., Emmanuel Jimenez and Lili Liu (1994c). 'Energy Pricing and Air Pollution: Econometric Evidence in Chile and Indonesia'. Working Paper No 1323, July, Policy Research Department, World Bank, Washington, D.C., U.S.A.

Eskeland, G.S., and A.Ten Kate (1993) *Environmental Protection under Economic Development: Selected Findings from Mexico*, from Workshop on Economywide Policies and the Environment. December 1993. Washington, D.C: The World Bank.

Fankhauser, S. and D. Pearce (1993) 'The Social Costs of Greenhouse Gas Abatement', in *The Economics of Climate Change*. Paris: Organization for Economic Cooperation and Development.

Fisher, A., L.G. Chestnut, and D.M. Violette (1989) 'The Value of Reducing Risks of Death: A Note on New Evidence', in *Journal of Policy Analysis and Management* 8 (Winter), pp. 88–100.

Fleming, W.M. (1983) 'Phewa Tal Catchment Management Program: Benefits and Costs of Forestry and Soil Conservation in Nepal', in L.S. Hamilton (ed.) *Forest and Watershed Development and Conservation in Asia and the Pacific*. Boulder, CO.: Westview Press.

Folke, C. and T. Kaberger (eds.) (1991) *Linking the Natural Environment and the Economy: Essays from the Eco-Eco Group*. Dordrecht, Netherlands: Kluwer Academic Publishers.

Folmer, H. and E. van Irland (eds.) (1989) *Valuation Methods and Policy Making in Environmental Economics*. New York: Elsevier.

Freeman, A.M. III (1979) *The Benefits of Environmental Improvement: Theory and Practice*. Baltimore: Johns Hopkins University Press.

Gittinger, J.P. (1982) *Economic Analysis of Agricultural Projects*. Baltimore: Johns Hopkins University Press.

Graham, D.A. (1981) 'Cost-Benefit Analysis Under Uncertainty'. *American Economic Review* 71, pp. 715–25.

Haimes, Y.Y. (ed.) (1981) *Risk Benefit Analysis in Water Resources Planning and Management*. New York: Plenum Press.

Hamilton, L.S. and S.C. Snedaker (eds.) (1984) *Handbook for Mangrove Area Management*. Honolulu: United Nations Environment Programme and East–West Center.

Hamilton, L.S., J.A. Dixon and G.O. Miller (1989) 'Mangrove Forests: An Undervalued Resource of the Land and of the Sea', in *Ocean Yearbook*, eds. E.M. Borgese, N. Ginsburg and J.R. Morgan, 8, pp. 254–88. Chicago:

The University of Chicago Press.

Harrison, D. Jr and D.L. Rubinfeld (1978a) 'Hedonic Housing Prices and the Demand for Clean Air'. *Journal of Environmental Economics and Management* 5, pp. 81–102.

—— (1978b) 'The Distribution of Benefits from Improvements in Urban Air Quality'. *Journal of Environmental Economics and Management* 5, pp. 313–32.

Haveman, R. (1969) 'The Opportunity Cost of Displaced Private Spending and the Social Discount Rate'. *Water Resources Research* 5, pp. 947–57.

Helmers, F.L.C.H. (1979) *Project Planning and Income Distribution*. The Hague: Martinus-Nijhoff.

Henry, C. (1974) 'Option Values in the Economics of Irreplaceable Assets'. *Review of Economic Studies*, Symposium on Exhaustible Resources, pp. 89–104.

Hicks, J.R. (1939) 'Foundations of Welfare Economics'. *Economic Journal* 49 (196).

Hodson, G. and J.A. Dixon (1988). *Logging versus Fisheries and Tourism in Palawan: An Environmental and Economic Analysis*. EAPI Occasional Paper No. 7. Honolulu: East–West Center.

Hodgson, G. and J.A. Dixon (1992) 'Sedimentation Damage to Marine Resources: Environmental and Economic Analysis', *Resources and Environment in Asia's Marine Sector*, ed. J.B. March. New York: Taylor and Francis.

Hufschmidt, M.M., D.E. James, A.D. Meister, B.T. Bower, and J.A. Dixon (1983) *Environment, Natural Systems and Development: An Economic Valuation Guide*. Baltimore: Johns Hopkins University Press.

Hyman, E.L. and M.M. Hufschmidt (1983) *The Relevance of Natural Resource Economics in Environmental Planning*. Working Paper. Honolulu: East–West Environment and Policy Institute.

International Union for the Conservation of Nature and Natural Resources (1980) *World Conservation Strategy*. Geneva: IUCN.

—— (1988) *Logging Versus Fisheries and Tourism in Palawan*. Occasional Paper No. 7. Honolulu: East-West Environment and Policy Institute.

International Union for the Conservation of Nature and Natural Resources (1980) *World Conservation Strategy*. Geneva: IUCN.

James, D.E., H.M.A. Jansen and J.B. Opschoor (1978) *Economic Approaches to Environmental Problems*. Amsterdam: Elsevier Scientific.

Jones-Lee, M.W. (1976) *The Value of Life: An Economic Analysis*. Chicago: University of Chicago Press.

Kahneman, D. and Knetsch, J.L (1992a) 'Valuing Public Goods: The Purchase of Moral Satisfaction', in *Journal of Environmental Economics and Management* 22, pp. 57–70.

—— (1992b). 'Contingent Valuation and the Value of Public Goods: Reply', in *Journal of Environmental Economics and Management* 22, pp. 90–94.

Kellenberg, J., and H. Daly (1994) *Counting User Cost in Evaluating Projects Involving Depletion of Natural Capital: World Bank Best Practice and Beyond*. Environment Department Working Paper No. 66. Washington, D.C: The World Bank.

Kim, S.H. and J.A. Dixon (1986) 'Economic Valuation of Environmental Quality Aspects of Upland Agricultural Projects in Korea', in *Economic Valuation Techniques for the Environment: A Case Study Workbook*, ed. J.A. Dixon and M.M. Hufschmidt. Baltimore: Johns Hopkins University Press.

Kneese, A.V. (1966) 'Research Goals and Progress Towards Them', in *Environmental Quality in a Growing Economy*, ed. H. Jarrett. Baltimore: Johns Hopkins University Press.

Knetsch, J.L. (1993) *Environmental Valuation: Some Practical Problems of Wrong Questions and Misleading Answers*. Resource Assessment Commission Occasional Publication No. 5. Canberra: Australian Government Publishing Service.

—— (1989) 'The Endowment Effect and Evidence of Nonreversible Indifference Curves'. *The American Economic Review* 79, pp. 1277–84.

Knetsch, J.L. and J.A. Sinden (1984) 'Willingness to Pay and Compensation Demanded: Experimental Evidence of an Unexpected Disparity in Measures of Value'. *Quarterly Journal of Economics* 99, pp. 507–21.

Kramer, R.A. (1993) *Tropical Forest Protection in Madagascar*. Prepared for Northeast Universities Development Consortium, Williams College, October 15–16.

Kramer, R., M. Munasinghe, N. Sharma, E. Mercer, and P. Shyamsundar (1992) *Valuing a Protected Tropical Forest: A Case Study in Madagascar*. Prepared for the IV World Congress on National Parks and Protected Areas, Caracas, Venezuela, February 10–21.

Kramer, R.A., M. Munasinghe, N. Sharma, E. Mercer and P. Shyamsundar (1993). Valuation of Biophysical Resources in Madagascar in M. Munasinghe (ed), *Environmental Economics and Sustainable Development*, World Bank Environment Paper No. 3. Washington, D.C.: The World Bank.

Kramer, R.A., N. Sharma, P. Shyamsundar and M. Munasinghe (1994) *Cost and Compensation Issues in Protecting Tropical Rainforests: Case Study of Madagascar*. Africa Technical Department, Environment Working Paper No. 62. Washington, D.C: The World Bank.

Krupnick, A.J. and P.R. Portney (1991) 'Controlling Urban Air Pollution: A Benefit-Cost Assessment', in *Science*, 252, pp. 522–528.

Krutilla, J.V. (1969) *On the Economics of Preservation or Development of the Lower Portion of Hell's Canyon*. Draft report to the Federal Power Commission. Washington, DC.

Krutilla, J.V. and A.C. Fisher (1985) *The Economics of Natural Environments* (revised edn). Baltimore: Johns Hopkins University Press for Resources for the Future.

Lal, P.N. (1990) *Conservation or Conversion of Mangroves in Fiji*. Occasional Paper No. 11, Environment and Policy Institute, East-West Center, Hawaii.

Lancaster, K.J. (1966) 'A New Approach to Consumer Theory,' *Journal of Political Economy,* 75:2.

Lave, L.B. and E.P. Seskin (1977) *Air Pollution and Human Health*. Baltimore: Johns Hopkins University Press for Resources for the Future.

References

Little, I.M.D. and J.A. Mirrlees (1974) *Project Appraisal and Planning for Developing Countries*. New York: Basic Books.

Lutz, E. (ed.) (1993) *Toward Improved Accounting for the Environment*. Washington, D.C: The World Bank.

Lutz, E. (1994). *Greening the National Accounts*. Environment Dissemination Note No. 7, Environment Department, Washington, D.C.: The World Bank.

Mahar, D.J. (1989) *Government Policies and Deforestation in Brazil's Amazon Region*. Washington, D.C: World Bank.

Magrath, W.B. (1992) 'Loess Plateau Soil Conservation Project, Sediment Reduction Benefit Analysis'. Manuscript, Agriculture and Natural Resources Department. Washington, D.C: The World Bank.

Magrath, W. and P. Arens (1989) *The Costs of Soil Erosion on Java: A Natural Resource Accounting Approach*. World Bank Environment Department Working Paper No. 18. Washington, D.C: The World Bank.

Mäler, K.G. (1977) 'A Note on the Use of Property Values in Estimating Marginal Willingness to Pay for Environmental Quality'. *Journal of Environmental Economics and Management* 4, pp. 355–69.

Mäler, K.G., and P. Dasgupta (eds.) (forthcoming 1994) *Environment and Emerging Development Issues*. Oxford: Clarendon Press.

Margulis, S. (1991) *Back of the Envelope Estimates of Environmental Damage Costs in Mexico*. Internal Discussion Paper, Report No. IDP-0104. Washington, D.C: The World Bank.

Markandya, A. and J. Richardson (eds.) (1992) *Environmental Economics: A Reader*. New York: St. Martin's Press.

Mercer, D.E and R.A. Kramer (1992) *An International Nature Tourism Travel Cost Model: Estimating the Recreational Use Value of a Proposed National Park in Madagascar*. Presented at Association of Environmental and Resource Economists Contributed Paper Session: Recreation Demand Models Allied Social Science Associations Annual Meeting, New Orleans, Louisiana.

Miller, J.R. and F. Lad (1984) 'Flexibility, Learning and Irreversibility in Economic Decisions: A Bayesian Approach'. *Journal of Environmental Economics and Management* 11, pp. 161–72.

Mishan, E.J. (1982) *Cost-Benefit Analysis* (3rd edn). London: Allen & Unwin.

Mitchell, R.C., and R.T. Carson (1989) *Using Surveys to Value Public Goods: The Contingent Valuation Method*. Washington, D.C: Resources for the Future.

Munasinghe, M., W. Cruz, and J. Warford (1993) 'Are Economywide Policies Good for the Environment?' *Finance and Development* 30:3, pp. 40–43.

Munasinghe, M. (ed.) (1993a) *Environmental Economics and Natural Resource Management in Developing Countries*. Washington, D.C: Committee of International Development Institutions on the Environment.

—— (1993b) *Environmental Economics and Sustainable Development*. World Bank Environment Paper No. 3. Washington, D.C: The World Bank.

—— (1993c) 'The Economist's Approach to Sustainable Development'. *Finance and Development* 30:3, pp. 16–19.

North, J.H. and C. Griffin (1991) 'Water Source as a Housing Characteristic:

Hedonic Property Valuation and Willingness to Pay for Water', in *Water Resources Research: Water Resources Issues and Problems in Developing Countries*. Charlottesville: American Geophysical Union. 29:7, pp. 1923–29.

Ostro, B. (1992a) *Generic Estimates of the Economic Effects of Criteria Air Pollutants: A Review and Synthesis*. Manuscript, Policy Research Department. Washington, D.C: The World Bank.

Ostro, B. (1992b). *Estimating the Health and Economic Effects of Particulate Matter in Jakarta: A Preliminary Assessment*. Paper presented at the Fourth Annual Meeting of the International Society for Environmental Epidemiology, 26–29 August, Cuernavaca, Mexico.

Ostro, B. (1994) *Estimating the Health Effects of Air Pollutants: A Methodology with an Application to Jakarta*. Policy Research Working Paper 1301. Policy Research Department, Public Economics Division. Washington, D.C: The World Bank.

Pearce, D.W. and C.A. Nash (1981) *The Social Appraisal of Projects: A Text in Cost-Benefit Analysis*. London: Macmillan.

Pearce, D.W. (1993) *Economic Values and the Natural World*. Cambridge: The Massachusetts Institute of Technology Press.

Pearce, D.W. and J.J. Warford (1993) *World Without End: Economics, Environment, and Sustainable Development*. New York: Oxford University Press.

Pearce, D., E. Barbier, A. Markandya, S. Barrett, R.K. Turner and T. Swanson (1991) *Blueprint 2: Greening the World Economy*. London: Earthscan Publications Limited.

Pearce, D.W., E.B. Barbier and A. Markandya (1990) *Sustainable Development: Economics and Environment in the Third World*. London: Earthscan Publications Limited.

Pearce, D.W. and R.K. Turner (1990) *Economics of Natural Resources and the Environment*. Baltimore: The Johns Hopkins University Press.

Pearce, D., A. Markandya and E.B. Barbier (1989) *Blueprint for a Green Economy: A Text for the Next Election*. The *Guardian*. London: Earthscan Publications Limited for the UK Department of the Environment.

Pearce, D.W. (ed.) (1978) *The Valuation of Social Cost*. London: Allen and Unwin.

Perrings, C., Mäler, K-G., Folke C., Holling, C.S. and Jansson, B.O. (eds) (1994) *Biodiversity Conservation: Problems and Policies*. Dordrecht, Netherlands: Kluwer Academic Press.

Pezzey, J. (1992) *Sustainable Development Concepts: An Economic Analysis*. World Bank Environment Paper No. 2. Washington, D.C: The World Bank.

Pigou, A.C. (1920) *The Economics of Welfare*. London: Macmillan.

Pouliquen, L.Y. (1970) *Risk Analysis in Project Appraisal*. Baltimore: Johns Hopkins University Press.

Raiffa, H. (1968). *Decision Analysis*. Reading: Addison-Wesley.

Ray, A. (1984) *Cost-Benefit Analysis: Issues and Methodologies*. Baltimore: Johns Hopkins University Press for The World Bank.

Rees, C.P. (1983) Environmental Management in the Project Cycle. *ADB Quarterly Review* QR-4-83. Manila: Asian Development Bank.

References

Repetto, R., W. Magrath, M. Wells, C. Beer and F. Rossini (1989) *Wasting Assets: Natural Resources in the National Income Accounts*. Washington, D.C: World Resources Institute.

Repetto, R., R.C. Dower, R. Jenkins and J. Geoghegan (1992) *Green Fees: How a Tax Shift Can Work for the Environment and the Economy*. Washington, D.C: World Resources Institute.

Ridker, R.G. (1967) *Economic Costs of Air Pollution: Studies and Measurement*. New York: Praeger.

Rosen, S. (1974). 'Hedonic Prices and Implicit Markets: Product Differentiation in Prefect Competition', *Journal of Political Economy* 82:1, pp. 34–55.

Rowe, R.D. and L.G. Chestnut (1982) *The Value of Visibility: Theory and Applications*. Cambridge MA: Abt Books.

Ruitenbeek, H.J. (1992). *Mangrove Management: An Economic Analysis of Management Options with a Focus on Bintuni Bay, Irian Jaya*. Environmental Management Development in Indonesia Project, Halifax: Dalhousie University.

Ruitenbeek, H.J. (1994). Modelling Ecology-wide Linkages in Mangroves: Economic Evidence for Promoting Conservation in Bintuni Bay, Indonesia. *Ecological Economics*, Vol. 10, No. 3, pp. 233–47.

Russell, C.S. (1973) *Residuals Management in Industry: A Case Study of Petroleum Refining*. Baltimore: Johns Hopkins University Press for Resources for the Future.

Russell, C.S. and W.J. Vaughan (1976) *Steel Production: Processes, Products, and Residuals*. Baltimore: Johns Hopkins University Press.

Samples, K.C., J.A. Dixon and M.M. Gowen (1986) 'Information Disclosure and Endangered Species Valuation', *Land Economics* 62:3, pp. 307–312.

Schneider, R. (1993) *Land Abandonment, Property Rights, and Agricultural Sustainability in the Amazon*. LATEN Dissemination Note No. 3. Washington, D.C: The World Bank.

Schramm, G. and J.J. Warford (eds.) (1989) *Environmental Management and Economic Development*. Baltimore: Johns Hopkins University Press for the World Bank.

Scura, L.F. and D. Maimon (1993) 'Economic Valuation of Surface Water Quality Improvements in the Metropolitan Region of Rio de Janeiro Using Objection and Subjective Valuation Approaches'. Consultancy report submitted to the World Bank Environment Department. Washington, D.C.

Scura, L.F., and T. van't Hof (1993) *The Ecology and Economics of Bonaire Marine Park*. Environment Department Divisional Paper No. 1993–44. Washington, D.C: The World Bank.

Sinden, J.A., and A.C. Worrell (1979) *Unpriced Values: Decisions Without Market Prices*. New York: Wiley.

Singh, B., R. Ramasubban, R. Bhatia, J. Briscoe, C.C. Griffin and C. Kim (1993) 'Rural Water Supply in Kerala, India: How to Emerge From a Low-Level Equilibrium Trap', in *Water Resources Research: Water Resources Issues and Problems in Developing Countries*. Charlottesville: American Geophysical Union. 29:7, pp. 1931–42.

References

Squire, L. and H.G. van der Tak (1975) *Economic Analysis of Projects.* Baltimore: Johns Hopkins University Press for The World Bank.

Steer, A., and E. Lutz (1993) 'Measuring Environmentally Sustainable Development'. *Finance and Development* 30:4, pp. 20–23.

Swanson, T.M. and E.B. Barbier (eds.) (1992) *Economics for the Wilds: Wildlife, Wildlands, Diversity and Development.* London: Earthscan Publications Limited.

Ten Kate, A. (1993) *Industrial Development and the Environment in Mexico.* Policy Research Working Paper No. WPS 1125. Policy Research Department. Washington, D.C: The World Bank.

Tietenberg, T. (1992) *Environmental and Natural Resource Economics.* Third Edition. New York: Harper Collins Publishers Inc.

Turner, K. and T. Jones (eds.) (1991) *Wetlands: Market and Intervention Failures – Four Case Studies.* London: Earthscan Publications Limited.

Van Houtven, G.L., and M.L. Cropper (1994) *When Is a Life Too Costly to Save?: Evidence from U.S. Environmental Regulations.* Policy Research Working Paper No. 1260. Washington, D.C: The World Bank.

van Pelt, M.J.F. (1993) *Ecological Sustainability and Project Appraisal: Case Studies in Developing Countries.* Avebury: Ashgate Publishing Limited.

van Tongeren, J., S. Schweinfest, E. Lutz, M.G. Luna and G. Martin (1993) 'Integrated Environmental and Economic Accounting: A Case Study for Mexico', in *Toward Improved Accounting for the Environment*, ed. by E. Lutz. A UNSTAT-World Bank Symposium. Washington, D.C: The World Bank.

Vincent, J.R., E.W. Crawford and J.P. Hoehn (eds.) (1991) 'Valuing Environmental Benefits in Developing Economies'. Proceedings of a Seminar Series held February–May 1990 at Michigan State University. *Special Report* No. 29. East Lansing: Michigan State University.

Viscusi, W.K. (1992) *Fatal Tradeoffs, Public and Private Responsibilities for Risk.* Oxford: Oxford University Press.

Ward, F.A. and J.B. Loomis (1986) 'The Travel Cost Demand Model as an Environmental Policy Assessment Tool: A Review of the Literature', *Western Journal of Agricultural Economics* 11:2, pp. 164–78.

Ward, W.A., B.J. Deren and E.H. D'Silva (1991) *The Economics of Project Analysis: A Practitioner's Guide.* Economic Development Institute. Washington, D.C: The World Bank.

Weiss, J. (ed) (1994) *The Economics of Project Appraisal and the Environment.* Vermont: Edward Elgar Publishing Limited.

Wells, M. and K. Brandon with L. Hannah (1992) *People and Parks: Linking Protected Area Management with Local Communities.* Washington, D.C: The World Bank, Worldwide Fund for Nature, and U.S. Agency for International Development.

Whelan, T. (ed) (1991) *Nature Tourism: Managing for the Environment.* Washington, D.C: Island Press.

Whittington, D., D. Lauria and X. Mu (1991). A Study of Water Vending and Willingness to Pay for Water in Onitsha, Nigeria. *World Development*, Vol 19, No. 2–3, pp. 179–198.

References

Whittington, D., D.T. Lauria, A.M. Wright, K. Choe, J.A. Hughes and V. Swarna (1991) 'Willingness to Pay for Improved Sanitation in Kumasi, Ghana: A Contingent Valuation Study', in Vincent *et al.* (1991). Proceedings of a Seminar Series Held February–May 1990 at Michigan State University. *Special Report No. 29*. East Lansing: Michigan State University.

Wilson, E.O. (ed.) (1988) *Biodiversity*. Washington, DC: National Academy Press.

Winpenny, J.T. (1991) *Values for the Environment: A Guide to Economic Appraisal*. Overseas Development Institute. London: Her Majesty's Stationery Office.

World Bank (1991) *Environmental Assessment Sourcebook*. Volumes I, II, III. Environment Department. Washington, D.C: The World Bank.

—— (1992) *World Development Report 1992: Development and the Environment*. New York: Oxford University Press.

—— (1993a). *Environment and Development in Latin America and the Caribbean: The Role of The World Bank*. Washington, D.C.: The World Bank.

—— (1993b) *Water Resources Management: A Policy Paper*. Washington, D.C: The World Bank.

—— (1993c) *World Development Report 1993: Investing in Health*. New York: Oxford University Press.

—— (1994) 'Project Management and Implementation', in *Staff Appraisal Report on China – Shanghai Environment Project*. Report No. 12386-CHA, pp. 27–30. Washington, D.C: The World Bank.

World Bank and Organization for Economic Cooperation and Development (1993). *Environmental Action Programme for Central and Eastern Europe: Setting Priorities*. Document of the Ministerial Conference, Lucerne, Switzerland.

Index

ECONOMIC ANALYSIS OF ENVIRONMENTAL IMPACTS

Sustainable economic development calls for sound environmental management. It is becoming increasingly acknowledged that thorough analysis and valuation of environmental impacts is an essential component of development projects.

This is a new edition of the classic text on the subject, first published in 1988 as *Economic Analysis of Environmental Impacts of Development Projects*. The authors have thoroughly revised the text, adding new case studies and references and organising the different valuation techniques to incorporate recent advances in applied research and thinking. The new title reflects the changed focus and broader scope of the new edition.

Part One sets out the theory and role of economic analysis, explaining how impacts can be measured, and describing both the available valuation techniques and their limitations. Part Two contains nine detailed case studies from around the world, which illustrate the full range of techniques in practice.

John A Dixon is Principal Environmental Economist and Chief, Indicators and Environmental Valuation Unit, with the World Bank Environment Department. **Louise Fallon Scura** is a Natural Resource Management Specialist in the same department. **Richard A Carpenter** is an independent consultant based in Virginia.

An Earthscan Original
Economics • Environment

£20.00

Published in association with the Asian Development Bank and The World Bank.

'. . . an excellent and welcome volume . . . clear, readable and interesting . . . commendably free from technical jargon and clutter . . . essential reading.'

Resources Policy

'. . . looks set to become even more influential than its predecessor . . . it deserves its fame.'

Development Policy Review

ISBN 1-85383-185-9

9 781853 831850